William Motherwell, Isaac Brown

Poetical Works

William Motherwell, Isaac Brown

Poetical Works

ISBN/EAN: 9783337777746

Printed in Europe, USA, Canada, Australia, Japan

Cover: Foto ©Thomas Meinert / pixelio.de

More available books at **www.hansebooks.com**

THE POETICAL WORKS

OF

WILLIAM MOTHERWELL.

WITH

MEMOIR BY JAMES M'CONECHY, Esq.

A NEW EDITION, WITH LARGE ADDITIONS.

PAISLEY: ALEXANDER GARDNER.
GLASGOW: D. ROBERTSON AND CO.
1881.

PREFACE.

The Poems of WILLIAM MOTHERWELL are well entitled to a place in the series of reprints already enriched by his *Minstrelsy* and by the *Harp of Renfrewshire*. Although not to be ranked in the first class of British poets, he must always stand very high among the minor minstrels of his native Scotland. MOTHERWELL'S mind was strongly imbued with the love of poetry. His *Minstrelsy* shows how dearly he loved a ballad; and those pieces it contains which are now, on good authority, believed to have been the products of his own muse, prove that he was not only a diligent collector and editor, but an able imitator of the old bards. In his poems, this sympathy, with the admiration which loved to enshrine the doughty deeds of old world warriors in song, finds frequent expression. The minstrel fire burns in the "Battle Flag of Sigurd," the "Sword Chant of Thorstein Raudi," and in the "Wooing Song of Jarl Egill Scallagrim." MOTHERWELL'S muse must have been sadly cribbed in the Sheriff-Clerk's office at Paisley, where dry legal forms and musty parchments called him from indulging flights of fancy to the most prosaic of all employments. Yet even here he wooed her persistently and successfully, and when he was appointed Sheriff-Clerk Depute of Renfrewshire his more abundant leisure was diligently consecrated to her service. His poems are nearly all of a ballad character. It was a mark of his wisdom that he knew the field which he could most successfully cultivate, and seldom passed beyond it. He is, perhaps, at his best in his martial pieces, which are instinct with life and action ; and yet, in " Jeanie Morrison" and "My Heid is like to rend, Willie," plaintive chords are touched by a master hand, and it would be hard to find lyrics of similar character, in the pages of any writer, more full of simple pathos than these poems.

The greater part of MOTHERWELL'S verse appeared in ephemeral provincial serials, and it was not until after his death that his poems were published in a collected form. The selection made in 1846 by his friend, Dr. M'Conechy, who succeeded him in the editor's chair of the *Glasgow Courier*, was most judicious ; and the Memoir attached to the volume by that gentleman, retained in the present edition, is marked by good taste and critical acumen. The first and second issues of the Poems were speedily exhausted, and a third edition, containing additional pieces, was published in 1848, under the supervision of the author's friend and brother poet, William Kennedy. The selections of Messrs. M'Conechy and Kennedy form the basis of the present edition of MOTHERWELL'S Works. The bulk of the volume might have been increased by additional unpublished poems which have come under observation at this time. With the judgment, however, which led preceding editors to reject these, we heartily concur. It is not desirable that every piece written by an author should be published. Even Burns has suffered at the hands of injudicious editors who have failed to respect his own desire that certain of his writings should pass into oblivion.

In one respect, however, this volume differs from preceding editions. Appended to it is the reprint of a scarce poem written by MOTHERWELL under the pseudonym of "Isaac Brown." MOTHERWELL more than once gave to the public under the cloak of a name that differed from his the effusions of his own pen. In the *Minstrelsy*, at least one ballad attributed to Lovelace had its origin in the Sheriff-Clerk's office at Paisley; and the carefully-elaborated account of the discovery by MOTHERWELL of the "Curious Poems" by James Macalpie* is now generally regarded as a fictitious narrative, by means of which the author desired to mislead and mystify the public mind.

Isaac Brown was no more a real personage than James Macalpie. The "ingenious hands" that had to do with *Renfrewshire Characters and Scenery* were none other than WILLIAM MOTHERWELL'S. The system of mystification adopted by the Poet was more fashionable then than now. It had the sanction of Sir Walter Scott's example, and was, no doubt, convenient in connection with a poem which dealt pawkily, humorously, and, though in kindly fashion, yet somewhat satirically withal, with living Renfrewshire characters as well as with scenery. The prose as well as the verse is admirable, and the production shows the author in a light somewhat different from that in which the pieces which precede exhibit the author. It has therefore been thought well to preserve *Renfrewshire Characters and Scenery* in the present edition of MOTHERWELL's Poems.

---

* See *Harp of Renfrewshire*, Second Series, Appendix, p. iii.

CONTENTS.

PREFACE,	v.
MEMOIR,	i.
The Battle Flag of Sigurd,	1
The Wooing Song of Jarl Egill Skallagrim,	8
The Sword Chant of Thorstein Raudi,	13
Jeanie Morrison,	17
My Heid is like to Rend, Willie,	20
The Madman's Love,	22
Halbert the Grim,	34
True Love's Dirge,	38
The Demon Lady,	41
Zara,	44
Ouglou's Onslaught,	46
Elfinland Wud,	49
Midnight and Moonshine,	53
The Water! The Water!	57
Three Fanciful Supposes,	60
A Caveat to the Wind,	61
What is Glory? What is Fame?	63
The Solemn Song of a Righteous Hearte,	65
Melancholye,	67
I am not Sad!	70
The Joys of the Wilderness,	72
A Solemn Conceit,	73
The Expatriated,	75
Facts from Fairyland,	77
Certain Pleasant Verses to the Lady of my Heart,	78
Beneath a Placid Brow,	80
The Covenanters' Battle Chant,	81
Tim the Tacket,	83
The Witches' Joys,	86
A Sabbath Summer Noon,	89
A Monody,	94
They come! the Merry Summer Months,	97
Change Sweepeth over All,	99

SONGS.

O Wae be to the Orders?	103
Wearie's Well,	104
Song of the Danish Sea-King,	106
The Cavalier's Song,	107
The Merry Gallant,	108
The Knight's Song,	109
The Trooper's Ditty,	111
He is Gone! He is Gone!	112
The Forester's Carol,	113
May-Morn Song,	114
The Bloom hath Fled thy Cheek, Mary,	116
In the Quiet and Solemn Night,	117
The Voice of Love,	118
Away! Away! O, do not Say,	119
O, Agony! keen Agony!	120
The Serenade,	121
Could Love Impart,	123
The Parting,	125
Love's Diet,	126
The Midnight Wind,	127

POSTHUMOUS PIECES.

Second Edition.

The Waithman's Wail,	131
The Troubadour's Lament,	134
When I beneath the Cold Red Earth am Sleeping,	135
Spirits of Light! Spirits of Shade!	137
The Crusader's Farewell,	142
The Midnight Lamp,	142
Come Down, ye Spirits!	143
Ding Dong!	144
Clerke Richard and Maid Margaret,	146
Lord Archibald: A Ballad,	148
And have I Gazed?	152
She is not Dead,	154
Sweet Earlsburn, Blythe Earlsburn,	155
Begone, Begone, thou Truant Tear,	156
O, Babble not to me, Gray Eild,	157

Sonnet: The Patriot's Death,	158
Sonnet: Pale Daughter of the Night,	159
Sonnet: The Hand's Wild Clasp,	160
Sonnet: Silvery Hairs,	160
Lady Margaret: A Ballad,	161

POSTHUMOUS PIECES.

Third Edition.

Cruxtoun Castle,	168
Roland and Rosabelle,	173
Song,	175
For Blyther Fields and Braver Bowers,	176
Hope and Love,	177
Song of the Schippe,	178
He stood alone,	180
Cupid's Banishment,	180
The Ship of the Desert,	181
The Poet's Wish,	182
Isabelle, (a Serenade),	183
What is this World to Me?	184
To a Lady's Bonnet,	185
The Wanderer,	186
Song,	188
The Hunter's Well,	189
It deeply wounds the Trusting Heart,	190
The Ettin o' Sillarwood,	191
Like a Worn Gray-haired Mariner,	197
Choice of Death,	197
Friendship and Love,	198
The Lay of Geoffroi Rudel,	199
Envie,	200
Love's Tokens,	201
O Say not pure Affections Change!	202
The Rose and the Fair Lilye,	203
Like Mist on a Mountain Top Broken and Gray,	204
Young Love,	206
To the Tempest,	207
Song,	208
And hae ye seen my ain True Luve?	208
Goe Cleed wi' Smylis the Cheek!	210

The Spell-bound Knight,	211
O that this weary War of Life!	212
The Poet's Destiny,	213
I met wi' her I Luved Yestreen,	214
To the Lady of my Heart,	215
The Fause Ladye,	216
My Ain Countrie,	217
To a Friend at Parting,	218
I Plucked the Berry,	220
Song,	220
To * * * *	221
The Knight's Requiem,	222
The Rocky Islet,	224
True Woman,	224
The Past and the Future,	226
Oh: Turn from me those Radiant Eyes,	227
O Think nae mair o' Me, Sweet May!	228
The Love-lorn Knight and the Damsel Pitiless,	229
Love in Worldlynesse,	230
A Night Vision,	232
This is no Solitude,	237
The Lone Thorn,	237
The Slayne Menstrel,	238
The Mermaiden,	240
Song,	241
The Lean Lover,	242
Affectest Thou the Pleasures of the Shade?	243
Music,	244
The Shipwrecked Lover,	245
Hollo, My Fancy!	247
Love's Potencie,	255
Life,	256
Superstition,	257
Ye Vernal Hours,	259
Come, Thou Bright Spirit,	260
LAYS OF THE LANG BEIN RITTERS:—	
The Ritters Ride Forth,	262
Lay of the Broken-Hearted and Hope-Bereaved Men,	263
Dream of Life's Early Day, Farewell for Ever,	264
The Ritters Ride Home,	266
Lines written on a Visit to the Grave of Motherwell, by WILLIAM KENNEDY,	268

POEMS BY ISAAC BROWN.

To the Public, ...	3
To the Reader, ...	7
Renfrewshire Scenery and Character, ...	13
Do. Notes, ...	28
Historia Sti. Mireni Confessoris, ...	47

MEMOIR

OF

WILLIAM MOTHERWELL.

MEMOIR.

WILLIAM MOTHERWELL was born at Glasgow on the thirteenth day of October, 1797.* He was the third son of William Motherwell, a native of Stirlingshire, who settled in that city about the year 1792, where he followed the business of an ironmonger.† His mother's name was Elizabeth Barnet, the daughter of William Barnet, a respectable farmer in the parish of Auchterarder, in Perthshire, who, at her father's death, inherited a little fortune of two thousand pounds. Early in the present century, his father removed with his family to Edinburgh, where his son was placed under the charge of Mr. William Lennie, an eminent teacher of English in that city, and the author of several useful and popular school books; and it was while attending this school that the boy met "Jeanie Morrison," a mild and bashful girl, whose name he afterwards immortalised, and of whose gentle nature he retained through life the most pleasing recollections. The first draught of his poem is said to have been made at fourteen years of age, and, as he has himself recorded, they never met after leaving school.‡ As

---

* The house in which this event took place was situated at the south corner of College Street, fronting High Street.

† Mr. Motherwell's family consisted of three sons—David, John, and William, and three daughters—Margaret, Amelia, and Elizabeth.

‡ O! dear, dear Jeanie Morrison,
  Since we were sindered young,
  I've never seen your face, nor heard
  The music o' your tongue.

the reader cannot fail to be gratified by an account of the poet's juvenile history, I transcribe the following details which have been obligingly communicated by Mr. Lennie himself :—

"WILLIAM MOTHERWELL entered my school, then kept at No. 8 Crichton Street, in the neighbourhood of George Square, on the 24th of April, 1805, and left it for the High School here on the first day of October, 1808. He was between seven and eight years old when he joined, an open-faced, firm, and cheerful-looking boy. He began at the alphabet, and though he did not at first display any uncommon ability his mind soon opened up, and as he advanced in his education he speedily manifested a superior capacity, and ultimately became the best scholar in the school ; yet he never showed any of that petulant or supercilious bearing which some children discover who see themselves taken notice of for the quickness of their parts ; he was, on the contrary, kind and accommodating, always ready to help those who applied to him for assistance, and a first-rate hand at carrying on sport during the hours of recreation. Besides acquiring a fair knowledge of geography, which was taught in the higher classes, and becoming well acquainted with the principles of English grammar, he, during the last twelve or eighteen months of his attendance at my school, devoted two separate hours daily to arithmetic and writing, in the latter of which especially he excelled. In the course of a single year he wrote an excellent small distinct hand ; so good, indeed, was it, that few are able to do anything like it even after several years' practice. He also filled up skeleton maps so neatly that at first sight they might have been mistaken for copper-plate engravings. During the last year he was with me, "Wilson's Sentimental Scenes" was introduced into the upper classes. The reading of these sketches delighted him exceedingly, and he entered so completely into the spirit of the pieces that he made the characters his own, and appeared to be a *Roscius* in miniature, a thing I have never found a boy to do but himself.

"Jane (Jeanie) Morrison was the daughter of one of the most respectable brewers and corn-factors then in Alloa. She came to Edinburgh to finish her education, and was in my school with WILLIAM MOTHERWELL during the last year of his course. She was about the same age with himself, a pretty girl, and of good capacity. Her hair was of a lightish brown, approaching to fair; her eyes were dark, and had a sweet and gentle expression; her temper was mild, and her manners unassuming. Her dress was also neat and tidy. In winter she wore a pale blue pelisse, then the fashionable colour, and a light-coloured beaver with a feather. She made a great impression on young MOTHERWELL, and that it was permanent his beautiful ballad shows. At the end of the season she returned to her parents at Alloa, with whom she resided till the time of her marriage. She is now a widow with a family of three children, all of whom are grown up, and, I believe, doing well."*

It would appear from this that MOTHERWELL was entered in the High School of Edinburgh as early as the year 1808, but

---

* I had the pleasure of a slight acquaintance with this lady in after life, as Mrs. Murdoch. Her husband was a respectable merchant in this city, and died about the year 1828. She was, when I knew her, a very elegant woman in her personal appearance, and seemed to have preserved those gentle and agreeable manners for which she had been distinguished in girlhood; but it is proper to remark, that she was wholly unconscious of the ardent interest which she had excited in the mind of her boyish admirer.

his attendance at that excellent institution could not have exceeded a few months, as I find that he was placed early in 1809 at the Grammar School of Paisley, then superintended by the late Mr. John Peddie. His father had not prospered in Edinburgh, and in consequence of the embarrassed state of his affairs his son WILLIAM was consigned to the care of his brother, Mr. John Motherwell, a respectable iron-founder in Paisley. The curriculum at the Paisley Grammar School extended over five years, and if WILLIAM MOTHERWELL completed it he must have enjoyed the full measure of elementary classical instruction, including in the fifth year the rudiments of Greek, which it was then customary to give to boys in Scotland. One of his surviving school companions* informs me that, in conjunction with the late Mr. William Bain, advocate, and a Mr. Lymburn, also deceased, he was a *dux* boy, and there seems to be no reason to doubt that he exhibited the same quickness of apprehension and readiness of parts in the Paisley Academy which he had displayed in other schools; but as his tastes were never scholastic, and as his knowledge of the dead tongues was always limited, the presumption is that he followed the prominent bias of his mind, and devoted to works of imagination the hours that should have been given to school exercises. I am fortified in this belief by the recollections of Mr. Crawford, who says, "What MOTHERWELL was most remarkable for was his gift of spinning long yarns about castles, and robbers, and strange out-of-the-way adventures, with which, while Mr. Peddie imagined he was assisting his class-fellows with their lessons, he would entertain them for hours, day after

---

* Mr. John Crawford, writer in Paisley.

day, like some of the famous story-tellers in the Arabian Nights; and these stories were retailed at second-hand by his class-fellows to those who had not the privilege of hearing them from the author himself."

In the year 1811, his mother died at Edinburgh, and after that melancholy event, his father, accompanied by his daughter, Amelia, retired to the village of Kilsyth, in Stirlingshire, where he dwelt till his death, which occurred in February, 1827.

The history of his ancestors possesses considerable interest. In a letter with which I have been favoured by my venerable and accomplished friend, Mr. Sheriff Campbell, of Paisley, they are thus spoken of :—

"Of his family I had occasion to learn something, in the course of a judicial inquiry concerning the succession of David Motherwell, his uncle, upwards of thirty years ago. That David Motherwell died possessed of a small estate on the banks of the Carron, in the Barony of Dundaff, in Stirlingshire, which, according to what I found to be the tradition of the neighbourhood, supported, to a certain extent, by the title deeds of the property, which I saw, had been in the possession of thirteen generations of the same family, all bearing the same name of David, with the surname variously spelled, being at one time Moderville, at another Moderell, and latterly Motherwell. His uncle, Alexander, set aside David's deed of settlement, and sold the property to his younger brother John, an extensive ironmonger in Paisley, who left it to trustees for behoof of his daughter."

The estate here spoken of was called Muirmill, and the name at once indicates the calling of the proprietors. They were the hereditary millars of Dundaff, and are so designated in a confirmatory charter granted in favour of the then possessor by James Graham, the celebrated Marquis of Montrose, in 1642, as will be seen by the following short extract from that document. It is to be observed that this extract has reference to 'an instrument of seizin,' dated 29th June, 1629, in favour of 'David Moddrell, in Spittal,* and Isabella Small, his wife, proceeding on a charter granted by James, Earl of Montrose, Lord Graham and Mugdock, of the lands of all and whole, that pendicle of land called Spittal,' &c. The deed of 1642, then, confirms the previous grant of 1629, to

"William Modrell, miller, at Dundaff, callit the Muir Mill,   , † his spouse, and David Modrell, their son, on the other part (of date at Drum-phad, 29th April, 1629 years), whereby, with consent aforesaid, set in feu farm to the said William Modrell, and his spouse above named, and the langest liver of them twa, in life-rent; and to David Modrell, their son, all and haill, the said mill, mill lands, and multures, &c., and pasturage for eight ky, all lying within the barony of Dundaff, and shire of Stirling."‡

Upon what conditions the lands in question were held before the year 1629 my ignorance of feudal law disables me from saying; but it is plain, both from the tradition mentioned by Mr. Campbell and the charters at present in my possession, that this family of Motherwells had been settled

---

* An abbreviation of Hospital, and a common designation of small farms in certain parts of Scotland. Lands so called had formed portions of the extensive possessions of the military order of KNIGHTS HOSPITALLERS.

† Blank in the original.

‡ I am indebted for the transcription of this passage to my friend Dr. John Smith, the well-known Secretary to the Maitland Club.

in that locality, and probably, on this very spot, for at least four hundred years—the land and the occupation descending in regular succession from father to son. The name itself is obviously a local surname, but it belongs to the county of Lanark, in the middle ward of which, and in the parish of Dalziel, there is a considerable village called Motherwell. The statistical accounts speak of a well or spring as still existing there, from which the inhabitants are supplied with water, and which, in the olden time, was called the "Well of our Ladye." It was probably believed to possess medicinal virtues, and was, therefore, placed under the immediate protection of the "Virgin Mother"—whence the name, Motherwell.* Its antiquity as a surname must be considerable, since it appears in the Ragman Rolls† for 1296, and also in the index to a chartulary of the Monastery of Paisley in 1490 ; and from what has been already stated it will be seen that that branch of the race from which the poet sprang had been planted in Stirlingshire as far back as the beginning of the fifteenth century. The name, however, is an uncommon one.‡

---

* Few towns where there has been an ecclesiastical establishment, such as Glasgow, for instance, want a LADY WELL.

† The title given to the list of the names of those who swore fealty to Edward I., which has now something of the character and interest of a "Domesday Book."

‡ In illustration of the history of the poet's family it may be mentioned, that there is extant a deed of "assignation and disposition," by his grandfather, David Motherwell, wherein he bequeaths to each of his "younger sons" (the number is not mentioned) £100 sterling ; and to each of his daughters, Elizabeth, Janet, and Amelia, 1000 merks Scots, or about £55 sterling.

Janet married	Henry Bannerman.
Elizabeth „	David Whyte.
Amelia „	John Barnet.

It having been resolved, I know not why, to devote this wayward and dreamy boy to the legal profession, he was placed, at the age of fifteen, in the office of the Sheriff-Clerk of Paisley, where he remained for many years; but, as may be readily conceived, the duties of such a situation were little congenial to his tastes. Notwithstanding his dislike to the duties of a writer's clerk, he contrived to turn his new position so far to account by bestowing great pains on the deciphering of ancient legal documents; an art in which he latterly excelled. I am indebted to Mr. Sheriff Campbell for the following interesting particulars concerning MOTHERWELL at this time:—

"When I first knew WILLIAM MOTHERWELL he was a very little boy in the Sheriff-Clerk's office here. I had observed his talent for sketching figures of men, in armour and other-

---

The latter was probably the poet's uncle. The descendants of Janet are now eminent merchants in Manchester, and the line of Motherwell is represented by the poet's nephew, the son of his elder brother, David, Mr. Charles M'Arthur Motherwell, who is a purser's clerk in the navy. The name of William Motherwell's grandmother was Amelia Monteath, the daughter of an old and respectable family settled at Dunblane, in Stirlingshire. A sister of his mother married a Mr. Ogilvie, who left a son, Major Ogilvie, now resident in Edinburgh.

John de Moderwell, chaplain, appears in the deed of 1460, as one of the Procurators of Henry of Livingston, Knight, Commander of the Temple of St. John; which Sir Henry was son of William, Lord of Kilsyth, and preceptor of Torphichen. He died in 1463. Edward, his elder brother, was the direct ancestor of the Viscount Kilsyth, who was attainted in 1715. There is no evidence of any relationship between this ancient priest and the poet's family; but his connection with Kilsyth, where a branch of the Motherwells has been planted for many centuries, might justify the suspicion that he was of the same lineage. This mention of him in so old a document is satisfactory evidence of the antiquity of the surname, whatever opinion we may form as to his probable affinity to the ancestors of the subject of this memoir.

For these details I am indebted chiefly to the diligence and antiquarian skill of my late amiable and lamented friend Mr. Philip Ramsay, of Edinburgh, S.S.C., who had collected some materials for a life of William Motherwell.

wise, and amongst the rest one of myself upon a blotter which I had occasion to use when sitting in the Sheriff-Court. I gave him a few ancient documents to copy for me; and, in place of an ordinary transcript, I received from him, with surprise and satisfaction, a *fac simile* so perfect that, except for the colour and texture of the paper, it would have been difficult to distinguish it from the original manuscript. Finding him a smart and intelligent boy, I asked him to give me a statement, in writing, of certain occurrences to which he had been a witness at a period when the peace of the district was threatened. This account was not confined to facts, but was interspersed with observations and reflections of his own, of a nature so unexpected and so curious, that I wished to preserve it; but I am sorry that, in a search made for it some years ago, I was unable to find it. The notions of the boy were then what would now be called *extremely* liberal. In process of time, however, his views changed, and I used to joke him upon the ground that his conversion had been beaten into him by a party of lads (Radicals), with whom he happened to get into conflict. On that occasion he was thrown down and trampled upon in the street, and received injuries so severe that his life was thought in imminent danger. This, I believe, was in 1818 or 1819, during a time of political excitement. He was appointed to the office of Sheriff-Clerk Depute of the county of Renfrew, under the late Robert Walkinshaw, of Parkhouse, the principal clerk, in May, 1819, and held that situation with credit till Nov. 1829.

"His talent for poetry was accompanied by a strong taste for the *antique*, and I cannot help thinking that the last may have had its origin in the copying of the ancient manuscript for me. While in office here he contributed articles to the *Paisley Advertiser,* and ultimately became its editor. He had also a chief hand in commencing and conducting a *Paisley Monthly Magazine,* which lived to attain to the size of a goodly volume. It contained many contributions from his pen, besides a number of curious extracts from documents which his researches among the records of the Sheriff-Clerk's office brought to light. At a recent sale of the library of a deceased Paisley gentleman this Magazine, though poorly bound, brought the respectable price of 22s. 6d. His temperament was enthusiastic, kind, and convivial. * * I had a great regard for him."

Upon this outline of MOTHERWELL's history from the age of fifteen to thirty-two, I would remark, in the first place, that we learn from it that eighteen of the most valuable years of his life were passed in an occupation which presented the fewest possible attractions for a man of his habits and pursuits ; and, in the second place, that if he attained to a certain measure of excellency in poetical composition in circumstances so unfavourable to the growth of a poetical temper, his merit was all the higher on that account. The incident to which Mr. Campbell refers, and which he supposes determined his future political creed, MOTHERWELL always spoke of with the strongest indignation. It occurred during the time of what was called the Radical War in the west country (1818), and when, as Sheriff-Clerk Depute, he was obliged, in obedience to the orders of his superiors, to perform many duties which rendered him unpopular. A deliberate attempt was made to murder him by throwing him over the bridge into the Cart, and he has often assured me that he was actually raised to the top of the parapet wall by the infuriated mob before he was rescued. That he should have abandoned liberalism after such treatment would not be surprising, but the truth is, his political belief was a part of his nature, and was very slightly modified by external considerations. His ideas of the constitution of civil society were chivalric, not philosophical: and if others undervalued the virtues of the middle ages he certainly over-rated them. It was not his custom to analyse his emotions too nicely at any period of his life; and I can perfectly understand how he may have been captivated as a boy with those showy notions which are more or less prevalent in all imperfectly-instructed societies, and which have so many charms for youthful imaginations. But MOTHERWELL was instinctively a Tory—all the tendencies of his mind gravitated towards the creed of that old and respectable party—and I am satisfied that his monarchical principles would have been just as high after he escaped from mere nonage had he never handled a truncheon in defence of the public peace on the streets of Paisley. His political convictions might be extreme, but they were honest. He firmly believed that his opinions were founded in truth, and that their vindication was essential to the well-being of his country; nor have I ever known a man who had more thoroughly identified himself with the doctrines which he maintained and promulgated.

There is another point noticed by Mr. Campbell, viz., his power of sketching. This was a faculty which he possessed in the highest perfection, so much so that had he not been a poet he might have been an artist. Many of his manuscripts are illustrated at the beginning after the manner of old black letter volumes and illuminated missals, and numerous scraps of paper attest his accurate perception of the ludicrous and the horrible by all sorts of queer and grotesque delineations. A few strokes of his pen were sufficient for this, and it is impossible not to admire the ease which attaches to these figures. His handwriting likewise partook of this peculiarity. It was formal and square, and, particularly in the capital letters, resembled the Chaldee character, constituting, in fact, a variety of painting.*

The winter session of 1818-19 he spent at Glasgow College, where he attended the Latin class, under the late Mr. Walker, and the Greek class under the late Mr. Young; but, as I have already stated, he never attained to ordinary proficiency in either language, and with the modern tongues he was wholly unacquainted. He manifested at this time a strong desire to repair the defects of his early education, and in a letter to his friend, the late Mr. Robert Walkinshaw, in March, 1818, he expresses a hope that, should he succeed to the office of Sheriff-Clerk Depute, then held by Mr. Walkinshaw, he might be able "to save some little money sufficient to re-launch his frail skiff once more on the *dead sea of the languages.*"

As the office of Sheriff-Clerk Depute brought him a considerable income he spent the greater part of it in the purchase of books, and long before his removal to Glasgow he had collected a large and miscellaneous library. Like most book-fanciers he sometimes sacrificed usefulness to the

---

* This seems to have been a very early habit; Mr. Crawford speaks of it in these terms:—"He was also remarkable for his talent for sketching figures of mailed knights, on foot and mounted, and all manner of caricatures, which were sketched with great life and spirit. The boards of his class-fellows' school-books were covered with Motherwell's sketches, and it was considered a great favour when he gave them one."

indulgence of a spirit of curiosity, but in that province of literature to which he was chiefly devoted—poetry and the historical romance—his library was rich. Its chief wants were in the department of modern history and moral and philosophical science, in none of which subjects can it be said that he took much pleasure. His knowledge of them was, consequently, defective, and this was both felt and seen when politics became his profession.

It may be naturally supposed of the man who at fourteen sketched the outline of "Jeanie Morrison," that if he did not actually lisp in numbers the art of versification must have been at least an irresistible habit, and that *sponte sua carmen numeros veniebat ad aptos*; but when he first committed himself publicly to the dangers and allurements of rhyme, or where, I have been unable satisfactorily to ascertain. In 1818 he contributed some little things to a small work published at Greenock, called the *Visitor*, and for several years afterwards he continued to furnish with pieces of original poetry such of his literary friends in Paisley and Glasgow as applied to him for assistance. In this respect his liberality was exemplary, if not prodigal, but he afterwards collected the best of these fugitive productions, and embodied them in that volume upon which his reputation as a poet must ultimately rest. In 1819, the HARP OF RENFREWSHIRE,* of which he was the editor, appeared at Paisley. This work is anonymous; but it is well known to have been brought out under MOTHERWELL's care, who supplied the in-

---

* THE HARP OF RENFREWSHIRE; a collection of songs and other poetical pieces, many of which are original; accompanied with notes, explanatory, critical, and biographical; and a short essay on the Poets of Renfrewshire, 1 vol. Paisley, 1819.

troductory essay, which was his first attempt at serious criticism. In it he gives a rapid sketch of the poets of Renfrewshire, beginning with Sir Hugh Montgomerie who died at a very advanced age in 1545, and ending with Robert Tannahill, whom he could not have known personally, but with whose melancholy history he had ample means of becoming acquainted. The notes are likewise by him, and are both numerous and valuable; and this little volume, which is now scarce, may be regarded as a favourable specimen of his zeal and diligence. Its chief merit, however, is, that it was the herald to a work of much larger pretensions, and with which his fame is now closely identified—MINSTRELSY, ANCIENT AND MODERN,* which was published at Glasgow in 1827, and which instantly secured for its author an honourable place among the commentators on our national poetry. The "Historical Introduction" is elaborate and full, but I must leave it to those who have made such subjects as it discusses a study to decide upon its merits; it is enough to state here that this work brought him into direct communication with some men of high distinction in the world of letters, and, amongst others, with Sir Walter Scott. The ancient ballad of "Gil Morrice" seems to have attracted much of MOTHERWELL's attention. It was the foundation of Home's celebrated tragedy of "Douglas," and the scene of the melancholy adventure which it relates was "Carronside," the home of his ancestors. He tells us, moreover, that "the green wood" of the ballad was the ancient forest of Dundaff, in Stirlingshire, and that "Lord Barnard's castle is said to have occupied a precipitous cliff

---

* Minstrelsy; Ancient and Modern: with an historical Introduction, and notes. By William Motherwell. John Wylie. Glasgow, 1827.

overhanging the water of Carron, on the lands of Halbertshire."* Earlsburn, a favourite name with him, is also a small stream in that locality which falls into the Carron and derives its appellation, according to him, from the Earl's son, who is the hero of this legendary poem. There is internal evidence in his writings to show that he had carefully inquired into this matter while residing with his uncle at Muirmill; but it was from an old woman at Paisley, who sang the verses to him, that he obtained that copy of the ballad which he considered the true one, and which led to his correspondence with Sir Walter. His idea was that GIL should have been written CHILD, and that MORRICE was an obvious corruption of NORYCE, the old English word for foster-child. Willie, the page, is called, in one of the versions (Mr. Jamieson's), his "foster-brither;" and MOTHERWELL's object would appear to have been to show that between the "child's" messenger and himself there existed a stronger bond of union than mere feudalism could create. In this way, it is to be presumed, he proposed to account for "Willie's" undertaking, though reluctantly, to deliver the message to Lady Barnard from her son, the ill-fated Gil, of whose relationship to that noble person the lad was ignorant. He accordingly wrote to Sir Walter Scott on the subject as early as April, 1825, two years before the Minstrelsy appeared, and received from that eminent man the following reply :—

"Abbotsford, 3rd May, 1825.

"SIR,

"I am honoured with your letter covering the curious old version of the ballad of Gil Morrice, which seems,

---

* Minstrelsy, p. 258.

according to your copy, to be a corruption of Child Norrice, or Child Nursling, as we would say. As I presume the ballad to be genuine, and, indeed, see no reason to suspect the contrary, the style being simple and ancient, I think you should print it exactly as you have taken it down, and with a reference to the person by whom it is preserved so special as to enable any one to ascertain its authenticity who may think it worth while. I have asked, at different times, the late Mr. John Home, concerning the ballad on which he was supposed to have founded 'Douglas,' but his memory was too imperfect when I knew him to admit of his giving me any information. I have heard my mother, who was fond of the ballad, say, that when 'Douglas' was in its height of popularity, 'Gil Morrice' was, to a certain extent, re-written, which renovated copy, of course, includes all the new stanzas about 'Minerva's loom,' and so forth. Yet there are so many fine old verses in the common set, that I cannot agree to have them mixed up even with your set, though more ancient, but would like to see them kept quite separate, like different sets of the same melody. In fact, I think I did wrong myself in endeavouring to make the best possible set of an ancient ballad out of several copies obtained from different quarters, and that, in many respects, if I improved the poetry, I spoiled the simplicity of the old song. There is no wonder this should be the case, when one considers that the singers or reciters by whom these ballads were preserved and handed down, must, in general, have had a facility, from memory at least, if not from genius (which they might often possess), of filling up verses which they had forgotten, or altering such as they might think they could improve. Passing through this process in different parts of the country, the ballads, admitting that they had one common poetical original (which is not to be inferred merely from the similitude of the story), became, in progress of time, totally different productions, so far as the tone and spirit of each is concerned. In such cases, perhaps, it is as well to keep them separate, as giving in their original state a more accurate idea of our ancient poetry, which is the point most important in such collections. There is room for a very curious essay on the relation which the popular poetry of the north of Europe bears to that of the south, and even to that of Asia; and the varieties of some of our ballads might be accounted for by showing that one edition had been derived from the French or Norman, another from the Danish, and so on; so that, though the substance of the dish be the same, the cookery is that of foreign and distant *cuisiniers*. This reasoning certainly does not apply to mere brief alterations and corruptions, which do not, as it were, change the tone and form of the original.

"You will observe that I have no information to give respecting 'GIL MORRICE,' so I might as well, perhaps, have saved you the trouble of this long letter.

"I am, SIR,
"Your obliged, humble servt.,
"WALTER SCOTT."

Sir Walter and MOTHERWELL never met, but after the death of that great man he performed a pilgrimage to Abbotsford, and, as I am informed, was wont to say that "nothing in that splendid mansion had affected him so much as Sir Walter's staff, with the bit dibble at the end of it." [*] Of course, in the forthcoming edition of the "Minstrelsy" he followed the advice of the illustrious critic, and kept his own copy of the ballad distinct from the others, and so it stands in the volume.

In 1828, the *Paisley Magazine* was begun by MOTHERWELL, and carried on by him, with the assistance of his friends, for a year. It is, undoubtedly, what Mr. Campbell represents it—a respectable provincial work; and in it, for

---

[*] Notes by Mr. Charles Hutchison.

the first time, appeared some of the poet's best pieces, such as The Sword Chant of Thorstein Raudi—Midnight and Moonshine—The Water! The Water!—The Wooing Song of Jarl Egill Skallagrim—and Wearie's Well. His position, however, had now changed, and it will be necessary to explain how this was brought about.

In the year 1826 a newspaper was begun in Paisley, called the *Paisley Advertiser*. Its politics were Conservative and Ministerial, and its first editor was a Mr. John Goldie, who had been formerly connected with an Ayr journal. He died suddenly within a year, and was succeeded in his office by Mr. William Kennedy, an Irish gentleman of distinguished poetical abilities, and the author of the pretty poem called "The Arrow and the Rose;" and also a little volume of poems entitled "Fitful Fancies."

Between Mr. Kennedy and MOTHERWELL there sprang up a strong friendship. They were both addicted to literature and poetry, they thought alike on matters political, and were nearly of an age. It is not surprising, therefore, that MOTHERWELL should have become a contributor and a proprietor, and still less so that, on the retirement of Mr. Kennedy, in 1828, he should have succeeded him as editor of that paper. What success he may have had in his new capacity I know not, but on the retirement of Mr. James M'Queen from the management of the *Glasgow Courier*, in 1830, Mr. MOTHERWELL was invited by the proprietors of that journal to take his place; and all things being satisfactorily arranged he left Paisley and took up his abode in Glasgow in the beginning of that year. The first number of the *Courier* which appeared after his accession to the office of editor has the date of 2nd Feb., 1830; and he continued in connection with that paper till his death in November, 1835.

Whether journalism was exactly the vocation that was best suited to a man of his tastes and peculiar acquirements I shall not take upon me to determine, but there can be no doubt that he entered upon his new duties at Glasgow at a time of great difficulty and considerable public danger. The political world was at that moment upheaved from its foundations, and the revolution in France, consequent upon the three glorious days of July, followed as that event was by the accession of Lord Grey's Administration, and the Reform Bill excitement, presented to a lover of the olden ways a mass of embarrassment which we may admit to have been unsurmountable. Whatever MOTHERWELL'S views may have been in boyhood they were now fixed. He saw one after another of his most cherished prejudices first derided and then destroyed. Change followed change with the rapidity of lightning, and in the midst of this universal whirlwind the only man in this immense community who was expected to keep himself free from the common contagion, and to observe the most philosophical abstinence in the discussion of passing events, was the Tory editor of *the* Tory newspaper! Mere humanity is not equal to so great a trial as this, and MOTHERWELL was not the man to affect to undergo it. He entered into the strife with all his soul, and whatever difference of opinion may have formerly prevailed as to his style of defence, it will not be denied by his bitterest political enemies (for I would persuade myself that, personally, he had and could have none), that he conducted his case for many years against frightful odds, with exemplary zeal, courage, and fidelity. It would be easy, no doubt, to select from his writings at that time passages which might appear to be objectionable, but the same remark would apply equally to his opponents; and those only who have had some experience of a controversial life, and of the perplexities which beset a writer for the public press in a provincial town, can form an adequate conception of the difficulties with which MOTHERWELL was at that juncture surrounded. The public mind is now comparatively cool; it was then at a boiling heat, and in the fierce contest of parties, passions were evoked which overmastered reason and laid judgment prostrate in the dust. That in such a tumult he, a man of warm and impetuous temperament, should have stood erect and looked down with complacent indifference on the scene below was impossible; nor did he make the attempt. He defended his principles from the assaults daily and hourly made upon them, and it was his duty to do so; but if, in the execution of that duty he transgressed the established laws of political warfare, or outraged any of the conventional courtesies of life, then he was blameable. I do not say that this was the case, because I do not think so; not that I would be understood as approving of all that he wrote in these times, but that, considering the circumstances in which he was placed, his abstinence from a certain measure of vehemence would have argued a neutrality of feeling on the great questions of the day which would have literally disqualified him for the office that he held. Let us be just to the dead, then, and grant that what was well was due to the man, and that what was amiss was chargeable upon the infirmity of our common nature.

In his editorial capacity MOTHERWELL occasionally drew upon his poetical faculty and in general successfully, as the following *jeu d'esprit* will show. It appeared early in 1833, when the Reform Bill was supposed to be in danger, and when its friends in Glasgow exhibited an unusual degree of anxiety respecting it. T—m A—k—n is the late Mr. Thomas Aitkinson, bookseller, who was a very keen Liberal politician. M'P—n was his neighbour Mr. M'Phun, likewise a bookseller and agent for the *Sun* newspaper. Sir D. K. S—f—d is the late Sir D. K. Sandford, the accomplished Professor of Greek in the University of Glasgow, who was at that time an ardent reformer, and whose premature and much-lamented death was probably accelerated by the excitement of that miserable period. With these explanations this clever trifle will be intelligible :—

THE REFORMER'S GARLAND.

AN EXCELLENT NEW SONG.

Tune—" Young Lochinvar."

T—m A—k—n mounted his berry brown steed,
Thro' all the West Country unequalled for speed ;
And, save an odd threepence to pay for the toll,
He carried no weight but a placard in scroll.
So lightly and jaunty he Eastward did hie,
With the Bill in his heart, and the Mail in his eye—
He swore that, for once, he would e-clipse the SUN, *
And darken the shine of his neighbour, M'P—n.
Camlachie folk stared, and Tollcross stood abeigh,
So rapid he rode, and the steed was so skeigh ;
But Tom did not value his horsemanlike skill,
His thoughts were " Reform," and " nought but the Bill."
Yea, even in passing the scene at Carmyle,†
The Whig field of honour seemed worthless the while—
For still he expected to e-clipse the SUN,
And darken the shine of his neighbour, M'P—n.

---

* This is an allusion to the *Sun*, London newspaper, at that time forwarded by special express to Glasgow.

† The scene of a recent duel, with the distance marked out by two bricks.

>   Then onward he sped, till he came to a turn
>   Of the road, when the Guard of the Mail cried—"Adjourn!"
>   And about ship went Tom, and the spur did apply,
>   And the *Stationer*, truly, for once seemed to *fly*.
>   His Tontine constituents soon did he hail,
>   For near eighteen minutes he distanc'd the Mail:
>   The 'Adjourn' was repeated, e-clipsed was the SUN,
>   The shine was o'erclouded of neighbour, M'P—n.
>   Sir D. K. S—f—d next mounted his beast,
>   With its tail to the West and its head to the East,
>   And on like a War Knight the brute he did urge,
>   To nose the effect of the fam'd "Russell Purge;"
>   But at Bothwell the Mail Guard roar'd out—"Lost by Eight!"
>   When about went the prad, as it had taken fright;
>   Sir Dan he stuck on, and again 'clipsed the SUN,
>   To the utter confounding of neighbour, M'P—n.

That MOTHERWELL'S prospects were improved by a removal to Glasgow may be admitted, since that city, from its greater size, would necessarily afford a wider field for the display of his abilities; but I have many doubts whether the change was friendly to the development and cultivation of his poetical faculty. The charge of a three-times-a-week paper leaves little leisure for the prosecution of a formal course of study, while the distracting anxieties which are inseparable from political warfare are altogether incompatible with that repose of mind which is essential to the achievement of distinction in any walk of literature. It is my impression, therefore, that his muse was comparatively idle in Glasgow, and that his attention was directed to the improvement of old rather than to the composition of new poems. This idea is partially confirmed by an inspection of two quarto volumes of manuscript pieces which he left behind him, the one of which is nearly a transcript of the other, and was obviously executed at Glasgow; and it is farther strengthened by the fact, that he published little after he came to this city which had not been written long before. It would be idle to talk of the *genius loci* in such circumstances, for the character of that mysterious lady must be much the same in both places, and it is not particularly spiritual in either ; but there may be something in the disruption of old and established ties—something in the absence of familiar faces and well-known voices, and something in the destruction of those secret and inexplicable material sympathies which make one spot of earth more than another the home of a man's soul. Whether any or all of these influences may have affected him I shall not take upon me positively to affirm, but I think myself so far justified in the conclusion at which I have arrived by the subsequent steps of his history, which indicate a sluggish action if not an absolute torpor of his creative energies.

In 1832 a publication was started in Glasgow, under the direction of Mr. John Strang, the author of two interesting volumes of Travels in Germany, called *The Day*, to which MOTHERWELL contributed largely. In that periodical there appeared for the first time the following poetical pieces from his pen :—The Serenade—The Solemn Song of a Righteous Hearte—Elfinland Wud—The Covenanters' Battle Chant—Caveat to the Wind—What is Glory ? What is Fame ?—A Solemn Conceit—The Parting—The Ettin Lang o' Sillarwood—and, Spirits of Light ! Spirits of Shade !—all of which, with the exception of the two last, he afterwards embodied in his volume.* He also communicated to that work a series

---

* It is needless to add, that these were gratuitous contributions, and that their author neither expected nor received anything for them. It was in this year that "Jeanie Morrison" appeared in an Edinburgh magazine, and for that exquisite lyrical composition he was paid—thirty shillings ! George Buchannan was not far wrong when he exclaimed three hundred years ago,

Denique quicquid agis, comes assidet improba egestas
Sive poema canis, sive poema doces.

of humorous papers in prose, entitled, "Memoirs of a Paisley Bailie," which afforded considerable amusement at the time; and towards the end of this year he collected his scattered poetical fragments, and formed them into a small volume with the title of "POEMS, NARRATIVE AND LYRICAL," which he dedicated to his friend Kennedy. Most of these pieces, if not the whole of them, were reprints. I am not quite sure about the "Battle Flag of Sigurd," but I rather think it appeared originally in the pages of the *Paisley Advertiser*.

This volume was, upon the whole, well received. There could be no doubt about the high quality of the poetry which an unknown author had ventured thus to submit to the world, but its character was peculiar, and for the most part not fitted for extensive popularity; and the season which was chosen for its introduction was eminently unfavourable to its chances of immediate success. No adventitious murmurs of applause had announced its approach, and at a time when little was heard but the noise of political contention, it was perhaps too much to expect that a comparatively obscure bard should draw towards himself a large share of the public notice, let his abilities be what they might. This work, however, gave MOTHERWELL, what it had been the object of his life to attain, a place among the poets of Britain; and it carried his name into quarters which it never would have otherwise reached. A commendatory criticism in *Blackwood's Magazine* for April, 1833, proclaimed his pretensions wherever the English language is read; and though his nature was too modest and too manly for the display of any open exultation at the triumph which he had so honourably won, he never ceased to feel the deepest gratitude to the distinguished reviewer whom he knew to be a consummate judge of poetical merit, and for whose genius and character he always felt and expressed the warmest admiration.

The last work in which MOTHERWELL engaged, and which he did not live to complete, was, a joint edition of Burns' works by him and James Hogg, the Ettrick Shepherd.* His share in this production consisted merely of occasional notes, critical and explanatory, which are marked with the letter M., and in which he exhibits much knowledge of the contemporary history of Burns' period, and his usual discrimination as a commentator. The fifth and last volume contains the life of the Ayrshire poet by Hogg; but before it appeared his comparatively youthful coadjutor was no more.†

In August, 1835, MOTHERWELL was summoned to London, to appear before a committee of the House of Commons which had been appointed to take evidence as to the constitution and practices of the Orange Society, with a view to its suppression. He had unluckily allowed himself to be enrolled as a member of that association, and was one of the district secretaries for the West of Scotland. There is no incident in his history which it more perplexes me to account for than this. He had no connexion with Ireland, direct or indirect, nor had he ever been in that island in his life, and

---

* The Works of Robert Burns, edited by the Ettrick Shepherd, and William Motherwell, Esq., 5 vols. Glasgow: Archd. Fullarton & Co., 1836.

† It should have been mentioned in its proper place that in the year 1832 Motherwell supplied a preface of some length to Henderson's volume of Scottish Proverbs. Andrew Henderson was a portrait painter of considerable celebrity in Glasgow and an intimate friend of the Poet. He was a man of abrupt manners, but of great honesty of nature, and capable of both steadfast and warm attachments. He pre-deceased Motherwell by about six months.

few men, in my opinion, were less qualified by previous habits of study to appreciate the value of the mixed questions of civil and ecclesiastical polity which that body professed to discuss: yet he entered with characteristic warmth into its schemes, and became one of the agents employed in the extension of its principles. To his mind Orangeism would seem to have presented itself under the guise of a wholesome influence of general applicability which it was desirable to perpetuate, instead of being, what it really was, a particular form of one of those numerous factions into which Irish society is divided. It would not appear to have occurred to him that whatever the merits, real or imaginary, of the Orange confederacy might be, its introduction into Scotland could be attended with no benefits whatever; and that if it was destined ever to achieve advantages of a permanent kind it was only on the soil which had generated and nourished it that this could happen. As an antagonist to Popery and Jacobitism it was certainly not wanted in Presbyterian Scotland: and a little reflection might have satisfied him that the civil and religious rights of the people of this country were not to be upheld through the instrumentality of an Hibernian political fraternity which had outlived the necessity that gave it birth, and which was now respectable only from the historical associations connected with its origin, and the recollection of the services which it had formerly rendered to the cause of constitutional government in Ireland. His adhesion to this body was, therefore, a decided error in judgment, while it was attended with this additional inconvenience that it gave rise to the suspicion that the party whose public representative he was had become favourable to a system of political propagandism, and was not unwilling to patronise, in an underhand way, that which its general creed repudiated. Legitimate and open combination it did not, because it could not, reject; but it professed to hold secret societies in abhorrence; and though the Orange body might not in strictness of speech deserve to be so called, it had too many of the characteristics of a sectarian club to be agreeable to sober-minded Scotchmen. This act, however, was purely personal, and was confined to MOTHERWELL and one or two of his more intimate friends; and I distinctly remember that there was no subject upon which he was more reserved, and none upon which he bore a little raillery with less equanimity, than upon his alliance with Irish Orangeism. By this time, however, the evil spirit of political acerbity had displaced the gentler impulses of his nature, and WILLIAM MOTHERWELL had exchanged the catholicity of poetry for the fanaticism of social exclusiveness!*

MOTHERWELL remained in London for about a week, and there can be no doubt that he exhibited great mental infirmity before the committee—in common speech, he "broke down." That this did not result from any want of courage on his part will be at once admitted by those who knew the man; but it is proper to observe that in such circumstances he was constitutionally "unready" and slow of utterance. He not only required time to arrange his ideas and to consolidate his thoughts on the most ordinary occasions, but he was habitually slow, and even confused, in the expression of them. No ordeal could, therefore, be more embarrassing to him than a formal examination before a body of sharp-

---

* That this incident was hurtful to his health was the general impression of his friends. Mr. Hutchison, who saw him frequently before he set out for London, says "that he was greatly depressed."

witted men whose pleasure it not infrequently is to lay snares for an inexperienced witness : but besides this I am convinced that on this particular point MOTHERWELL was at fault as to knowledge—that he had never seriously inquired of himself what Orangeism was, or what object was to be gained by its propagation—and that, consequently, he must have failed when rigorously interrogated by an intelligent and authoritative tribunal about these matters. Let me farther add, in explanation of this melancholy occurrence, that it has been long my fixed impression that he was labouring under the effects of the approaches of that insidious disease (softening of the brain), which destroyed him a few months afterwards : and those who remember the circumstances attendant upon his visit to the Metropolis, and the strange fancies which haunted him while there, will probably have little hesitation in accepting this apology for what we may now call an involuntary weakness. The indications of this mental debility did not escape the observation of the gentlemen composing the committee ; and Mr. Wallace, of Kelly, at that time Member for Greenock, with a kindness which was the more honourable to him that MOTHERWELL had frequently spoken of him in his editorial capacity with considerable severity, paid him marked attention ; and, perceiving how matters really stood, lost no time in getting his bewildered countryman shipped off to Scotland.

On his return he resumed his old habits of life, and was, to all outward appearance, in perfect health. On Saturday, the 31st day of October, 1835, he dined and spent the evening at the house of a gentleman in the suburbs of Glasgow. There was dancing, and it was observed that he bled freely at the nose, which was attributed to the heated state of the apartments. On going into the open air for a short time the bleeding stopped, and at half-past ten he left his friend's house in the company of the late Mr. Robert M'Nish (better known as the Modern Pythagorean), and the late Mr. Philip Ramsay, and from these gentlemen he parted about eleven o'clock. At four o'clock on the morning of the 1st of November he was suddenly struck while in bed with a violent shock of apoplexy, which almost instantly deprived him of consciousness. He had simply time to exclaim, "My head! My head!" when he fell back on the pillow and never spoke more. I saw him in my professional capacity about half-past six, having been sent for by the medical man who was first called in, but the case was then hopeless and had been obviously so from the first; knowing, however, that a deep interest was felt in his fate, and anxious that he should have the benefit of the advice of a senior practitioner, I sent for my late friend, Dr. William Young, but before he arrived he was dead. He expired quietly and without suffering at eight o'clock, thus closing a life of incessant labour, and of some anxiety not unmixed with enjoyment, at the early age of thirty-seven.

He was buried in the Necropolis, a new cemetery, situated over-against the Cathedral, on Thursday, the 5th of November; and his remains were followed to the grave by a large assemblage of friends of all shades of political opinion; nor were the compositors and pressmen of the *Courier* office, headed by their foreman, the late Mr. Andrew Tough, the least interesting part of that procession. The body was borne to the ground on men's shoulders, and the pall-bearers were—head, Mr. C. A. Motherwell, his nephew;

foot, Mr.—now Sir James Campbell; sides, Mr. Whyte, Mr M'Laren, Mr. M'Arthur, Mr. Philip Ramsay, Captain Andrew Hamilton, Sheriff Campbell.*

MOTHERWELL's death was deeply regretted by the citizens of Glasgow generally, and with unaffected sorrow by his more immediate relatives, friends, and associates. Its suddenness invested it with a melancholy interest, and in the presence of that dread messenger whose approach no eye can detect, and whose stern impartiality makes no distinction of age, sex, or condition, it was felt that the tempest of political warfare should be stilled, and that those hollow differences which so often separate kindred spirits in life should be buried in that grave which now contained the mortal remains of a man of genius and of worth. The records of his demise which appeared in the different newspapers were creditable to their conductors, and indicated an anxious desire to do honour to his merits; and I have sincere pleasure in reproducing, after the lapse of eleven years, the handsome testimony which was at that time borne to his character by his public opponent, but private friend, Mr. Wm. Weir, then editor of the Glasgow *Argus*:—

"This accomplished gentleman died suddenly on Sunday morning. Mr. MOTHERWELL's antiquarian knowledge was extensive; and, as the bent of his mind towards the past

---

* It is painful to be obliged to state that MOTHERWELL's grave cannot be discovered without the assistance of a guide, not being marked by even a headstone and the initials W. M. This is not as it should be, and I am sure that it is only necessary to call the attention of his surviving friends to a circumstance so little creditable to all of us, to have this reproach immediately removed. The grave is situated at the north-eastern corner of the burying ground, and at the bend of the road which leads up the hill, to the right hand. It is a little triangular space covered with weeds, lying between the tombs of Mr. Wm. Sloan, on the right, and Mr. Alex. Patrick, on the left.

tinged his poetry, so his imagination lent grace and vitality to his knowledge. A small volume of lyrical poems, published some years back by Mr. MOTHERWELL, is full of tender and unobtrusive beauty. There are few pieces more touching in the whole range of Scottish poetry than his 'Jeanie Morrison.' A series of papers published in *The Day*, entitled 'Memoirs of a Paisley Bailie,' are full of grave, quiet, exquisite humour. In addition to these, we have had occasion to see fragments of a prose work of some extent, which Mr. MOTHERWELL had, we believe, almost completed for the press. It is an embodiment of the old wild legends of the Norsemen (always a favourite theme with the author), and contains passages of surpassing splendour, animated by a wayward spirit, half merriment, half pathos. Mr. MOTHERWELL was also engaged in making collections for a life of Tannahill—a work much wanted, and which, since we have lost him, we know of no other man alive able to supply. Mr. MOTHERWELL is a loss in his own peculiar circle of literature. He will be missed by his antiquarian and poetical associates. But he will be more deeply and lastingly missed in the circle of his personal friends, and of the already too much narrowed circle of his family. This hurried and inadequate tribute is paid to him by one who, decidedly opposed to him on public grounds, and placed in immediate collision with him, was yet proud to call him his friend, and laments his loss."

In personal appearance MOTHERWELL was under-sized, not exceeding, I should think, five feet five or thereby, in height; but he was vigorously and well formed, and possessed great muscular strength. His bust was that of a large manly figure, the deficiency in his stature being, as generally happens in such cases, in his limbs, which, though gracefully turned, were short. His head was large and his brow ample. His eyes, which were small and deeply-set, were surmounted by bushy eyebrows. His face was square with prominent cheek bones, and his nose wanting in symmetry. His mouth was perhaps the most unexceptionable feature of his countenance, and indicated great firmness as well as benevolence of character. His hair was of a dark brown colour, and besides being abundant in quantity, inclined to curl. In his dress he was neat and plain, and scrupulously clean. The *vignette* affixed to this volume is an excellent likeness, and is fitted to convey a faithful impression of his general appearance.

In his manners he was modest and unpretending, and in general society he spoke little. His conversational powers, in fact, were not high ; but in the company of his more intimate friends he was free and unreserved, and entered with a keen relish into the amusements of the hour. When excited, as he was apt occasionally to be when the conversation turned upon any subject in which he took an interest, he displayed much enthusiasm, and threw into his action considerable energy—but this seldom happened, and only in moments of total relaxation from all restraint. He was decidedly social in his tastes, and had nothing of the anchorite about him ; and at one period of his life he was addicted to practical joking. Some of his exploits in this way were amusing enough, but the habit was ultimately abandoned, as it threatened to lead to disagreeable consequences, and was improper in itself. He was fond of manly exercises, such as boxing, in which he took lessons from a Negro pugilist, and sword-playing, in the niceties of which he was instructed He was also a passionate admirer of the military art, and there can be no doubt that had circumstances admitted of his exhibiting his military virtues he would have made a good soldier. In 1820 he served in the Paisley Rifle corps as a serjeant, and latterly as a trooper in the regiment of Renfrewshire Yeomanry Cavalry which was commanded by the late Sir Michael Shaw Stewart. He was fond of this kind of life, and was punctual in his attendance upon the Yeomanry balls which were given in the county. It would seem, likewise, that he was a good rower, but I do not think that the ocean had many attractions for him.

In his relations as brother and friend his conduct was irreproachable. I have known few equally disinterested men, and none more upright or honourable in their dealings with others. He could not but be aware that he possessed great and peculiar powers, but he never betrayed any consciousness of this, and was utterly free from literary vanity. Of jealousy, that abiding reproach to men of letters, he had not one particle ; nor do I remember ever to have heard him utter a harsh sentence respecting any human being. His political antipathies were strong, but his personal animosities were weak ; not that he had not his likings and dislikings like other men, but that his nature was too generous to adopt, and still more to cherish, unkindly feelings towards any one. No better proof of this quality could be given than this, that many of his most intimate and best loved friends were his political antagonists, and that his premature death was regretted by none more sincerely than by those gentlemen, who knew him well and esteemed him highly. Of this fine trait of character the following letter affords a pleasing illustration. Mr. Carrick, in whose behalf it was written, was a meritorious but unsuccessful literary man,* who was an applicant for the office of editor to a Kilmarnock journal; and it will be seen from it that MOTHERWELL, though decidedly opposed to him in politics, exerted himself strenuously in his favour.

" COURIER OFFICE, GLASGOW,
" November 28, 1833.

" To MR. DAVID ROBERTSON.

"MY DEAR SIR,—Understanding that a newspaper is about to be established in Kilmarnock, and that my friend Mr. Mr. J. D. Carrick (present editor of the *Perthshire Advertiser*) has offered himself as a candidate for its editorship, I wish you would interest yourself on his behalf among those who may have the appointment in their hands.

"Unfortunately, I neither know the proprietors of the projected journal, nor any person of influence in Kilmarnock having a likelihood of being connected with it, otherwise I should have preferred addressing them personally on this subject, in place of through you. Be this as it may, I would fain trust that my disinterested and unsolicited opinion of the talents and literary attainments of Mr. Carrick, in whatever shape laid before the proprietors, may be of some use to a most deserving individual in his canvass.

"With Mr. Carrick and with his writings, both as a literary character, and as the conductor of a very intelligent weekly paper, I have been long familiar; and to the taste, tact, judgment, knowledge, and research displayed in these writings, I can bear the most unqualified testimony. Mr. Carrick and I, as you well know, have the misfortune to be opposed to each other in political sentiments, but that circumstance detracts nothing from his merits in my eyes. Perhaps, in the present case, it may even advance his interest; for I am given to understand, that the Kilmarnock

---

* Author of the Life of Sir William Wallace, which was written for *Constable's Miscellany* in 1825.

paper is to be conducted on what are called Liberal or Reform principles, and to these, in their popular acceptation, I have never, either in my public or private capacity, concealed my most rooted hostility. If I am well informed, then, as to the political views entertained by the proprietors of the contemplated journal, my decided conviction is, that they never could light upon a more energetic and uncompromising, and, at the same time, prudent, sagacious, and enlightened advocate of their principles, than they will find in the person of Mr. Carrick.

"In the management of a paper he has had large experience: his taste in selection is excellent; and, in getting up some of those witty and good-humoured paragraphs which conduce so much to the interest of the columns of a provincial paper, and, in consequence, extends its circulation, I scarcely know his equal. My friend, Macdiarmid, of the *Dumfries Courier*, has, in his own peculiar walk, a formidable rival in Mr. Carrick. As to his eminent qualifications in a higher point of view, his historical works and political essays afford the best of all evidence; but as these, in all probability, will be submitted to the committee entrusted with the nomination of editor, I need not further enlarge on them, for sure I am, that the committee will think with me, that they every way support Mr. Carrick's claims to extensive literary and political acquirements, and furnish the best of all guarantees for the creditable discharge of his duties as an editor.

"My dear Sir, in conclusion, I have only again to beg, that you will use your best influence to back the feeble and inadequate testimony I have borne to the abilities of a common friend—of one who, in every relation of life, has always shown himself a most estimable character.

"Yours faithfully,
"W. MOTHERWELL."

It would be easy to multiply instances of this kind were I not afraid of trespassing upon the indulgence of the reader, for his correspondence abounds in them; but I cannot pass over in silence his intimacy with R. A. Smith, a man to whom he was sincerely attached, and with whom till his death he cultivated a friendship which was unbroken by even a passing cloud.

Smith was born at Reading, in Berkshire, in 1779. His father was a native of West Calder, in Lanarkshire, and his mother an Englishwoman of respectable connections. In the year 1773, his father emigrated to England in consequence of the dulness of the silk-weaving trade, but returned to Paisley in 1800 after an absence of seventeen years, bringing with him his son, whom he intended to educate to the loom. This, however, was found to be impossible. Nature had furnished the lad with the most delicate musical sensibilities, and after an ineffectual struggle with the ruling passion, music became the business of his life. He attained to considerable provincial distinction, and composed original music for the following songs of the poet Tannahill, whose intimate friend he was:—Jessie the Flower o' Dunblane—The Lass of Arranteenie—The Harper of Mull—Langsyne beside the Woodland Burn—Our Bonnie Scots Lads—Despairing Mary—Wi' waefu' heart and sorrowin' ee—The Maniac's Song—Poor Tom's Farewell—The Soldier's Widow—and, We'll Meet beside the Dusky Glen.

In 1823 he removed to Edinburgh at the solicitation of the late Rev. Dr. Andrew Thomson, where he led the choir of St. George's Church, of which Dr. Thomson was the incumbent, and where he died in January, 1829. Between him and MOTHERWELL there existed a warm friendship arising no doubt from a congeniality of tastes on many points; but, on the part of the latter, strengthened by a sincere respect for the virtues as well as the genius of the man. Smith had to contend through life not only with narrow means and domestic discomfort, but against the pressure of a constitutional melancholy which occasionally impaired the vigour of his fine faculties. His real griefs—of which he had a full share, were, therefore, increased by some that were imaginary, and he was obviously accustomed not only to lean upon the stronger mind of his friend in his moments of depression, but to seek for sympathy in his distress, which, it is needless to add, was never refused. In November, 1826, Smith thus writes to him :—

"I would have written you long ere this, but have been prevented by an amount of domestic distress sufficient to drive all romance out of the mind ; and you must be aware that without a considerable portion of that delightful commodity no good music can be engendered. To be serious, my dear friend, two of my family, my eldest daughter and youngest son, are at this moment lying dangerously ill of the typhus fever. I hope that I may escape the contagion, but I have sometimes rather melancholy forebodings ; and in the midst of all this, I am obliged to sing professionally every day, and mask my face with smiles to cover the throbbings of a seared and lonely heart."

To this sad effusion MOTHERWELL returned the following characteristic reply :—

"Your domestic afflictions deeply grieve me. I trust by this time, however, that your children have mended, and that you are no sufferer by their malady. Kennedy and I have been shedding tears over your calamities, and praying to Heaven that you may have strength of spirits to bear up under such severe dispensations. We both, albeit we have no family afflictions to mourn over, have yet much to irritate and vex us—much, much indeed, to sour the temper and sadden the countenance—but these things must be borne with patiently. It is folly of the worst description to let thought kill us before our time. * * * I hope to hear from you soon, and to learn that you are in better spirits, and that the causes which have depressed them are happily removed. Kennedy joins me in warm and sincere prayers that this may speedily be the case."

MOTHERWELL was decidedly superstitious; that is, he had an absolute and unqualified belief in the reality of those spectral illusions which, under whatever name designated, have played so important a part in the history of human credulity from the dawn of time downwards Upon this point he was tenacious, and as he fortified himself by what he supposed to be facts, he was wont to wax warm in defence of his Rosicrucian theory when it chanced to be assailed. It is no reproach to his memory to say that his logic upon such a subject was necessarily defective, and it would be altogether unjust to condemn as a weakness his participation in an infirmity which has so often attached itself to the highest created intelligences.

His habits of poetical composition were, I suspect, slow and even laborious, and there is ample evidence in his manuscripts to show that the divine *œstrum* was not always at command when most needed. That he prepared his productions with great care before he committed them to the press, or even inserted them in any of his common-place books, is certain; and the history of many of his freest compositions, could it be obtained, would demonstrate that he never forgot the Horatian precept, but wisely remembered that *nescit vox missa reverti.* Of "Jeanie Morrison," for example, there exist at least two rough draughts, if not more, in which this process of elaboration is very distinct, and out of which the poem as it now stands was wrought. There are, of course, different versions of particular stanzas, but the leading ideas and images are the same in all; and as he was thirty-four years of age when he published the ballad in its present form, we thus see that this single production was, in a certain sense, the work of a life.*

In his habits of study he was necessarily desultory. No one who is engaged in the active business of the world can be otherwise; but except in that particular and somewhat narrow department of literature for which he had contracted so strong a partiality in early life, it cannot be said of MOTHERWELL that he was a "well-read" man. With physical science he was but slightly acquainted, and he had neglected general history, including even that of his own country, to an extraordinary degree. From some peculiarity of temperament which is not easily explained he preferred such writers as Holinshed and Stowe to Hume and Hallam; and the only modern historical work of any note that I ever recollect to have heard him speak of, was Sharon Turner's History of the Anglo-Saxons. He had likewise a strong distaste to what is commonly called metaphysics, and particularly for the writers of the Scotch school, of whom he sometimes spoke in terms of greater confidence than his acquaintance with their works entitled him to do; but he professed a deep reverence for Coleridge, whose "Friend" he considered a master-piece of philosophy. I do not recollect of ever having heard him even allude to

---

* I would not be understood as disputing the fact that he sketched the outline of this poem at 14, because I see no just reason to doubt it; but the earliest copy now existing was written when he was 18, or perhaps 20.

Burke, and for Sir James Mackintosh he had conceived an unreasonable dislike. These carelessnesses and prejudices are to be regretted, since they tended to abridge his knowledge and to impair his usefulness, but they are probably to be referred to the circumstances in which he was placed rather than to any defect in his mental constitution. A more liberal intercourse with mankind would have disabused him of many of those prepossessions which he had hastily adopted and had little temptation to abandon, and his better nature would have done the rest.

In his personal tastes and feelings he was essentially and ardently Scottish. The language and literature of his native country he had studied with care and success, and to her legendary poetry and metrical traditions he attached a high value. The land was also beautiful in his eyes, and no wandering minstrel of ancient times could have been impressed with a loftier sense of the valour of the men or the virtue of the women who dwelt within its limits. That he was a devout admirer of external nature his poems amply testify. The vast solitude of the universe and the sublime depths of space filled his soul with a holy awe; and whether he looked upon the heavens above with their countless myriads of stars, or upon the earth beneath with its garment of green, and its hills, and valleys, and running streams, his mind was equally impressed with the majesty and power of that great Being who made and sustains all things.

> O God! this is an holy hour:—
>   Thy breath is o'er the land:
> I feel it in each little flower
>   Around me where I stand.
> In all the moonshine scattered fair,
> Above, below me, everywhere—

> In every dew-bead glistening sheen,
> In every leaf and blade of green—
> And in this silence grand and deep,
> Wherein thy blessed creatures sleep.*

An elaborate analysis of MOTHERWELL's character as a poet would not be compatible with the objects and limits of this slight sketch; but it is fortunately rendered unnecessary by the criticism of Professor Wilson, which appeared in *Blackwood's Magazine* for April, 1833.

"All his perceptions are clear, for all his senses are sound; he has fine and strong sensibilities, and a powerful intellect. He has been led by the natural bent of his genius to the old haunts of inspiration—the woods and glens of his native country—and his ears delight to drink the music of her old songs. Many a beautiful ballad has blended its pensive and plaintive pathos with his day-dreams, and while reading some of his happiest effusions, we feel—

> " The ancient spirit is not dead,—
> Old times, we say, are breathing there."

"His style is simple, but in his tenderest movements, masculine; he strikes a few bold knocks at the door of the heart, which is instantly opened by the master or mistress of the house, or by son or daughter, and the welcome visitor at once becomes one of the family."†

This is generous praise, but not more generous than just, and it places the whole case before us by a few vivid strokes. It may be remarked, however, that the field which he chose for the exercise of the higher efforts of his genius was unappropriated by any name of marked celebrity, and that there was both originality and boldness in the thought that he

---

* Midnight and Moonshine.
† Blackwood's Magazine, Vol. xxxiii. p. 670.

could win his way to fame through apparently so unpromising a channel as the Scandinavian mythology, and by the adaptation to modern verse of the stern thoughts and sanguinary aspirations of the northern Scalds. It is obvious that in so daring an enterprise anything short of entire success would have been fatal to the reputation of its author, and that upon a theme, at once so novel and so vast, mediocrity would not have been tolerated ; and it has always appeared to me, that to have triumphed so completely over the latent prejudices of society, and to have extorted the reluctant praise of the critical world, was, in MOTHERWELL'S circumstances, the strongest proof he could give of the vigour and elasticity of his powers. Such men as Wordsworth, Southey, and Coleridge could afford some abatement from that full harvest of renown which they had accumulated ; but to a person in MOTHERWELL'S position the case was widely different, and the punishment of failure would have been proportioned in its severity to the alleged presumption of the attempt. He did not fail, however, nor—as the result showed—was his confidence in himself over-rated ; and his metrical imitations of the Sagas are not only distinguished by an exact fidelity of tone and sentiment, but are considered by competent judges to be fine heroic ballads, which display energetic powers of description united to a high dramatic faculty. Had Gray followed out his original intention, and given to the world that "History of Poetry" of which he had at one time meditated the composition, his successor would have had to encounter a much more formidable competition than that which actually awaited him ; but he, as is well known, abandoned the design, and except "The Fatal Sisters" and the "Descent of Odin," I cannot call to mind any other purely English poems constructed upon a northern basis. It may argue an undue partiality, but I prefer "The Battle Flag of Sigurd" to either of Gray's odes.*

That the manners of the Valhalla and the exploits of the Vikingr had made a lasting impression upon MOTHERWELL'S imagination we have abundant proof in the first three poems of this volume; and my own impression is, that in future times his fame will rest in a great measure on these splendid specimens of warlike invocation. As he comes nearer to

---

* Had the intellect of Collins preserved its balance the Norse legends would have afforded an inexhaustible supply of those materials in which his genius most delighted. "He loved fairies, genii, giants, and monsters; he delighted to rove through the meanders of enchantment, to gaze on the magnificence of golden palaces, to repose by the waterfalls of Elysian gardens."—(Johnson). His ode on "The Passions" shows how familiar his mind was with those terrible images in which we naturally, as it were, involve the harsher emotions of the soul; and it is probable, from the extent and variety of his attainments, and his allusion in the ode on the popular superstitions of the Highlands of Scotland, inscribed to Mr. Home, to those—

"Old Runic bards . . . . .
With uncouth lyres, in many colour'd vest,"

that he was not unacquainted with the mythical treasures of the Sagas. There is nothing finer or more vigorous in the language than his description of "Revenge":—

"He threw his blood-stained sword in thunder down,
    And, with a withering look,
The war-denouncing trumpet took,
And blew a blast so loud and dread,
Were ne'er prophetic sound so full of woe.
    And ever and anon he beat
    The doubling drum with furious heat;
And though, sometimes, each dreary pause between,
    Dejected Pity at his side
    Her soul-subduing voice applied,
Yet still he kept his wild unaltered mien,
While each strained ball of sight seem'd bursting from his head."

ordinary life his poetical individuality insensibly disappears, and the "uncouth lyre" of the "Runic bard" is exchanged for the softer harp of the modern minstrel. The old Scottish ballad might be as successfully imitated, perhaps, by men of far inferior capacity, and exquisite as some of his lyrical compositions are, they might likewise be approached, if not excelled; but for the conception and execution of the "Battle Flag of Sigurd," "The Wooing Song of Jarl Egill Skallagrim," and the "Sword Chant of Thorstein Raudi," a special inspiration and peculiar powers were required—and I will venture to predict that they will survive the changes of time and the caprices of fashion.

One of his most prominent defects as a lyrical poet is, in my opinion, the assumption—for it was no more—of a morbid tone of feeling respecting the world and its ways. Doubtless—

> " pictoribus atque poetis
> Quidlibet audendi semper fuit æqua potestas :"

but there is a natural limit to even this proverbial licence, and a perpetual dirge about broken vows, slighted love, and human selfishness, is apt to engender the idea that the man who thus indulges in habitual lamentation over his own misfortunes, must have been less discriminating in his friendships, or less deserving of regard, than we could wish him to have been. But this was not the case with WILLIAM MOTHERWELL. Few men have enjoyed, and few men have more entirely merited, the strong and steady attachment of those with whom they associated ; and if life brought to him its share of sorrow and anxiety it likewise afforded many and solid compensations for his sufferings, of which, I have not a doubt, he was fully sensible, and for which, I have as little doubt, he was truly thankful. I would not have noticed this peculiarity had it not communicated to some of his effusions an air of harsh exaggeration which was really foreign to his modest and uncomplaining nature, and did it not tend to create the belief that my late friend, with all his gifts, was deficient in that humility of mind which should characterise a wise and a good man. This was not so, and when passages—I regret to say that they are too numerous—do occur which might encourage this notion, let me hope that they will not be construed to his prejudice, but that they may be looked upon as mere poetical embellishments.

For the occasional defects which may be discovered in the mechanical structure of his verse no very satisfactory explanation can be offered. He had made poetry and its laws the business of his life, yet imperfect lines and prosaic expressions do occur more frequently than could be desired to mar the harmony of some of his best pieces, and, in certain cases, even to impair their sense. The only account that I can give of this infirmity is, that his ear wanted rhythmical accuracy, and that from some peculiarity of his physical organisation he was unable to appreciate the more delicate modulations of sound. He was eminently unmusical —not that he disliked music, far from it—but that his love of melody did not counterbalance his unacquaintance with the rules of harmony, of breaches of which he was often, though unintentionally, guilty.

Upon the whole, his place as a minor poet is a distinguished one. He has undoubtedly enriched the language with many noble specimens of manly song; and when it is remembered that he prosecuted his poetical studies in silence and retirement, animated alone by the love of his art, and sustained through many long years of trial and of toil by the distant gleam of posthumous fame, it will not be disputed that his motives to action were exalted, and his exertions in the cause of human improvement disinterested.

Ossa quieta, precor, tuta requiescite in urna ;
Et sit humus cineri non onerosa tuo.

J. M‘C.

GLASGOW, DEC. 23, 1846.

POEMS.

I.

THE BATTLE-FLAG OF SIGURD.

I.

THE eagle hearts of all the North
Have left their stormy strand;
The warriors of the world are forth
To choose another land!
Again, their long keels sheer the wave,
Their broad sheets court the breeze;
Again, the reckless and the brave,
Ride lords of weltering seas.
Nor swifter from the well-bent bow
Can feathered shaft be sped,
Than o'er the ocean's flood of snow
Their snoring galleys tread.
Then lift the can to bearded lip,
And smite each sounding shield,
Wassaile! to every darked-ribbed ship,
To every battle-field!
So proudly the Skalds raise their voices of triumph,
As the Northmen ride over the broad-bosom'd billow.

II.

Aloft, Sigurdir's battle-flag
Streams onward to the land,
Well may the taint of slaughter lag
On yonder glorious strand.
The waters of the mighty deep,
The wild birds of the sky,
Hear it like vengeance shoreward sweep,
Where moody men must die.
The waves wax wroth beneath our keel—
The clouds above us lower,
They know the battle sign, and feel
All its resistless power!
Who now uprears Sigurdir's flag,
Nor shuns an early tomb?
Who shoreward through the swelling surge,
Shall bear the scroll of doom?
So shout the Skalds as the long ships are nearing
The low-lying shores of a beautiful land.

III.

Silent the Self-devoted stood
Beside the massive tree;
His image mirror'd in the flood
Was terrible to see!
As leaning on his gleaming axe,
And gazing on the wave,
His fearless soul was churning up,
The death-rune of the brave.
Upheaving then his giant form
Upon the brown bark's prow,
And tossing back the yellow storm
Of hair from his broad brow;
The lips of song burst open, and
The words of fire rushed out,
And thundering through that martial crew
Pealed Harald's battle shout;—

It is Harald the dauntless that lifteth his great voice,
As the Northmen roll on with the Doom-written banner.

IV.

"I bear Sigurdir's battle-flag
  Through sunshine or through gloom;
Through swelling surge on bloody strand
  I plant the scroll of doom!
On Scandia's lonest, bleakest waste,
  Beneath a starless sky,
The shadowy Three like meteors passed,
  And bade young Harald die;—
They sang the war-deeds of his sires,
  And pointed to their tomb;
They told him that this glory-flag
  Was his by right of doom.
Since then, where hath young Harald been,
  But where Jarl's son should be?
'Mid war and waves—the combat keen
  That raged on land or sea!"
So sings the fierce Harald, the thirster for glory,
As his hand bears aloft the dark death-laden banner.

V.

"Mine own death's in this clenched hand!
  I know the noble trust;
These limbs must rot on yonder strand—
  These lips must lick its dust,
But shall this dusky standard quail
  In the red slaughter day;
Or shall this heart its purpose fail—
  This arm forget to slay?
I trample down such idle doubt;
  Harald's high blood hath sprung
From sires whose hands in martial bout
  Hath ne'er belied their tongue;—

  Nor keener from their castled rock
   Rush eagles on their prey,
  Than, panting for the battle-shock,
   Young Harald leads the way."
It is thus that tall Harald, in terrible beauty,
Pours forth his big soul to the joyaunce of heroes.

VI.

  " The ship-borne warriors of the North,
   The sons of Woden's race,
  To battle as to feast go forth,
   With stern, and changeless face ;
  And I, the last of a great line—
   The Self-devoted, long
  To lift on high the Runic sign
   Which gives my name to song.
  In battle-field young Harald falls
   Amid a slaughtered foe,
  But backward never bears this flag,
   While streams to ocean flow ;
  On, on above the crowded dead
   This Runic scroll shall flare,
  And round it shall the lightnings spread,*
   From swords that never spare."
So rush the hero-words from the Death-doomed one,
While Skalds harp aloud the renown of his fathers.

VII.

  " Flag ! from your folds, and fiercely wake
   War-music on the wind,
  Lest tenderest thoughts should rise to shake
   The sternness of my mind ;
  Brynhilda, maiden meek and fair,
   Pale watcher by the sea,

---

*And round it shall PALE lightnings spread.—*MS. copy.*

I hear thy wailings on the air,
Thy heart's dirge sung for me ;—
In vain thy milk-white hands are wrung
Above the salt sea foam ;
The wave that bears me from thy bower,
Shall never bear me home ;
Brynhilda ! seek another love,
But ne'er wed one like me,
Who death foredoomed from above
Joys in his destiny."
Thus mourned young Harald as he thought on Brynhilda,
While his eyes filled with tears which glittered, but fell not.

VIII.

" On sweeps Sigurdir's battle-flag,
The scourge of far from shore ;
It dashes through the seething foam,
But I return no more !
Wedded unto a fatal bride—
Boune for a bloody bed—
And battling for her, side by side,
Young Harald's doom is sped !
In starkest fight, where kemp on kemp,
Reel headlong to the grave,
There Harald's axe shall ponderous ring,
There Sigurd's flag shall wave ;—
Yes, underneath this standard tall,
Beside this fateful scroll,
Down shall the tower-like prison fall
Of Harald's haughty soul."
So sings the Death-seeker, while nearer and nearer
The fleet of the Northmen bears down to the shore.

IX.

" Green lie those thickly-timbered shores
Fair sloping to the sea :

>   They're cumbered with the harvest stores
>   That wave but for the free :
>   Our sickle is the gleaming sword,
>   Our garner the broad shield
>   Let peasants sow, but still he's lord
>   Who's master of the field ;
>   Let them come on, the bastard-born,
>   Each soil-stain'd churle !—alack !
>   What gain they but a splitten skull,
>   A sod for their base back ?
>   They sow for us these goodly lands,
>   We reap them in our might,
>   Scorning all title but the brands
>   That triumph in the fight !"

It was thus the land-winners of old gained their glory,
And grey stones voiced their praise in the bays of far isles.

X.

>   " The rivers of yon island low,
>   Glance redly in the sun,
>   But ruddier still they're doomed to glow,
>   And deeper shall they run ;
>   The torrent of proud life shall swell
>   Each river to the brim,
>   And in that spate of blood, how well
>   The headless corpse will swim !
>   The smoke of many a shepherd's cot
>   Curls from each peopled glen ;
>   And, hark ! the song of maidens mild,
>   The shout of joyous men !
>   But one may hew the oaken tree,
>   The other shape the shroud ;
>   As the LANDEYDA o'er the sea
>   Sweeps like a tempest cloud :"—

So shouteth fierce Harald—so echo the Northmen,
As shoreward their ships like mad steeds are careering.

XI.

"Sigurdir's battle-flag is spread
 Abroad to the blue sky,
And spectral visions of the dead
 Are trooping grimly by;
The spirit heralds rush before
 Harald's destroying brand,
They hover o'er yon fated shore
 And death-devoted band.
Marshall, stout Jarls, your battle fast!
 And fire each beacon height,
Our galleys anchor in the sound,
 Our banner heaves in sight!
And through the surge and arrowy shower
 That rains on this broad shield,
Harald uplifts the sign of power
 Which rules the battle-field!"
So cries the Death-doomed on the red strand of slaughter
While the helmets of heroes like anvils are ringing.

XII.

On rolled the Northmen's war, above
 The Raven Standard flew,
Nor tide nor tempest ever strove
 With vengeance half so true.
'Tis Harald—'tis the Sire-bereaved—
 Who goads the dread career,
And high amid the flashing storm
 The flag of Doom doth rear.
"On, on," the tall Death-seeker cries,
"These earth-worms soil our heel,
 Their spear-points crasp like crisping ice
On ribs of stubborn steel!"
Hurra! hurra! their whirlwinds sweep,
 And Harald's fate is sped;

    Bear on the flag—he goes to sleep
    With the life-scorning dead.
Thus fell the young Harald, as of old fell his sires,
And the bright hall of heroes bade hail to his spirit.

II.

THE WOOING SONG OF JARL EGILL SKALLAGRIM.

    BRIGHT maiden of Orkney,
    Star of the blue sea!
    I've swept o'er the waters
    To gaze upon thee;
    I've left spoil and slaughter,
    I've left a far strand,
    To sing how I love thee,
    To kiss thy small hand!
    Fair Daughter of Einar,
    Golden-haired maid!
    The lord of yon brown bark,
    And lord of this blade;
    The joy of the ocean—
    Of warfare and wind,
    Hath boune him to woo thee,
    And thou must be kind.
So stoutly Jarl Egill wooed Torf Einar's daughter.

    In Jutland—in Iceland
    On Neustria's shore,
    Where'er the dark billow
    My gallant bark bore,
    Songs spoke of thy beauty,
    Harps sounded thy praise,
    And my heart loved thee long ere
    It thrilled in thy gaze;

Ay, Daughter of Einar,
Right tall may'st thou stand,
It is a Vikingir
Who kisses thy hand;
It is a Vikingir
That bends his proud knee,
And swears by Great Freya,
His bride thou must be!
So Jarl Egill swore when his great heart was fullest.

Thy white arms are locked in
Broad bracelets of gold;
Thy girdle-stead's gleaming
With treasures untold:
The circlet that binds up
Thy long yellow hair,
Is starred thick with jewels,
That bright are and rare;
But gifts yet more princely
Jarl Egill bestows,
For girdle, his great arm
Around thee he throws;
The bark of a sea-king
For palace, gives he,
While mad waves and winds shall
Thy true subjects be.
So richly Jarl Egill endowed his bright bride.

Nay, frown not, nor shrink thus,
Nor toss so thy head,
'Tis a Vikingir asks thee,
Land-maiden, to wed!
He skills not to woo thee,
In trembling and fear,
Though lords of the land may
Thus troop with the deer.

The cradle he rock'd in
So sound and so long,
Hath framed him a heart
And a hand that are strong :
He comes then as Jarl should,
Sword belted to side,
To win thee and wear thee
With glory and pride.
So sternly Jarl Egill wooed, and smote his long brand.

Thy father, thy brethren,
Thy kin keep from me,
The maiden I've sworn shall
Be Queen of the sea !
A truce with that folly—
Yon sea-strand can show
If this eye missed its aim,
Or this arm failed its blow :
I had not well taken
Three strides on this land
Ere a Jarl and his six sons
In death bit the sand.
Nay, weep not, pale maid, though
In battle should fall
The kemps who would keep thy
Bridegroom from the hall.
So carped Jarl Egill and kissed the bright weeper.

Through shadows and horrors,
In worlds underground,
Through sounds that appal
And through sights that confound,
I sought the Weird women
Within their dark cell,
And made them surrender
Futurity's spell ;

I made them rune over
The dim scroll so free,*
And mutter how Fate sped
With lovers like me.
Yes, maiden, I forced them
To read forth my doom,
To say how I should fare
As jolly bridegroom.
So Jarl Egill's love dared the world of grim shadows.

They waxed and they waned,
They passed to and fro,
While lurid fires gleamed o'er
Their faces of snow;
Their stony eyes moveless,
Did glare on me long,
Then sullen they chanted:
"The Sword and the Song
Prevail with the gentle,
Sore chasten the rude,
And sway to their purpose
Each evil-shaped mood!"
Fair Daughter of Einar,
I've sung the dark lay
That the Weird sisters runed, and
Which thou must obey.
So fondly Jarl Egill loved Einar's proud daughter.

The curl of that proud lip,
The flash of that eye,
The swell of that bosom,
So full and so high,
Like foam of sea-billow,
Thy white bosom shows,

---

* The dim scroll TO ME.—*MS. copy.*

Like flash of red levin
Thine eagle eye glows :
Ha ! firmly and boldly,
So stately and free,
Thy foot treads this chamber,
As bark rides the sea :
This likes me—this likes me,
Stout maiden of mould,
Thou wooest to purpose ;
Bold hearts love the bold.
So shouted Jarl Egill, and clutched the proud maiden.

Away and away then,
I have thy small hand ;
Joy with me—our tall bark
Now bears toward the strand ;
I call it The Raven,
The wing of black night,
That shadows forth ruin
O'er islands of light :
Once more on its long deck,
Behind us the gale,
Thou shalt see how before it
Great kingdoms do quail ;
Thou shalt see then how truly,
My noble-souled maid,
The ransom of kings can
Be won by this blade.
So bravely Jarl Egill did soothe the pale trembler.

Ay, gaze on its large hilt,
One wedge of red gold ;
But doat on its blade, gilt
With blood of the bold.
The hilt is right seemly,
But nobler the blade,

   That swart Velint's hammer
   With cunning spells made ;
   I call it the Adder,
   Death lurks in its bite,
   Through bone and proof-harness
   It scatters pale light.
   Fair Daughter of Einar,
   Deem high of the fate
   That makes thee, like this blade
   Proud Egill's loved mate !
So Jarl Egill bore off Torf Einar's bright daughter.

III.

THE SWORD CHANT OF THORSTEIN RAUDI.

  'Tis not the grey hawk's flight
   O'er mountain and mere ;
  'Tis not the fleet hound's course
   Tracking the deer ;
  'Tis not the light hoof print
   Of black steed or grey,
  Though sweltering it gallop
   A long summer's day,
  Which mete forth the Lordships
   I challenge as mine ;
  Ha ! ha ! 'tis the good brand
  I clutch in my strong hand,
  That can their broad marches
   And numbers define.
  LAND GIVER ! I kiss thee.

  Dull builders of houses,
   Base tillers of earth,
  Gaping, ask me what lordships
   I owned at my birth ;

But the pale fools wax mute
   When I point with my sword
East, west, north, and south,
   Shouting, "There am I Lord!"
Wold and waste, town and tower,
   Hill, valley, and stream,
Trembling, bow to my sway
In the fierce battle fray,
When the star that rules Fate, is
   This falchion's red gleam.
MIGHTY GIVER! I kiss thee.

I've heard great harps sounding,
   In brave bower and hall,
I've drank the sweet music
   That bright lips let fall,
I've hunted in greenwood,
   And heard small birds sing;
But away with this idle
   And cold jargoning;
The music I love, is
   The shout of the brave,
The yell of the dying,
The scream of the flying,
When this arm weilds Death's sickle,
   And garners the grave.
JOY GIVER! I kiss thee.

Far isles of the ocean
   Thy lightning have known,
And wide o'er the main land
   Thy horrors have shone.
Great sword of my father,
   Stern joy of his hand,
Thou hast carved his name deep on
   The stranger's red strand,

And won him the glory
   Of undying song.
Keen cleaver of gay crests,
Sharp piercer of broad breasts,
Grim slayer of heroes,
   And scourge of the strong.
FAME GIVER! I kiss thee.

In a love more abiding
   Than that the heart knows,
For maiden more lovely
   Than summer's first rose,
My heart's knit to thine,
   And lives but for thee;
In dreamings of gladness,
   Thou'rt dancing with me,
Brave measures of madness
   In some battle-field,
Where armour is ringing,
And noble blood springing,
And cloven, yawn hemlet,
   Stout hauberk and shield.
DEATH GIVER! I kiss thee.

The smile of a maiden's eye
   Soon may depart;
And light is the faith of
   Fair woman's heart;
Changeful as light clouds,
   And wayward as wind,
Be the passions that govern
   Weak woman's mind.
But thy metal's as true
   As its polish is bright;
When ills wax in number,
Thy love will not slumber,

But starlike, burns fiercer,
　　The darker the night.
Heart Gladdener ! I kiss thee.

My kindred have perished
　　By war or by wave—
Now, childless and sireless,
　　I long for the grave.
When the path of our glory
　　Is shadowed in death,
With me thou wilt slumber
　　Below the brown heath ;
Thou wilt rest on my bosom,
　　And with it decay—
While harps shall be ringing,
And Scalds shall be singing
The deeds we have done in
　　Our old fearless day.
Song Giver ! I kiss thee.

IV.

JEANIE MORRISON.

I'VE wandered east, I've wandered west,
   Through mony a weary way ;
But never, never can forget
   The luve o' life's young day !
The fire that's blawn on Beltane e'en,
   May weel be black gin Yule ;
But blacker fa' awaits the heart
   Where first fond luve grows cule.

O dear, dear Jeanie Morrison,
   The thochts o' bygane years
Still fling their shadows ower my path,
   And blind my een wi' tears :
They blind my een wi' saut, saut tears,
   And sair and sick I pine,
As memory idly summons up
   The blithe blinks o' langsyne.

'Twas then we luvit ilk ither weel,
   'Twas then we twa did part ;
Sweet time—sad time ! twa bairns at scule,
   Twa bairns, and but ae heart !
'Twas then we sat on ae laigh bink,
   To leir ilk ither lear ;
And tones, and looks, and smiles were shed,
   Remembered evermair.

I wonder, Jeanie, aften yet,
   When sitting on that bink,
Cheek touchin' cheek, loof lock'd in loof,
   What our wee heads could think ?

When baith bent doun ower ae braid page,
   Wi' ae buik on our knee,
Thy lips were on thy lesson, but
   My lesson was in thee.

Oh, mind ye how we hung our heads,
   How cheeks brent red wi' shame,
Whene'er the scule-weans laughin' said,
   We cleek'd thegither hame?
And mind ye o' the Saturdays,
   (The scule then skail't at noon,)
When we ran aff to speel the braes—
   The broomy braes o' June?

My head rins round and round about,
   My heart flows like a sea,
As ane by ane the thochts rush back
   O' scule-time and o' thee.
Oh, mornin' life! oh, mornin' luve!
   Oh lichtsome days and lang,
When hinnied hopes around our hearts
   Like simmer blossoms sprang!

O mind ye, luve, how aft we left
   The deavin' dinsome toun,
To wander by the green burnside,
   And hear its waters croon?
The simmer leaves hung ower our heads,
   The flowers burst round our feet,
And in the gloamin o' the wood,
   The throssil whusslit sweet;

The throssil whusslit in the wood,
   The burn sang to the trees,
And we with Nature's heart in tune,
   Concerted harmonies;

And on the knowe abune the burn,
   For hours thegither sat
In the silentness o' joy, till baith
   Wi' very gladness grat.

Aye, aye, dear Jeanie Morrison,
   Tears trinkled doun your cheek,
Like dew-beads on a rose, yet nane
   Had ony power to speak !
That was a time, a blessed time,
   When hearts were fresh and young,
When freely gushed all feelings forth,
   Unsyllabled—unsung !

I marvel, Jeanie Morrison,
   Gin I hae been to thee
As closely twined wi' earliest thochts,
   As ye hae been to me ?
Oh ! tell me gin their music fills
   Thine ear as it does mine ;
Oh ! say gin e'er your heart grows grit
   Wi' dreamings o' langsyne ?

I've wandered east, I've wandered west,
   I've borne a weary lot ;
But in my wanderings, far or near,
   Ye never were forgot.
The fount that first burst frae this heart,
   Still travels on its way ;
And channels deeper as it rins,
   The luve o' life's young day.

O dear, dear Jeanie Morrison,
   Since we were sindered young,
I've never seen your face, nor heard
   The music o' your tongue ;

But I could hug all wretchedness,
   And happy could I die,
Did I but ken your heart still dreamed
   O' bygane days and me !

---

v.

MY HEID IS LIKE TO REND, WILLIE.

My heid is like to rend, Willie,
   My heart is like to break—
I'm wearin' aff my feet, Willie,
   I'm dyin' for your sake !
Oh lay your cheek to mine, Willie,
   Your hand on my briest-bane—
Oh say ye'll think on me, Willie,
   When I am deid and gane !

It's vain to comfort me, Willie,
   Sair grief maun hae its will—
But let me rest upon your briest,
   To sab and greet my fill.
Let me sit on your knee, Willie,
   Let me shed by your hair,
And look into the face, Willie,
   I never sall see mair !

I'm sittin' on your knee, Willie,
   For the last time in my life—
A puir heart-broken thing, Willie,
   A mither, yet nae wife.
Ay, press your hand upon my heart,
   And press it mair and mair—
Or it will burst the silken twine
   Sae strang is its despair !

MY HEID IS LIKE TO REND, WILLIE.

Oh wae's me for the hour, Willie,
    When we thegither met—
Oh wae's me for the time, Willie,
    That our first tryst was set !
Oh wae's me for the loanin' green
    Where we were wont to gae—
And wae's me for the destinie,
    That gart me love thee sae!

Oh ! dinna mind my words, Willie,
    I downa seek to blame—
But oh ! it's hard to live, Willie,
    And dree a warld's shame !
Het tears are hailin' ower your cheek,
    And hailin' ower your chin ;
Why weep ye sae for worthlessness,
    For sorrow and for sin ?

I'm weary o' this warld, Willie,
    And sick wi' a' I see—
I canna live as I hae lived,
    Or be as I should be.
But fauld unto your heart, Willie,
    The heart that still is thine—
And kiss ance mair the white, white cheek,
    Ye said was red langsyne.

A stoun' gaes through my heid, Willie,
    A sair stoun' through my heart—
Oh ! haud me up and let me kiss
    Thy brow ere we twa pairt.
Anither, and anither yet !—
    How fast my life-strings break !
Fareweel! fareweel! through yon kirk-yaird
    Step lichtly for my sake !

The lav'rock in the lift, Willie,
    That lilts far ower our heid,
Will sing the morn as merrilie
    Abune the clay-cauld deid;
And this green turf we're sittin' on,
    Wi' dew-draps' shimmerin' sheen,
Will hap the heart that luvit thee
    As warld has seldom seen.

But oh! remember me, Willie,
    On land where'er ye be—
And oh! think on the leal, leal heart,
    That ne'er luvit ane but thee!
And oh! think on the cauld, cauld mools,
    That file my yellow hair—
That kiss the cheek, and kiss the chin,
    Ye never sall kiss mair!

VI.

THE MADMAN'S LOVE.

Ho! Flesh and Blood! sweet Flesh and Blood
    As ever strode on earth!
Welcome to Water and to Wood—
    To all a Madman's mirth.
This tree is mine, this leafless tree
    That's writhen o'er the linn;
The stream is mine that fitfully
    Pours forth its sullen din.
Their lord am I; and still my dream
Is of this Tree—is of that Stream.

The Tree, the Stream—a deadly Twain!
    They will not live apart;
The one rolls thundering through my brain,
    The other smites my heart:

Ay, this same leafless fire-scathed tree,
   That groweth by the rock,
Shakes its old sapless arms at me,
   And would my madness mock!
The slaves are saucy—well they know
Good service did they long ago.

I've lived two lives : The first is past
   Some hundred years or more;
But still the present is o'ercast
   With visionings of yore.
This tree, this rock that's cushioned sweet
   With tufts of savoury thyme,
That unseen river which doth greet
   Our ears with its rude rhyme,
Were then as now—they form the chain
That links the present with past pain.

Sweet Flesh and Blood! how deadly chill
   These milk-white fingers be!
The feathery ribs of ice-bound rill
   Seem not so cold to me;—
But press them on this burning brow
   Which glows like molten brass,
'Twill thaw them soon; then thou shalt know
   How ancient visions pass
Before mine eyes, like shapes of life,
Kindling old loves and deadly strife.

Drink to me first!—nay do not scorn
   These sparkling dews of night;
I pledge thee in the silver horn
   Of yonder moonlet bright:
'Tis stinted measure now, but soon
   Thy cup shall overflow;

It half was spilled two hours agone,
   That little flowers might grow,
And weave for me fine robes of silk ;
For which good deeds, stars drop them milk.

Nay, take the horn into thy hand,
   The goodly silver horn,
And quaff it off. At my command
   Each flower-cup, ere the morn,
Shall brimful be of glittering dews,
   And then we'll have large store
Of heaven's own vintage ripe for use,
   To pledge our healths thrice o'er ;
So skink the can as maiden free,
Then troll the merry bowl to me !

Hush—drink no more ! for now the trees,
   In yonder grand old wood,
Burst forth in sinless melodies
   To cheer my solitude ;
Trees sing thus every night to me,
   So mournfully and slow—
They think, dear hearts, 'twere well for me,
   Could large tears once forth flow
From this hard frozen eye of mine,
As freely as they stream from thine.

Ay, ay, they sing right passing well,
   And pleasantly in tune,
To midnight winds a canticle
   That floats up to the moon ;
And she goes wandering near and far
   Through yonder vaulted skies,
No nook whereof but hath a star
   Shed for me from her eyes ;—
She knows I cannot weep, but she
Weeps worlds of light for love of me !

Yes, in her bower of clouds she weeps
    Night after night for me—
The lonely man that sadly keeps
    Watch by the blasted tree.
She spreads o'er these lean ribs her beams,
    To scare the cutting cold;
She lends me light to read my dreams,
    And rightly to unfold
The mysteries that make men mad,
Or wise, or wild, or good, or bad.

So lovingly she shines through me,
    Without me and within,
That even thou, methinks, might'st see,
    Beneath this flesh so thin,
A heart that like a ball of fire
    Is ever blazing there,
Yet dieth not; for still the lyre
    Of heaven soothes its despair—
The lyre that sounds so sadly sweet,
When winds and woods and waters meet.

Hush! hush! so sang yon ghastly wood,
    So moaned the sullen stream
One night, as TWO on this rock stood
    Beneath this same moonbeam:—
Nay, start not!—one was Flesh and Blood,
    A dainty straight-limbed dame,*
That clung to me and sobbed—O God!
    Struggling with maiden shame,
She faltered forth her love, and swore—
"ON LAND OR SEA, THINE EVERMORE!"

---

* A dainty WELL-LIMBED dame.—*MS. copy.*

By Wood, by Water, and by Wind;
   Yea, by the blessed light
Of the brave moon, that maiden kind
   Eternal faith did plight;
Yea, by the rock on which we stood—
   This altar-stone of yore—
That loved one said, "On land or flood,
   Thine, thine for evermore!"
The earth reeled round, I gasped for breath,
I loved, and was beloved till death!

I felt upon my brow a kiss,
   Upon my cheek a tear;
I felt that now life's sum of bliss
   Was more than heart could bear.
Life's sum of bliss? say rather pain,
   For heart to find its mate,
To love, and be beloved again,
   Even when the hand of Fate
Motions farewell!—and one must be
A wanderer on the faithless sea.

Ay, Land or Sea! for, mark me now,
   Next morrow o'er the foam,
Sword girt to side, and helm on brow,
   I left a sorrowing home;
Yet still I lived as very part
   Even of this sainted rock,
Where first that loved one's tristful heart
   Its secret treasure broke *
In my love-thirsting ear alone,
Here, here, on this huge altar-stone.

---

* Its TREASURED SECRET broke.—*MS. copy.*

Hear'st thou the busy sounds that come
    From yonder glittering shore :
The madness of the doubling drum,
    The naker's sullen roar—
The wild and shrilly strains that swell
    From each bright brassy horn—
The fluttering of each penoncel
    By knightly lance upborne—
The clear ring of each tempered shield,
And proud steeds neighing far afield ?

Sweet Flesh and Blood ! my tale's not told,
    'Tis scantly well begun :—
Our vows were passed, in heaven enrolled,
    And then next morrow's sun
Saw banners waving in the wind,*
    And tall barks on the sea : †
Glory before, and Love behind,
    Marshalled proud chivalrie,
As every valour-freighted ship
Its gilt prow in the wave did dip.

And then passed o'er a merry time—
    A roystering gamesome life,
Till cheeks were tanned with many a clime,
    Brows scarred in many a strife.
But what of that ? Year after year,
    In every battle's shock,
Or 'mid the storms of ocean drear,
    My heart clung to this rock ;
Was with its very being blent,
Sucking from it brave nourishment.

---

* Saw PENNONS waving in the wind.—*MS. copy.*
† And GREAT SHIPS on the sea.—*MS. copy.*

All life, all feeling, every thought
    Was centred in this spot;
The Unforgetting being wrought
    Upon the Unforgot.
Time fleeted on; but time ne'er dimmed
    The picturings of the heart *—
Freshly as when they first were limned,
    Truth's fadeless tints would start;
Yes! wheresoe'er Life's bark might steer,
This changeless heart was anchored here.

Ha! laugh sweet Flesh and Blood, outright,
    Nor smother honest glee,
Your time is now; but ere this night
    Hath travelled over me,
My time shall come; and then, ay, then
    The wanton stars shall reel
Like drunkards all, when we madmen
    Upraise our laughter-peal.
I see the cause: the TWAIN—the ONE—
The SHAPE that gibbered in the sun!

You pinch my wrist, you press my knee,
    With fingers long and small;
Light fetters these—not so on me
    Did heathen shackles fall,
When I was captived in the fight
    On Candy's fatal shore;
And paynims won a battered knight,
    A living well of gore;—
How the knaves smote me to the ground,
And hewed me like a tree all round!

---

* The picturings of THIS heart.—*MS. copy.*

They hammered irons on my hand,
    And irons on my knee ;
They bound me fast with many a band,
    To pillar and to tree ;
They flung me in a loathsome pit,
    Where loathly things were rife—
Where newte, and toad, and rat would sit,
    Debating for my life,
On my breast-bone ; while one and all
Hissed, fought, and voided on their thrall.

Yet lived I on, and madman-like,
    With unchanged heart I lay ;
No vemon to its core could strike,
    For it was far away :—
'Twas even here beside this Tree,
    Its Trysting-place of yore,
Where that fond maiden swore to me,
    "Thine, thine, for evermore."
Faith in her vow made that pit seem
The palace of Arabian dream.

And so was passed a weary time,
    How long I cannot tell,
'Twas years ere in that sunny clime
    A sunbeam on me fell.
But from that tomb I rushed in tears,
    The fetters fell from me,
They rusted through with damp and years,
    And rotted was the tree,
When the undying crawled from night—
From loathsomeness, into God's light.

O Lord ! there was a flood of sound
    Came rushing through my ears,
When I arose from underground,
    A wild thing shedding tears :—

The voices of glad birds and brooks,
　　And eke of greenwood tree,
With all the long-remembered looks*
　　Of earth, and sky, and sea,
Danced madly through my 'wildered brain,
And shook me like a wind-swung chain.

Men marvelled at the ghastly form
　　That sat before the sun—
That laughed to scorn the pelting storm,
　　Nor would the thunders shun;
The bearded Shape that gibbered sounds
　　Of uncouth lore and lands,
Struck awe into these Heathen hounds,
　　Who, lifting up their hands,
Blessed the wild prophet, and then brought
Raiment and food unthanked, unsought.

I have a dreaming of the sea—
　　A dreaming of the land—
A dreaming that again to me
　　Belonged a good knight's brand—
A dreaming that this brow was pressed
　　With plumed helm once more,
That linked mail reclad this breast
　　When I retrod the shore,
The blessed shores of my father-land,
And knelt in prayer upon its strand.

"Years furrow brows and channel cheeks,
　　But should not chase old loves away;
The language which true heart first speaks,
　　That language must it hold for aye."

---

* And all the long-remembered looks. - *MS. copy.*

This poesie a war-worn man
    Did mutter to himself one night,
As upwards to this cliff he ran,
    That shone in the moonlight ;
And by the moonlight curiously,
He scanned the bark of this old tree.

" No change is here, all things remain
    As they were years ago ;
With selfsame voice the old woods playne,
    When shrilly winds do blow—
Still murmuring to itself, the stream
    Rolls o'er its rocky bed—
Still smiling in its quiet dream,
    The small flower nods its head ;
And I stand here," the War-worn said,
" Like Nature's heart, unaltered."

Now, Flesh and Blood, that sits by me
    On this bare ledge of stone,
So sat that Childe of chivalrie,
    One summer eve alone.
I saw him, and methought he seemed
    Like to the Bearded Form
That sat before the sun, and gleamed
    Defiance to the storm ;
I saw him in his war-weed sit,
And other Two before him flit.

Yes, in the shadow of that tree,
    And motionless as stone,
Sat the War-worn, while mirthfully
    The other Two passed on ;—
By heaven ! one was a comely bride,
    Her face gleamed in the moon,

As richly as in full-fleshed pride,
   Bright roses burst in June;
Methought she was the maiden mild,*
That whilome loved the wandering Childe!

But it was not her former love
   That wandered with her there—
Oh, no! long absence well may move
   A maiden to despair;
Old loves we cast unto the winds,
   Old vows into the sea,
'Tis lightsome for all gentle minds,
   To be as fancy free.
So the Vow-pledged One loved another,
And wantoned with a younger brother.

I heard a dull, hoarse, chuckle sound,
   Beside that trysting-tree;
I saw uprising from the ground,
   A ghastly shape like me.
But no! it was the War-worn wight,
   That pale as whited wall,
Strode forth into the moonshine bright,
   And let such hoarse sounds fall.
A voice uprushing from the tomb
Than his, were less fulfilled with doom.

"Judgment ne'er sleeps!" the War-worn said,
   As striding into light,
He stood before that shuddering maid,
   Between her and that knight.
Judgment ne'er sleeps! 'tis wondrous odd,
   One gurgle, one long sigh,

---

* Methought she SEEMED the maiden mild.—*MS. copy.*

Ended it all. Upon this sod
  Lay one with unclosed eye,
And then the boiling linn that night,
Flung on its banks a lady bright.

She tripped towards me as you have tripped,
  Pale maiden! and as cold;
She sipped with me as you have sipped,
  Night dews, and then I told
To her as you my weary tale
  Of double life and pain;
And thawed her fingers chill and pale
  Upon my burning brain;—
That daintiest piece of Flesh on earth,
I welcomed her to all my mirth.

And then I pressed her icy hand
  Within my burning palm,
And told her tales of that far land,
  Of sunshine, flowers, and balm;
I told her of the damp, dark hole,
  The fetters and the tree,
And of the slimy things that stole
  O'er shuddering flesh so free:
Yea, of the Bearded Ghastliness,
That sat in the sun's loveliness.

I welcomed her, I welcome thee,
  To sit upon this stone,
And meditate all night with me,
  On ages that are gone:
To dream again each marvellous dream,
  Of passion and of truth,
And re-construct each shattered beam
  That glorified glad youth.
These were the days!—hearts then could feel,
Eyes weep, and slumbers o'er them steal.

But not so now.   The second life
   That wearied hearts must live,
Is woven with that thread of strife—
   Forget not, nor Forgive !
Fires, scorching fires run through our veins,
   Our corded sinews crack,
And molten lead boils in our brains,
   For marrow to the back.
Ha ! ha ! What's life ?   Think of the joke,
The fiercest fire still ends in smoke.

Fill up the cup ! fill up the can !
   Drink, drink, sweet Flesh and Blood,
The health of the grim-bearded man
   That haunteth solitude ;—
The wood pours forth its melodies,
   And stars whirl fast around ;
Yon moon-ship scuds before the breeze—
   Hark, how sky-billows sound !
Drink, Flesh and Blood ! then trip with me,
One measure round the Madman's Tree !

VII.

HALBERT THE GRIM.

THERE is blood on that brow,
   There is blood on that hand ;
There is blood on that hauberk,
   And blood on that brand.

Oh ! bloody all o'er is
   His war-cloak, I weet ;
He is wrapped in the cover
   Of murder's red sheet.

There is pity in man—
   Is there any in him?
No! ruth were a strange guest
   To Halbert the Grim.

The hardest may soften,
   The fiercest repent;
But the heart of Grim Halbert
   May never relent.

Death doing on earth is
   For ever his cry;
And pillage and plunder
   His hope in the sky!

'Tis midnight, deep midnight,
   And dark is the heaven;
Sir Halbert, in mockery,
   Wends to be shriven.

He kneels not to stone,
   And he bends not to wood;
But he swung round his brown blade,
   And hewed down the Rood!

He stuck his long sword, with
   Its point in the earth;
And he prayed to its cross hilt,
   In mockery and mirth.

Thus lowly he louteth,
   And mumbles his beads;
Then lightly he riseth,
   And homeward he speeds.

His steed hurries homewards,
    Darkling and dim ;
Right fearful it prances
    With Halbert the Grim.

Still fiercer it tramples,
    The spur gores its side ;
Now downward and downward
    Grim Halbert doth ride.

The brown wood is threaded,
    The grey flood is past,
Yet hoarser and wilder
    Moans ever the blast.

No star lends its taper,
    No moon sheds her glow ;
For dark is the dull path
    That Baron must go.

Though starless the sky, and
    No moon shines abroad,
Yet, flashing with fire, all
    At once gleams the road.

And his black steed, I trow,
    As it galloped on,
With a hot sulphur halo,
    And flame-flash all shone.

From eye and from nostril,
    Out gushed the pale flame,
And from its chafed mouth, the
    Churned fire-froth came.

They are two ! they are two !—
  They are coal-black as night,
That now staunchly follow
  That grim Baron's flight.

In each lull of the wild blast,
  Out breaks their deep yell :
'Tis the slot of the Doomed One,
  These hounds track so well.

Ho ! downward, still downward,
  Sheer slopeth his way ;
No let hath his progress,
  No gate bids him stay.

No noise had his horse-hoof
  As onward it sped ;
But silent it fell, as
  The foot of the dead.

Now redder and redder
  Flares far its bright eye,
And harsher these dark hounds
  Yell out their fierce cry.

Sheer downward ! right downward !
  Then dashed life and limb,
As careering to hell,
  Sunk Halbert the Grim !

VIII.

TRUE LOVE'S DIRGE.

Some love is light and fleets away,
   Heigho! the Wind and Rain;
Some love is deep and scorns decay,
   Ah, well-a-day! in vain.

Of loyal love I sing this lay,
   Heigho! the Wind and Rain;
'Tis of a knight and lady gay,
   Ah! well-a-day! bright twain.

He loved her—heart loved ne'er so well,
   Heigho! the Wind and Rain;
She was a cold and proud damsel,
   Ah, well-a-day! and vain.

He loved her—oh, he loved her long,
   Heigho! the Wind and Rain;
But she for love gave bitter wrong,
   Ah, well-a-day! Disdain!

It is not meet for knight like me,
   Heigho! the Wind and Rain;
Though scorned, love's recreant to be,
   Ah, well-a-day! Refrain.

That brave knight buckled to his brand,
   Heigho! the Wind and Rain;
And fast he sought a foreign strand,
   Ah, well-a-day! in pain.

He wandered wide by land and sea,
   Heigho ! the Wind and Rain ;
A mirror of bright constancye,
   Ah, well-a-day ! in vain.

He would not chide, he would not blame,
   Heigho ! the Wind and Rain ;
But at each shrine he breathed her name,
   Ah, well-a-day ! Amen !

He would not carpe, he would not sing,
   Heigho ! the Wind and Rain ;
But broke his heart with love-longing,
   Ah, well-a-day ! poor brain.*

He scorned to weep, he scorned to sigh,
   Heigho ! the Wind and Rain ;
But like a true knight he could die—
   Ah, well-a-day ! life's vain.

The banner which that brave knight bore,
   Heigho ! the Wind and Rain ;
Had scrolled on it " 𝔉𝔞𝔦𝔱𝔥 𝔈𝔟𝔢𝔯𝔪𝔬𝔯𝔢,"
   Ah, well-a-day ! again.

That banner led the Christian van,
   Heigho ! the Wind and Rain ;
Against Seljuck and Turcoman,
   Ah, well-a-day ! bright train.†

---

   * Ah, well-a-day ! SAD PAIN.—*MS. copy.*

   † Ah, well-a-day ! THE SLAIN.—*MS. copy.*

The fight was o'er, the day was done,
   Heigho ! the Wind and Rain ;
But lacking was that loyal one—
   Ah, well-a-day ! sad pain.

They found him on the battle-field,
   Heigho ! the Wind and Rain ;
With broken sword and cloven shield,
   A well-a-day ! in twain.

They found him pillowed on the dead,
   Heigho ! the Wind and Rain ;
The blood-soaked sod his bridal bed,
   Ah, well-a-day ! the Slain.

On his pale brow, and paler cheek,
   Heigho ! the Wind and Rain ;
The white moonshine did fall so meek—
   Ah, well-a-day ! sad strain.*

They lifted up the True and Brave,
   Heigho ! the Wind and Rain ;
And bore him to his lone cold grave,
   Ah, well-a-day ! in pain.

They buried him on that far strand,
   Heigho ! the Wind and Rain ;
His face turned towards his love's own land,
   Ah, well-a-day ! how vain.

The wearied heart was laid at rest,
   Heigho ! the Wind and Rain ;
To dream of her it liked best,
   Ah, well-a-day ! again.

---

* Ah, well-a-day ! IN VAIN.—*MS. copy.*

They nothing said, but many a tear,
   Heigho ! the Wind and Rain ;
Rained down on that knight's lowly bier,
   Ah, well-a-day ! amain.*

They nothing said, but many a sigh,
   Heigho ! the Wind and Rain ;
Told how they wished like him to die,
   Ah, well-a-day ! sans stain.†

With solemn mass and orison,
   Heigho ! the Wind and Rain,
They reared o'er him a cross of stone,
   Ah, well-a-day ! in pain.

And on it graved with daggers bright,
   Heigho ! the Wind and Rain ;
Here lies a true and gentle Knight,
   Ah, well-a-day ! Amen !

requiescat. in. pace.

IX.

THE DEMON LADY.

Again in my chamber !
   Again at my bed !
With thy smile sweet as sunshine,
   And hand cold as lead !

---

* This stanza is left out altogether in the MS. copy.

† Ah, well-a-day ! LIFE'S VAIN.—*MS. copy.*

F

I know thee, I know thee !—
    Nay, start not, my sweet !
These golden robes shrank up,
    And showed me thy feet ;
These golden robes shrank up,
    And taffety thin,
While out crept the symbols
    Of Death and of Sin !

Bright, beautiful Devil !
    Pass, pass from me now ;
For the damp dew of death
    Gathers thick on my brow ;
And bind up thy girdle,
    Nor beauties disclose,
More dazzlingly white
    Than the wreath-drifted snows :
And away with thy kisses ;
    My heart waxes sick,
As thy red lips, like worms,
    Travel over my cheek !

Ha ! press me no more with
    That passionless hand,
'Tis whiter than milk, or
    The foam on the strand ;
'Tis softer than down, or
    The silken-leafed flower ;
But colder than ice thrills
    Its touch at this hour.
Like the finger of Death
    From cerements unrolled,
Thy hand on my heart falls
    Dull, clammy, and cold.

Nor bend o'er my pillow—
    Thy raven black hair

O'ershadows my brow with
  A deeper despair;
These ringlets thick falling
  Spread fire through my brain,
And my temples are throbbing
  With madness again.
The moonlight! the moonlight!
  The deep-winding bay!
There are TWO on that strand,
  And a ship far away!

In its silence and beauty,
  Its passion and power,
Love breathed o'er the land,
  Like the soul of a flower.
The billows were chiming
  On pale yellow sands;
And moonshine was gleaming
  On small ivory hands.
There were bowers by the brook's brink,
  And flowers bursting free;
There were hot lips to suck forth
  A lost soul from me!

Now, mountain and meadow,
  Frith, forest, and river,
Are mingling with shadows—
  Are lost to me ever.
The sunlight is fading,
  Small birds seek their nest;
While happy hearts flower-like,
  Sink sinless to rest.
But I!—'tis no matter;
  Ay, kiss cheek and chin;
Kiss—kiss—thou hast won me,
  Bright, beautiful Sin!

X.

ZARA.

" A SILVERY veil of pure moonlight
　Is glancing o'er the quiet water,
　And oh! 'tis beautiful and bright
　As the soft smile of Selim's daughter.

" Sleep, moonlight! sleep upon the wave,
　And hush to rest each rising billow,
　Then dwell within the mountain cave,
　Where this fond breast is Zara's pillow.

" Shine on, thou blessed moon! brighter still,
　Oh, shine thus ever night and morrow;
　For day-break mantling o'er the hill,
　But wakes my love to fear and sorrow."

'Twas thus the Spanish youth beguiled
The rising fears of Selim's daughter;
And on their loves the pale moon smiled,
Unweeting of the morrow's slaughter.

Alas! too early rose that morn
On harnessed knight and fierce soldada—
Alas! too soon the Moorish horn
And tambour rang in Old Grenada.

The dew yet bathes the dreaming flower,
The mist yet lingers in the valley,
When Selim and his Zegris' power
From port and postern sternly sally.

Marry! it was a gallant sight
To see the plain with armour glancing,
As on to Alpuxara's height
Proud Selim's chivalry were prancing.

The knights dismount; on foot they climb
The rugged steeps of Alpuxara;
In fateful and unhappy time,
Proud Selim found his long-lost Zara.

They sleep—in sleep they smile and dream
Of happy days they ne'er shall number;
Their lips breathe sounds,—their spirits seem
To hold communion while they slumber.

A moment gazed the stern old Moor,
A scant tear in his eye did gather,
For as he gazed, she muttered o'er
A blessing on her cruel father.

The hand that grasped the crooked blade,
Relaxed its gripe, then clutched it stronger;
The tear that that dark eye hath shed
On the swart cheek, is seen no longer.

'Tis past!—the bloody deed is done,
A father's hand hath sealed the slaughter!
Yet in Grenada many a one
Bewails the fate of Selim's daughter.

And many a Moorish damsel hath
Made pilgrimage to Alpuxara;
And breathed her vows where Selim's wrath
O'ertook the Spanish youth and Zara.

XI.

OUGLOU'S ONSLAUGHT.

A TURKISH BATTLE-SONG.

Tchassan Ouglou is on !
Tchassan Ouglou is on !
And with him to battle
The faithful are gone.
  Allah, il allah !
The tambour is rung ;
Into his war-saddle
Each Spahi hath swung ;—
Now the blast of the desert
Sweeps over the land,
And the pale fires of heaven
Gleam in each Damask brand.
  Allah, il allah !

Tchassan Ouglou is on !
Tchassan Ouglou is on !
Abroad on the winds, all
His horse-tails are thrown.
'Tis the rush of the eagle
Down cleaving through air,—
'Tis the bound of the lion
When roused from his lair.
Ha ! fiercer and wilder
And madder by far,—
On thunders the might
Of the Moslemite war.
  Allah, il allah !

Forth lash their wild horses,
With loose-flowing rein ;

O'er the thunder of cannon
Swells proudly their shout,—
And sheeted with foam,
Like the surge of the sea,
Over wreck, death, and woe, rolls
Each fierce Osmanli.
   Allah, il allah !

Fast forward, still forward,
Man follows on man,
While the horse-tails are dashing
Afar in the van ;—
See where yon pale crescent
And green turban shine,
There, smite for the Prophet,
And Othman's great line !
   Allah, il allah !
The fierce war-cry is given,—
For the flesh of the Giaour
Shriek the vultures of heaven.
   Allah, il allah !

   Allah, il allah !
How thick on the plain,
The infidels cluster
Like ripe, heavy grain.
The reaper is coming,
The crooked sickle's bare,
And the shout of the Faithful
Is rending the air.
Bismillah ! Bismillah !
Each far-flashing brand
Hath piled its red harvest
Of death on the land !
   Allah, il allah !

Mark, mark yon green turban
That heaves through the fight,

Like a tempest-tost bark
'Mid the thunders of night ;
See parting before it,
On right and on left,
How the dark billows tumble,—
Each saucy crest cleft !
Ay, horseman and footman
Reel back in dismay,
When the sword of stern Ouglou
Is lifted to slay.
    Allah, il allah !

    Allah, il allah !
Tchassan Ouglou is on !
O'er the Infidel breast
Hath his fiery barb gone :—
The bullets rain on him,
They fall thick as hail ;
The lances crash round him
Like reeds in the gale,—
But onward, still onward,
For God and his law,
Through the dark strife of Death
Bursts the gallant Pacha.
    Allah, il allah !

In the wake of his might,
In the path of the wind,
Pour the sons of the Faithful,
Careering behind ;
And bending to battle
O'er each high saddle-bow,
With the sword of Azrael,
They sweep down the foe.
    Allah, il allah !

'Tis Ouglou that cries,—
In the breath of his nostril
The Infidel dies!
Allah, il allah!

XII.

ELFINLAND WUD.

AN IMITATION OF THE ANCIENT SCOTTISH ROMANTIC BALLAD.

Erl William has muntit his gude grai stede,
  (Merrie lemis munelicht on the sea,)
And graithit him in ane cumli weid.
  (Swa bonilie blumis the hawthorn tree.)

Erl William rade, Erl William ran,—
  (Fast they ryde quha luve trewlie,)
Quhyll the Elfinland wud that gude Erl wan—
  (Blink ower the burn, sweit may, to mee.)

Elfinland wud is dern and dreir,
  (Merrie is the grai gowkis sang,)
Bot ilk ane leafis quhyt as silver cleir,
  (Licht makis schoirt the road swa lang.)

It is undirnith ane braid aik tree,
  (Hey and a lo, as the leavis grow grein,)
Thair is kythit ane bricht ladie,
  (Manie flouris blume quhilk ar nocht seen.)

Around hir slepis the quhyte muneschyne,
  (Meik is mayden undir kell,)
Hir lips bin lyke the blude reid wyne;
  (The rois of flouris hes sweitest smell.)

It was al bricht quhare that ladie stude,
  (Far my luve, fure ower the sea.)
Bot dern is the lave of Elfinland wud,
  (The knicht pruvit false that ance luvit me.)

The ladie's handis were quhyte als milk,
  (Ringis my luve wore mair nor ane.)
Her skin was safter nor the silk;
  (Lilly bricht schinis my luvis halse bane.)

Save you, save you, fayr ladie,
  (Gentil hert schawis gentil deed.)
Standand alane undir this auld tree;
  (Deir till knicht is nobil steid.)

Burdalane, if ye dwall here,
  (My hert is layed upon this land.)
I wuld like to live your fere;
  (The schippis cum sailin to the strand.)

Nevir ane word that ladie sayd;
  (Schortest rede hes least to mend.)
Bot on hir harp she evir playd;
  (Thare nevir was mirth that had nocht end.)

Gang ye eist, or fare ye wast,
  (Ilka stern blinkis blythe for thee,)
Or tak ye the road that ye like best,
  (Al trew feeris ryde in cumpanie.)

Erl William loutit doun full lowe;
  (Luvis first seid bin courtesie.)
And swung hir owir his saddil bow,
  (Ryde quha listis, ye'll link with mee.)

Scho flang her harp on that auld tree,
  (The wynd pruvis aye ane harpir gude.)
And it gave out its music free ;
  (Birdis sing blythe in gay green wud.)

The harp playde on its leeful lane,
  (Lang is my luvis yellow hair.)
Quhill it has charmit stock and stane,
  (Furth by firth, deir lady fare.)

Quhan scho was muntit him behynd,
  (Blyth be hertis quhilkis luve ilk uthir.)
Awa thai flew like flaucht of wind ;
  (Kin kens kin, and bairnis thair mither.)

Nevir ane word that ladie spak ;
  (Mim be maydens men besyde.)
But that stout steid did nicher and schaik ;
  (Small thingis humbil hertis of pryde.)

About his breist scho plet her handis ;
  (Luvand be maydens quhan thai lyke.)
Bot they were cauld as yron bandis.
  (The winter bauld bindis sheuch and syke.)

Your handis ar cauld, fayr ladie, sayd hee,
  (The caulder hand the trewer hairt.)
I trembil als the leif on the tree ;
  (Licht caussis muve ald friendis to pairt.)

Lap your mantil owir your heid,
  (My luve was clad in the red scarlett,)
And spredd your kirtil owir my stede ;
  (Thair nevir was joie that had nae lett.)

The ladie scho wald nocht dispute ;
  (Nocht woman is scho that laikis ane tung.)
But caulder her fingeris about him cruik.
  (Some sangis ar writt, bot nevir sung.)

This Elfinland wud will neir haif end ;
  (Hunt quha listis, daylicht for mee.)
I wuld I culd ane strang bow bend,
  (Al undirneth the grene wud tree.)

Thai rade up, and they rade doun,
  (Wearilie wearis wan nicht away.)
Erl William's heart mair cauld is grown ;
  (Hey, luve mine, quhan dawis the day ?)

Your hand lies cauld on my briest-bane,
  (Smal hand hes my ladie fair,)
My horss he can nocht stand his lane,
  (For cauldness of this midnicht air.)

Erl William turnit his heid about ;
  (The braid mune schinis in lift richt cleir.)
Twa Elfin een are gleutin owt,
  (My luvis een like twa sternis appere.)

Twa brennand eyne, sua bricht and full,
  (Bonnilie blinkis my ladeis ee,)
Flang fire flauchtis fra ane peelit skull ;
  (Sum sichts ar ugsomlyk to see.)

Twa rawis of quhyt teeth then did say,
  (Cauld the boysteous windis sal blaw,)
Oh, lang and weary is our way,
  (And donkir yet the dew maun fa'.)

Far owir muir, and far owir fell,
  (Hark the sounding huntsmen thrang ;)
Thorow dingle, and thorow dell,
  (Luve, come list the merlis sang.)

Thorow fire, and thorow flude,
  (Mudy mindis rage lyk a sea ;)
Thorow slauchtir, thorow blude,
  (A seamless shrowd weird schaipis for me !)

And to rede aricht my spell,
  Eerilie sal night wyndis moan,
Quhill fleand Hevin and raikand Hell,
  Ghaist with ghaist maun wandir on.

XIII.

MIDNIGHT AND MOONSHINE.

ALL earth below, all heaven above,
In this calm hour, are filled with Love ;
All sights, all sounds, have throbbing hearts,
In which its blessed fountain starts,
And gushes forth so fresh and free,
Like a soul-thrilling melody.

Look ! look ! the land is sheathed in light,
  And mark the winding stream,
How, creeping round yon distant height,
  Its rippling waters gleam.
Its waters flash through leaf and flower—
  Oh ! merrily they go ;
Like living things, their voices pour
  Dim music as they flow.

Sinless and pure they seek the sea,
As souls pant for eternity ;—
Heaven speed their bright course till they sleep
In the broad bosom of the deep.

High in mid air, on seraph wing,
The paley moon is journeying
In stillest path of stainless blue ;
Keen, curious stars are peering through
Heaven's arch this hour ; they doat on her
With perfect love ; nor can she stir
Within her vaulted halls a pace,
Ere rushing out, with joyous face,
   These Godkins of the sky
Smile, as she glides in loveliness ;
   While every heart beats high
With passion, and breaks forth to bless
   Her loftier divinity.

It is a smile worth worlds to win—
So full of love, so void of sin,
The smile she sheds on these tall trees,
Stout children of past centuries.
Each little leaf, with feathery light,
   Is margined marvellously ;
Moveless all droop, in slumberous quiet ;
   How beautiful they be !
And blissful as soft infants lulled
   Upon a mother's knee.

Far down yon dell the melody
   Of a small brook is audible ;
The shadow of a thread-like tone,—
It murmurs over root and stone,
   Yet sings of very love its fill ;—
And hark ! even now, how sweetly shrill
   It trolls its fairy glee,

Skywards unto that pure bright one;
  O! gentle heart hath she,
For, leaning down to earth, with pleasure,
She lists its fond and prattling measure.

It is indeed a silent night
Of peace, of joy, and purest light;—
No angry breeze, in surly tone,
Chides the old forest till it moan;
Or breaks the dreaming of the owl,
  That, warder-like, on yon gray tower,
Feedeth his melancholy soul
  With visions of departed power;
And o'er the ruins Time hath sped,
Nods sadly with his spectral head.

And lo! even like a giant wight
  Slumbering his battle toils away,
The sleep-locked city, gleaming bright
  With many a dazzling ray,
Lies stretched in vastness at my feet;
Voiceless the chamber and the street,
  And echoless the hall;—
Had Death uplift his bony hand
And smote all living on the land,
  No deeper quiet could fall.
In this religious calm of night,
Behold, with finger tall and bright,
Each tapering spire points to the sky,
In a fond, holy ecstacy;—
Strange monuments they be of mind,—
Of feelings dim and undefined,
Shaping themselves, yet not the less,
In forms of passing loveliness.

O God! this is a holy hour :—
   Thy breath is o'er the land ;
I feel it in each little flower
   Around me where I stand,—
In all the moonshine scattered fair,
Above, below me, everywhere,—
In every dew-bead glistening sheen,
In every leaf and blade of green,—
And in this silence grand and deep,
Wherein thy blessed creatures sleep.

The trees send forth their shadows long
   In gambols o'er the earth,
To chase each other's innocence
   In quiet, holy mirth ;
O'er the glad meadows fast they throng,
   Shapes multiform and tall ;
And lo! for them the chaste moonbeam,
   With broadest light doth fall.
Mad phantoms all, they onward glide,—
On swiftest wind they seem to ride
   O'er meadow, mount, and stream :
And now, with soft and silent pace,
   They walk as in a dream,
While each bright earth-flower hides its face
Of blushes, in their dim embrace.

Men say, that in this midnight hour,
The disembodied have power
To wander as it liketh them,
By wizard oak and fairy stream,—
   Through still and solemn places,
And by old walls and tombs, to dream,
   With pale, cold, mournful faces.
I fear them not ; for they must be
Spirits of kindest sympathy,

Who choose such haunts, and joy to feel
The beauties of this calm night steal
Like music o'er them, while they woo'd
   The luxury of Solitude.

Welcome, ye gentle spirits ! then,
Who love and feel for earth-chained men,—
Who, in this hour, delight to dwell
By moss-clad oak and dripping cell,—
Who joy to haunt each age-dimmed spot,
Which ruder natures have forgot ;
And, in majestic solitude,
Feel every pulse-stroke thrill of good
To all around, below, above ;—
Ye are the co-mates whom I love !
While, lingering in this moonshine glade,
I dream of hopes that cannot fade ;
And pour abroad those phantasies
That spring from holiest sympathies
With Nature's moods, in this glad hour
Of silence, moonshine, beauty, power,
When the busy stir of man is gone,
And the soul is left with its God alone !

XIV.

THE WATER! THE WATER!

The Water ! the Water !
  The joyous brook for me,
That tuneth, through the quiet night,
  Its ever-living glee.
The Water ! the Water !
  That sleepless merry heart,
Which gurgles on unstintedly,
  And loveth to impart

To all around in some small measure
Of its own most perfect pleasure.

The Water! the Water!
   The gentle stream for me,
That gushes from the old gray stone,
   Beside the alder tree.
The Water! the Water!
   That ever-bubbling spring
I loved and looked on while a child,
   In deepest wondering,—
And asked it whence it came and went,
And when its treasures would be spent.

The Water! the Water!
   The merry, wanton brook,
That bent itself to pleasure me,
   Like mine own shepherd crook.
The Water! the Water!
   That sang so sweet at noon,
And sweeter still at night, to win
   Smiles from the pale proud moon,
And from the little fairy faces
That gleam in heaven's remotest places.

The Water! the Water!
   The dear and blessed thing
That all day fed the little flowers
   On its banks blossoming.
The Water! the Water!
   That murmured in my ear,
Hymns of a saint-like purity,
   That angels well might hear;
And whisper in the gates of heaven,
How meek a pilgrim had been shriven.

The Water ! the Water !
  Where I have shed salt tears,
In loneliness and friendliness,
  A thing of tender years.
The Water ! the Water !
  Where I have happy been,
And showered upon its bosom flowers
  Culled from each meadow green,
And idly hoped my life would be
So crowned by love's idolatry.

The Water ! the Water !
  My heart yet burns to think
How cool thy fountain sparkled forth,
  For parched lip to drink.
The Water ! the Water !
  Of mine own native glen ;
The gladsome tongue I oft have heard,
  But ne'er shall hear again ;
Though fancy fills my ear for aye
With sounds that live so far away !

The Water ! the Water !
  The mild and glassy wave,
Upon whose gloomy banks I've longed*
  To find my silent grave.
The Water ! the Water !
  O bless'd to me thou art ;
Thus sounding in life's solitude,
  The music of my heart,
And filling it, despite of sadness,
With dreamings of departed gladness.

---

* Upon whose BROOMY banks I've longed.—*MS. copy.*

The Water! the Water!
  The mournful pensive tone,
That whispered to my heart how soon
  This weary life was done.
The Water! the Water!
  That rolled so bright and free,
And bade me mark how beautiful
  Was its soul's purity;
And how it glanced to heaven its wave,
As wandering on it sought its grave.

XV.

THREE FANCIFUL SUPPOSES.

WERE I a breath of viewless wind,
  As very spirits be,
Where would I joy at length to find
  I was no longer free?
Oh, Margaret's cheek,
Whose blushes speak
  Love's purest sympathies,
Would be the site,
Where gleaming bright,
  My prison-dome should rise:
I'd live upon that rosy shore,
  And fan it with soft sighs,
Nor other paradise explore
  Beneath the skies.

Were I a pranksome Elfin knight,
  Or eke the Faerye king,

Who, when the moonshine glimmers bright,
   Loves to be wandering ;
Where would I ride,
In all the pride
   Of Elfin Chivalry,
With each sweet sound
Far floating round,
   Of Faerye minstrelsy ?—
'Tis o'er her neck of drifted snow,
   Her passion-breathing lip,
Her dainty chin and noble brow,
   That I would trip.

Were I a glossy plumaged bird,
   A small glad voice of song,
Where would my love-lays aye be heard—
   Where would I nestle long ?—
In Margaret's ear
When none were near,
   I'd strain my little throat,
To sing fond lays
In Margaret's praise,
   That could not be forgot ;
Then on her bosom would I fall,
   And from it never part—
Dizzy with joy, and proud to call
   My home her heart !

XVI.

A CAVEAT TO THE WIND.

Sing high, sing low, thou moody wind,
   It skills not—for thy glee
Is ever of a fellow-kind
   With mine own fantasy.

Go, sadly moan or madly blow
  In fetterless free will,
Wild spirit of the clouds! but know
  I ride thy comrade still;
Loving thy humours, I can be
Sad, wayward, wild, or mad, like thee.

Go, and with light and noiseless wing,
  Fan yonder murmuring stream—
Brood o'er it, as the sainted thing,
  The spirit of its dream;
Give to its voice a sweeter tone
  Of calm and heartfelt gladness;
Or, to those old trees, woe-begone,
  Add moan of deeper sadness,—
It likes me still; for I can be
All sympathy of heart, like thee.

Rush forth, in maddest wrath, to rouse
  The billows of the deep;
And in the blustering storm, carouse
  With fiends that never weep.
Go, tear each fluttering rag away,
  Outshriek the mariner,
And hoarsely knell the mermaid's lay
  Of death and shipwreck drear;—
What reck I, since I still dare be
Harsh, fierce, and pitiless, like thee?

I love thy storm-shout on the land,
  Thy storm-shout on the sea;
Though shapes of death rise on each hand,
  Dismay troops not with me.
With iron-cheek, that never showed
  The channel of a tear,

With haughty heart, that never bowed
   Beneath a dastard fear,
I rush with thee o'er land and sea,
Rejoicing in thy thundering glee.

Lovest thou those cloisters, old and dim,
   Where ghosts at midnight stray,
To pour abroad unearthly hymn,
   And fright the stars away ? *
Add to their sighs thy hollow tone
   Of saddest melancholy—
For I, too, love such places lone,
   And court such guests unjolly :
Such haunts, such mates, in sooth, to me
Be welcome as they are to thee.

Blow as thou wilt, blow any where,
   Wild spirit of the sky,
It matters not—earth, ocean, air,
   Still echoes to my cry,
"I follow thee ;" for, where thou art,
   My spirit, too, must be,
While each chord of this wayward heart,
   Thrills to thy minstrelsy ;
And he that feels so sure must be
   Meet co-mate for a shrew like thee !

XVII.

WHAT IS GLORY ? WHAT IS FAME ?

What is Glory ? What is Fame ?
The echo of a long lost name ;

---

* And fright PALE stars away.—*MS. copy.*

A breath, an idle hour's brief talk;
The shadow of an arrant nought;
A flower that blossoms for a day,
    Dying next morrow;
A stream that hurries on its way,
    Singing of sorrow;—
The last drop of a bootless shower,
Shed on a sere and leafless bower;
A rose, stuck in a dead man's breast—
This is the World's fame at the best!

What is Fame? and what is Glory?
A dream—a jester's lying story,
To tickle fools withal, or be
A theme for second infancy;
A joke scrawled on an epitaph;
A grin at Death's own ghastly laugh;
A visioning that tempts the eye,
But mocks the touch—nonentity;
A rainbow, substanceless as bright,
    Flitting for ever
O'er hill-top to more distant height,
    Nearing us never;
A bubble, blown by fond conceit,
In very sooth itself to cheat;
The witch-fire of a frenzied brain;
A fortune, that to lose were gain;
A word of praise, perchance of blame;
The wreck of a time-bandied name,—
Ay, This is Glory! this is Fame!

XVIII.

THE SOLEMN SONG OF A RIGHTEOUS HEARTE.

AFTER THE FASHION OF AN EARLY ENGLISH POET.

There is a mightie Noyse of Bells,
    Rushing from the turret free ;
A solemn tale of Truthe it tells,
    O'er Land and Sea,
How heartes be breaking fast, and then
    Wax whole againe.

Poor fluttering Soule ! why tremble soe,
    To quitt Lyfe's fast decaying Tree ;
Time wormes its core, and it must bowe
    To Fate's decree ;
Its last branch breakes, but Thou must soare,
    For Evermore.

Noe more thy wing shal touch grosse Earth ;
    Far under shal its shadows flee,
And al its sounds of Woe or Mirth
    Growe strange to thee.
Thou wilt not mingle in its noyse,
    Nor court its Joies.

Fond One ! why cling thus unto Life,
    As if its gaudes were meet for thee ;
Surely its Follie, Bloodshed, Stryfe,
    Liked never thee ?
This World growes madder each newe daie,
    Vice beares such sway.

Couldst thou in Slavish artes excel,
    And crawle upon the supple knee—
Couldst thou each Woe-worn wretch repel,—
    This Worldes for Thee.
Not in this Spheare Man ownes a Brother :
    Then seek another.

Couldst thou bewraie thy Birthright soe
    As flatter Guilt's prosperitye,
And laude Oppressiounes iron blowe—
    This Worldes for Thee.
Sithence to this thou wilt not bend,
    Life's at an end.
Couldst thou spurn Vertue meanly clad,
    As if 'twere spotted Infamy,
And prayse as Good what is most Bad—
    This Worldes for Thee.
Sithence thou canst not will it soe,
    Poor Flutterer, goe !

If Head with Hearte could so accord,
    In bond of perfyte Amitie,
That Falsehood raigned in Thoughte, Deed, Word—
    This Worldes for Thee.
But scorning guile, Truth-plighted one !
    Thy race is run.

Couldst thou laughe loude, when grieved hearts weep
    And Fiendlyke probe theire Agonye,
Rich harvest here thou soon wouldst reape—
    This Worldes for Thee ;
But with the Weeper thou must weepe,
    And sad watch keep.

Couldst thou smyle swete when Wrong hath wrung
    The withers of the Poore but Prowde,
And by the rootes pluck out the tongue
    That dare be lowde

In Righteous cause, whate'er may be—
    This Worldes for Thee.

This canst thou not ! Then fluttering thing
    Unstained in thy puritye,
Sweep towards heaven with tireless wing—
    Meet Home for Thee.
Feare not, the crashing of Lyfe's Tree—
    God's Love guides Thee.

And thus it is :—these solemn bells,
    Swinging in the turret free,
And tolling forth theire sad farewells,
    O'er Land and Sea,
Tell how Hearts breake, full fast, and then
    Growe whole againe.

XIX.

MELANCHOLYE.

ADIEU ! al vaine delightes
Of calm and moonshine nightes ;
Adieu ! al pleasant shade
That forests thicke have made ;
Adieu ! al musick swete
    That little fountaynes poure,
When blythe theire waters greete
    The lovesick lyly-flowre.

Adieu ! the fragrant smel
Of flowres in boskye dell ;
And all the merrie notes
That tril from smal birdes' throates ;

Adieu ! the gladsome lighte
　　Of Day, Morne, Noone, or E'en ;
And welcome gloomy Nighte,
　　When not one star is seen.

Adieu ! the deafening noyse
Of cities, and the joyes
Of Fashioun's sicklie birth ;
Adieu ! al boysterous mirthe,
Al pageant, pompe, and state,
　　And every flauntynge thing
To which the would-be-great
　　Of earth in madness cling.

Come with me, Melancholye,
We'll live like eremites holie,
In some deepe uncouthe wild
Where sunbeame never smylde :
Come with me, pale of hue,
　　To some lone silent spot,
Where blossom never grewe,
　　Which man hath quite forgot.

Come with thy thought-filled eye,
That notes no passer by,
And drouping solemne head,
Where phansyes strange are bred,
And saddening thoughts doe brood,
　　Which idly strive to borrow
A smyle to vaile thy moode
　　Of heart-abyding sorrow.

Come to yon blasted mound
Of phantom-haunted ground,
Where spirits love to be ;
And list the moody glee

Of night-windes as they moane,
   And the ocean's sad replye
To the wild unhallowed tone
   Of the wandering sea-bird's cry.

There sit with me and keep
Vigil when al doe sleepe ;
And when the curfeu bell
Hath rung its mournfull knel,
Let us together blend
   Our mutual sighes and teares,
Or chaunt some metre penned,
   Of the joies of other yeares !

Or in cavern hoare and damp,
Lit by the glow-worm's lamp,
We'll muse on the dull theme
Of Life's heart-sickening dreame—
Of Time's resistlesse powre—
   Of Hope's deceitful lips—
Of Beauty's short-lived houre—
   And Glory's dark eclipse !

Or, wouldst thou rather chuse
This World's leaf to peruse,
Beneath some dripping vault
That scornes rude Time's assaulte ;
Whose close-ribbed arches still
   Frown in their green old age,
And stamp an awfull chill
   Upon that pregnant page ?

Yes, thither let us turne,
To this Time-shattered urne,
And quaintly carved stone—
(Dim wrackes of ages gone ;)

  Here on this mouldering tomb
   We'll con that noblest truth,
  The Flesh and Spirit's doome—
   Dust and Immortall Youthe.

XX.

I AM NOT SAD!

I AM not sad, though sadness seem
 At times to cloud my brow;
I cherished once a foolish dream—
 Thank Heaven, 'tis not so now.
  Truth's sunshine broke,
  And I awoke
 To feel 'twas right to bow
To Fate's decree, and this my doom,
The darkness of a Nameless Tomb.

I grieve not, though a tear may fill
 This glazed and vacant eye;
Old thoughts will rise, do what we will,
 But soon again they die;
  An idle gush,
  And all is hush,
 The fount is soon run dry:
And cheerly now I meet my doom,
The darkness of a Nameless Tomb.

I am not mad, although I see
 Things of no better mould
Than I myself am, greedily
 In Fame's bright page enrolled,

That they may tell
The story well,
What shines may not be gold.
No, no! content I court my doom,
The darkness of a Nameless Tomb.

The luck is theirs—the loss is mine,
And yet no loss at all;
The mighty ones of eldest time,
I ask where they did fall?
Tell me the one
Who e'er could shun
Touch with Oblivion's pall?
All bear with me an equal doom,
The darkness of a Nameless Tomb.

Brave temple and huge pyramid,
Hill sepulchred by art,
The barrow acre-vast, where hid
Moulders some Nimrod's heart;
Each monstrous birth
Cumbers old earth,
But acts a voiceless part,
Resolving all to mine own doom,
The darkness of a Nameless Tomb.

Tradition with her palsied hand,
And purblind History, may
Grope and guess well that in this land
Some great one lived his day;
And what is this,
Blind hit or miss,
But labour thrown away,
For counterparts to mine own doom,
The darkness of a Nameless Tomb?

I do not peak and pine away,
  Lo ! this deep bowl I quaff ;
If sigh I do, you still must say
  It sounds more like a laugh.
    'Tis not too late
    To separate
  The good seed from the chaff ;
And scoff at those who scorn my doom,
The darkness of a Nameless Tomb.

I spend no sigh, I shed no tear,
Though life's first dream is gone ;
And its bright picturings now appear
  Cold images of stone ;
    I've learned to see
    The vanity
  Of lusting to be known,
And gladly hail my changeless doom,
The darkness of a Nameless Tomb !

XXI.

THE JOYS OF THE WILDERNESS.

I HAVE a wish, and it is this, that in some uncouth glen,
It were my lot to find a spot unknown by selfish men ;
Where I might be securely free, like Eremite of old,
From Worldly guile, from Woman's wile, and Friend-
    ships brief and cold ;
And where I might, with stern delight, enjoy the varied
    form
Of Nature's mood, in every rude burst of the thundering
    storm.

Then would my life, lacking fierce strife, glide on in
    dreamy gladness,
Nor would I know the cark and woe which come of this
    world's madness;
While in a row, like some poor show, its pageantries
    would pass,
Without a sigh, before mine eye, as shadows o'er a
    glass:
Nonentity these shadows be,—and yet, good Lord! how
    brave
That knavish rout doth strut and flout, then shrink into
    the grave!

The Wilderness breathes gentleness;—these waters
    bubbling free,
The gallant breeze that stirs the trees, form Heaven's
    own melody;
The far-stretched sky, with its bright eye, pours forth
    a tide of love
On every thing that here doth spring, on all that glows
    above.
But live with man,—his dark heart scan,—its paltry
    selfishness
Will show to thee, why men like me, love the lone
    Wilderness!

XXII.

A SOLEMN CONCEIT.

STATELY trees are growing,
Lusty winds are blowing,
And mighty rivers flowing
    On, for ever on.
As stately forms were growing,
As lusty spirits blowing,

And as mighty fancies flowing
    On, for ever on ;
But there has been leave-taking,
Sorrow and heart-breaking,
And a moan, pale Echo's making,
    For the gone, for ever gone !

Lovely stars are gleaming,
Bearded lights are streaming,
And glorious suns are beaming
    On, for ever on.
As lovely eyes were gleaming,
As wondrous lights were streaming,
And as glorious minds were beaming
    On, for ever on ;—
But there has been soul-sundering,
Wailing, and sad wondering ;
For graves grow fat with plundering
    The gone, for ever gone !

We see great eagles soaring,
We hear deep oceans roaring,
And sparkling fountains pouring
    On, for ever on.
As lofty ones were soaring,
As sonorous voices roaring,
And as sparkling wits were pouring
    On, for ever on ;—
But, pinions have been shedding,
And voiceless darkness spreading,
Since a measure Death's been treading
    O'er the gone, for ever gone !

Every thing is sundering,
Every one is wondering,
And this huge globe goes thundering
    On, for ever on.

But, 'mid this weary sundering,
Heart-breaking and sad wondering,
And this huge globe's rude thundering
    On, for ever on,
I would that I were dreaming,
Where little flowers are gleaming,
And the long green grass is streaming
    O'er the gone, for ever gone !

XXIII.

THE EXPATRIATED.

No BIRD is singing
   In cloud or on tree,
No eye is beaming
   Glad welcome to me ;
The forest is tuneless ;
   Its brown leaves fast fall—
Changed and withered, they fleet
   Like hollow friends all.

No door is thrown open,
   No banquet is spread ;
No hand smoothes the pillow
   For the Wanderer's head ;
But the eye of distrust
   Sternly measures his way,
And glad are the cold lips
   That wish him—good day !

Good day !—I am grateful
   For such gentle prayer,
Though scant be the cost
   Of that morsel of air.

Will it clothe, will it feed me,
  Or rest my worn frame?
Good day! wholesome diet,
  A proud heart to tame.

Now the sun dusks his glories
  Below the blue sea,
And no star its splendor
  Deems worthy of me;
The path I must travel,
  Grows dark as my fate,
And nature, like man, can
  Wax savage in hate.

My country! my country!
  Though step-dame thou be,
Yet my heart in its anguish,
  Cleaves fondly to thee;
Still in fancy it lingers
  By mountain and stream,
And thy name is the spirit
  That rules its wild dream.

This heart loved thee truly,—
  And O! it bled free,
When it led on to glory
  Thy proud chivalry;
And O! it gained much from
  Thy prodigal hand,—
The freedom to break in
  The stranger's cold land!

XXIV.

FACTS FROM FAIRYLAND.

"Oh then, I see, Queen Mab hath been with you!"

Wouldst thou know of me
Where our dwellings be?
'Tis under this hill,
Where the moonbeam chill
Silvers the leaf and brightens the blade,—
'Tis under this mound
Of greenest ground,
That our crystal palaces are made.

Wouldst thou know of me
What our food may be?
'Tis the sweetest breath
Which the bright flower hath
That blossoms in wilderness afar,—
And we sip it up,
In a harebell cup,
By the winking light of the tweering star.

Wouldst thou know of me
What our drink may be?
'Tis the freshest dew,
And the clearest, too,
That ever hung on leaf or flower;
And merry we skink
That wholesome drink,
Thorough the quiet of the midnight hour.

Wouldst thou know of me,
What our pastimes be?

'Tis the hunt and halloo,
The dim greenwood through;
O, bravely we prance it with hound and horn,
O'er moor and fell,
And hollow dell,
Till the notes of our Woodcraft wake the morn.

Wouldst thou know of me
What our garments be?
'Tis the viewless thread,
Which the gossamers spread
As they float in the cool of summer eve bright,
And the down of the rose,
Form doublet and hose
For our Squires of Dames on each festal night.

Wouldst thou know of me
When our revelries be?
'Tis in the still night,
When the moonshine white
Glitters in glory o'er land and sea,
That, with nimble foot,
To tabor and flute,
We whirl with our loves round yon glad old tree.

XXV.

CERTAIN PLEASANT VERSES TO THE LADY OF MY HEART.

The murmur of the merry brook,
As gushingly and free
It wimples with its sun-bright look,
Far down yon sheltered lea,

Humming to every drowsy flower
   A low, quaint lullaby,
Speaks to my spirit, at this hour,
   Of Love and thee.

The music of the gay green wood,
   When every leaf and tree
Is coaxed by winds of gentlest mood,
   To utter harmony;
And the small birds that answer make
   To the wind's fitful glee,
In me most blissful visions wake,
   Of Love and thee.

The rose perks up its blushing cheek,
   So soon as it can see
Along the eastern hills, one streak
   Of the Sun's majesty:
Laden with dewy gems, it gleams
   A precious freight to me,
For each pure drop thereon me seems
   A type of thee.

And when abroad in summer morn,
   I hear the blythe bold bee
Winding aloft his tiny horn,
   (An errant knight perdy,)
That winged hunter of rare sweets
   O'er many a far country,
To me a lay of love repeats,
   Its subject—thee.

And when, in midnight hour, I note
   The stars so pensively,
In their mild beauty, onward float
   Through heaven's own silent sea:

My heart is in their voyaging
  To realms where spirits be,
But its mate, in such wandering,
  Is ever thee!

But O, the murmur of the brook,
  The music of the tree;
The rose with its sweet shamefast look,
  The booming of the bee;
The course of each bright voyager
  In heaven's unmeasured sea,
Would not one heart-pulse of me stir,
  Loved I not thee!

XXVI.

BENEATH A PLACID BROW.

Beneath a placid brow,
  And tear-unstained cheek,
To bear as I do now
  A heart that well could break;
To simulate a smile
  Amid the wrecks of grief,—
To herd among the vile,
  And therein seek relief,—
For the bitterness of thought
Were joyance dearly bought.

When will man learn to bear
  His heart nailed on his breast,
With all its lines of care
  In nakedness confessed?—

Why, in this solemn mask
  Of passion-wasted life,
Will no one dare the task,
  To speak his sorrows rife ?—
Will no one bravely tell,
His bosom is a hell ?

I scorn this hated scene
  Of masking and disguise,
Where men on men still gleam,
  With falseness in their eyes ;
Where all is counterfeit,
  And truth hath never say ;
Where hearts themselves do cheat,
  Concealing hope's decay.
And writhing at the stake,
Themselves do liars make.

Go, search thy heart, poor fool !
  And mark its passions well ;
'Twere time to go to school,—
  'Twere time the truth to tell,—
'Twere time this world should cast
  Its infant slough away,
And hearts burst forth at last
  Into the light of day ;—
'Twere time all learned to be
  Fit for Eternity !

XXVII.

THE COVENANTER'S BATTLE CHANT.

To BATTLE ! to battle !
  To slaughter and strife !
For a sad, broken Covenant
  We barter poor life.

The great God of Judah
  Shall smite with our hand,
And break down the idols
  That cumber the land.

Uplift every voice
  In prayer, and in song;
Remember! the battle
  Is not to the strong:—
Lo, the Ammonites thicken!
  And onward they come,
To the vain noise of trumpet,
  Of cymbal and drum.

They haste to the onslaught,
  With hagbut and spear;
They lust for a banquet
  That's deathful and dear.
Now, horseman and footman,
  Sweep down the hill-side:
They come, like fierce Pharaohs,
  To die in their pride!

See, long plume and pennon
  Stream gay in the air;
They are given us for slaughter—
  Shall God's people spare?
Nay, nay; lop them off—
  Friend, father, and son;
All earth is athirst till
  The good work be done.

Brace tight every buckler,
  And lift high the sword!
For biting must blades be
  That fight for the Lord.

Remember, remember,
　　How Saints' blood was shed, .
As free as the rain, and
　　Homes desolate made!

Among them!—among them!
　　Unburied bones cry;
Avenge us—or like us,
　　Faith's true martyrs die.
Hew, hew down the spoilers!
　　Slay on, and spare none:
Then shout forth in gladness,
　　Heaven's battle is won!

XXVIII.

TIM THE TACKET.

A LYRICAL BALLAD, SUPPOSED TO BE WRITTEN BY W. W.

A BARK is lying on the sands,
No rippling wave is sparkling near her;
She seems unmanned of all her hands—
There's not a soul on board to steer her!

'Tis strange to see a ship-shape thing
Upon a lonely beach thus lying,
While mystic winds for ever sing
Among its shrouds like spirits sighing.

Oh! can it be a spectre-ship,
Forwearied of the storm and ocean,
That here hath ended its last trip,
And sought repose from ceaseless motion?

I deem amiss : for yonder, see,
A sailor struts in dark-blue jacket—
A little man with face of glee—
His neighbours call him Tim the Tacket.

I know him well; the master he
Of a small bark—an Irish coaster ;
His heart is like the ocean, free,
And like the breeze his tongue's a boaster.

He is a father, too, I'm told,
Of children ten, and some say twenty ;
But it's no matter, he's grown old,
And, ten or more, he has got plenty !

List ! now he sings a burly stave
Of waves and wind, and shipwrecks many,
Of flying fish and dolphins brave,
Of mermaids lovely but uncanny.

Right oft, I ween, he joys to speak
Of slim maids in the green waves dancing,
Or singing in some lonesome creek,
While kembing locks like sunbeams glancing.

Oh, he hath tales of wondrous things
Spied in the vast and gousty ocean ;
Of monstrous fish whose giant springs
Give to the seas their rocking motion ;

And serpent huge, whose rings embrace
Some round leagues of the great Pacific ;
And men of central Ind, sans face,
But not on that head less terrific !

Lo ! he hath lit a brown cigar,
A special smooth-skinned real Havannah,

And swirling smoke he puffs afar—
'Tis sweet to him as desert manna !

Away, away the reek doth go,
In wiry thread or heavy volume ;
Now black, now blue, gold, grey, or snow
In colour and in height a column !

His little eyes, deep-set and hedged
All round and round with bristles hoary,
Do twinkle like a hawk's new-fledged—
Sure he hath dreams of marvellous glory !

Well, I would rather be that wight,
Contented, puffing, midst his tackling,
Than star-gemmed lord or gartered knight,
In masquerade or senate cackling.

He suns his limbs upon the deck,
He hears the music of the ocean ;
He lives not on another's beck,
He pines not after court promotion.

He is unto himself—he is
A little world within another ;
And furthermore he knoweth this,
That all mankind to him is brother.

He sings his songs and smokes his weed,
He spins his yarn of monstrous fables,
He cracks his biscuit, and at need
Can soundly sleep on coiled-up cables.

Although the sea be sometimes rough,
His bark is stout, its rudder steady,
At other whiles 'tis calm enough,
And buxom as a gentle lady.

In sooth, too, 'tis a pleasant thing,
To sail and feel the sea-breeze blowing
About one's cheek—oh! such doth bring
Full many a free-born thought and glowing.

For who upon the deep, deep sea,
Ere dwelt and saw its great breast heaving,
But by a kindred sympathy
Felt his own heart its trammels leaving?

The wide and wild, the strange and grand,
Commingle with his inmost spirit;
He feels a riddance from the land—
A boundlessness he may inherit.

Good night, thou happy ancient man!
Farewell, thou mariner so jolly!
I pledge thee in this social can,
Thou antipode of melancholy!

XXIX.

THE WITCHES' JOYS.

A RHAPSODY MOST PLEASANT AND MERRY.

When night winds rave
O'er the fresh scooped grave,
And the dead therein that lie,
Glare upward to the sky;
When gibbering imps sit down,
To feast on lord or clown,
And tear the shroud away
From their lithe and pallid prey;

Then clustering close, how grim
They munch each withered limb !
Or quarrel for dainty rare,
The lip of lady fair—
The tongue of high-born dame,
That never would defame,
And was of scandal free
As any mute could be !
Or suck the tintless cheek
Of maiden mild and meek ;
And when in revel rout
They kick peeled skulls about,
And shout in maddest mirth—
"These dull toys awed the earth !"
 Oh then, oh then, oh then,
  We hurry forth amain ;
For with such eldritch cries,
Begin our revelries !

II.

When the murderer's blanched corse
Swings with a sighing hoarse
From gibbet and from chain,
As the bat sucks out his brain,
And the owlet pecks his eyes,
And the wild fox gnaws his thighs ;
While the raven croaks with glee,
Lord of the dead man's tree ;
And rock on that green skull,
With sated look and dull,
In gloomy pride looks o'er
The waste and wildered moor,
And dreams some other day
Shall bring him fresher prey ;
When over bog and fen,
To lure wayfaring men,

Malicious spirits trail
A ground-fire thin and pale,
Which the belated wight
Pursues the livelong night,
Till in the treacherous ground
An unmade grave is found,—
  Oh then, oh then, oh then,
  We hurry forth amain,
Ha! ha! his feeble cries
Begin our revelries.

III.

When the spirits of the North,
Hurl howling tempests forth;
When seas of lightning flare,
And thunders choke the air;
When the ocean starts to life,
To madness, horror, strife,
And the goodly bark breaks up,
Like ungirded drinking cup,
And each stately mast is split
In some rude thunder-fit;
And like feather on the foam,
Float shattered plank and boom;
When, midst the tempest's roar,
Pale listeners on the shore
Hear the curse and shriek of men,
As they sink and rise again
On the gurley billow's back,
And their strong broad breast-bones crack
On the iron-ribbed coast,
As back to hell they're toss'd,
  Oh then, oh then, oh then,
  We hurry forth again!
For amid such lusty cries,
Begin our revelries.

IV.

When aged parents flee
The noble wreck to see,
And mark their sons roll in
Through foam and thundering din,
All mottled black and blue—
Their icy lips cut through
In the agony of death,
While drifting on their path;
When gentle maidens stand
Upon the wreck-rich strand,
And every labouring wave
That doth their small feet lave,
Gives them a ghastly lover
To wring their white hands over,
And tear their spray-wet hair
In the madness of despair;—
  Oh then, oh then, oh then,
  We hurry home amain;
For their heart-piercing cries,
Shame our wild revelries!

XXX.

A SABBATH SUMMER NOON.

THE calmness of this moontide hour,
  The shadow of this wood,
The fragrance of each wilding flower,
  Are marvellously good;
Oh, here crazed spirits breathe the balm
  Of nature's solitude!

It is a most delicious calm
   That resteth everywhere—
The holiness of soul-sung psalm,
   Of felt but voiceless prayer!
With hearts too full to speak their bliss,
   God's creatures silent are.

They silent are; but not the less,
   In this most tranquil hour,
Of deep unbroken dreaminess,
   They own that Love and Power
Which, like the softest sunshine, rests
   On every leaf and flower.

How silent are the song-filled nests
   That crowd this drowsy tree—
How mute is every feathered breast
   That swelled with melody!
And yet bright bead-like eyes declare
   This hour is ecstasy.

Heart forth! as uncaged bird through air,
   And mingle in the tide
Of blessed things that, lacking care,
   Now full of beauty glide
Around thee, in their angel hues
   Of joy and sinless pride.

Here, on this green bank that o'er-views
   The far retreating glen,
Beneath the spreading beech-tree muse,
   On all within thy ken;
For lovelier scene shall never break
   On thy dimmed sight again.

Slow stealing from the tangled brake
   That skirts the distant hill,
With noiseless hoof two bright fawns make
   For yonder lapsing rill ;
Meek children of the forest gloom,
   Drink on and fear no ill !

And buried in the yellow broom
   That crowns the neighbouring height,
Couches a loutish shepherd groom,
   With all his flocks in sight ;
Which dot the green braes gloriously
   With spots of living light.

It is a sight that filleth me
   With meditative joy,
To mark these dumb things curiously,
   Crowd round their guardian boy ;
As if they felt this Sabbath hour
   Of bliss lacked all alloy.

I bend me towards the tiny flower,
   That underneath this tree
Opens its little breast of sweets
   In meekest modesty,
And breathes the eloquence of love
   In muteness, Lord ! to thee.

There is no breath of wind to move
   The flag-like leaves that spread
Their grateful shadow far above
   This turf-supported head ;
All sounds are gone—all murmurings
   With living nature wed.

The babbling of the clear well-springs,
   The whisperings of the trees,
And all the cheerful jargonings
   Of feathered hearts at ease ;
That whilome filled the vocal wood,
   Have hushed their minstrelsies.

The silentness of night doth brood
   O'er this bright summer noon ;
And nature, in her holiest mood
   Doth all things well attune
To joy, in the religious dreams
   Of green and leafy June.

Far down the glen in distance gleams
   The hamlet's tapering spire,
And glittering in meridial beams,
   Its vane is tongued with fire ;
And hark how sweet its silvery bell—
   And hark the rustic choir !

The holy sounds float up the dell
   To fill my ravished ear,
And now the glorious anthems swell
   Of worshippers sincere—
Of hearts bowed in the dust, that shed
   Faith's penitential tear.

Dear Lord ! thy shadow is forth spread
   On all mine eye can see ;
And filled at the pure fountain-head
   Of deepest piety,
My heart loves all created things,
   And travels home to Thee.

Around me while the sunshine flings
  A flood of mocky gold,
My chastened spirit once more sings
  As it was want of old,
That lay of gratitude which burst
  From young heart uncontrolled,

When, in the midst of nature nursed,
  Sweet influences fell
On childly hearts that were athirst,
  Like soft dews in the bell
Of tender flowers that bowed their heads
  And breathed a fresher smell.

So, even now this hour hath sped,
  In rapturous thought o'er me,
Feeling myself with nature wed—
  A holy mystery—
A part of earth, a part of heaven,
  A part, great God! of Thee.

Fast fade the cares of life's dull sweven,
  They perish as the weed,
While unto me the power is given,
  A moral deep to read
In every silent throe of mind
  External beauties breed.

XXXI.

A MONODY.

I.

Hour after hour,
  Day after day,
Some gentle flower
  Or leaf gives way
Within the bower
  Of human hearts ;—
Tear after tear
  In anguish starts,
For, green or sere,
  Some loved leaf parts
From the arbère
  Of human hearts ;
The keen winds blow ;
Rain, hail and snow
  Fall everywhere !
And one by one,
As life's sands run,
  These loved things fare
Till plundered hearts at last are won,
  To woo despair.

II.

Why linger on,
  Fate's mockery here,
When each is gone,
  Heart-loved, heart-dear ?
Stone spells to stone
  Its weary tale,

How graves were filled,
　　How cheeks waxed pale,
How hearts were chilled
　　With biting gale,
And life's strings thrilled
　　With sorrow's wail.
Flower follows flower
In the heart's bower,
　　To fleet away;
While leaf on leaf,
Sharp grief on grief,—
　　Night chasing day,
Tell as they fall, all joy is brief,
　　Life but decay.

III.

The sea-weed thrown
　　By wave or wind,
On strand unknown,
　　Lone grave to find;
Methinks may own,
　　Of kindred more
Than I dare claim
　　On life's bleak shore.
Name follows name
　　For evermore,
As swift waves shame
　　Slow waves before;—
For keen winds blow;
Rain, hail, and snow
　　Fall everywhere,
Till life's sad tree,
In mockery,
　　Skeletoned bare
Of every leaf, is left to be
　　Mate of despair.

IV.

The world is wide,
  Is rich and fair,
Its things of pride
  Flaunt everywhere;
But can it hide
  Its hollowness,
One mighty shell
  Of bitterness,
One grand farewell
  To happiness,
One solemn knell
  To love's caress,
It seems to me.
The shipless sea
  Hath bravery more
Than this waste scene,
Where what hath been
  Beloved of yore,
In the heart's bower so fresh and green,
  Fades evermore!

V.

From all its kind,
  This wasted heart—
This moody mind
  Now drifts apart;
It longs to find
  The tideless shore,
Where rests the wreck
  Of Heretofore,—
The glorious wreck
  Of mental ore;
The great heartbreak
  Of loves no more.

> I drift alone,
> For all are gone
>   Dearest to me ;
> And hail the wave
> That to the grave
>   On hurrieth me :
> Welcome, thrice welcome, then, thy wave,
>   Eternity !

XXXII.

THEY COME ! THE MERRY SUMMER MONTHS.

They come ! the merry summer months of Beauty, Song,
    and Flowers ;
They come ! the gladsome months that bring thick leafiness
    to bowers.
Up, up, my heart, and walk abroad, fling cark and care aside,
Seek silent hills, or rest thyself where peaceful waters glide ;
Or, underneath the shadow vast of patriarchal tree,
Scan through its leaves the cloudless sky in rapt tranquility.

The grass is soft, its velvet touch is grateful to the hand,
And, like the kiss of maiden love, the breeze is sweet and
    bland ;
The daisy and the buttercup are nodding courteously,
It stirs their blood with kindest love, to bless and welcome
    thee :
And mark how with thine own thin locks,—they now are
    silvery grey,—
That blissful breeze is wantoning, and whispering "Be gay !"

There is no cloud that sails along the ocean of yon sky,
But hath its own winged mariners to give it melody :

Thou see'st their glittering fans outspread all gleaming like
    red gold,
And hark! with shrill pipe musical, their merry course they
    hold.
God bless them all, these little ones, who far above this earth,
Can make a scoff of its mean joys, and vent a nobler mirth.

But soft! mine ear upcaught a sound, from yonder wood it
    came;
The spirit of the dim green glade did breathe his own glad
    name;—
Yes, it is he! the hermit bird, that apart from all his kind,
Slow spells his beads monotonous to the soft western wind;
Cuckoo! Cuckoo! he sings again,—his notes are void of art,
But simplest strains do soonest sound the deep founts of the
    heart!

Good Lord! it is a gracious boon for thought-crazed wight
    like me,
To smell again these summer flowers beneath this summer
    tree!
To suck once more in every breath their little souls away,
And feed my fancy with fond dreams of youth's bright summer
    day,
When rushing forth like untamed colt, the reckless truant boy
Wandered through green woods all day long, a mighty heart
    of joy!

I'm sadder now, I have had cause; but O! I'm proud to think
That each pure joy-fount loved of yore, I yet delight to drink;—
Leaf, blossom, blade, hill, valley, stream, the calm unclouded
    sky,
Still mingle music with my dreams as in the days gone by.
When summer's loveliness and light fall round me dark and
    cold,
I'll bear indeed life's heaviest curse,—a heart that hath waxed
    old!

XXXIII.

CHANGE SWEEPETH OVER ALL.

CHANGE sweepeth over all!
In showers leaves fall
From the tall forest tree;
On to the sea
Majestic rivers roll,
It is their goal.
Each speeds to perish in man's simple seeming,—
Each disappears;
One common end o'ertakes life's idle dreaming—
Dust, darkness, tears!

Day hurries to its close:
The sun that rose
A miracle of light,
Yieldeth to night;*
The skirt of one vast pall
O'ershadows all,
Yon firmamental cresset lights forth shining,
Heaven's highest born!
Droop on their thrones, and, like pale spirits pining,
Vanish with morn.

O'er cities of old days,
Dumb creatures graze;
Palace and pyramid
In dust are hid;
Yea, the sky-searching tower
Stands but its hour.

---

* Is CAPTIVE to night.—*MS. copy*

Oceans their wide-stretched beds are ever shifting,
    Sea turns to shore,
And stars and systems through dread space are drifting,
    To shine no more.

    Names perish that erst smote
      Nations remote,
    With panic, fear, or wrong ;
      Heroic song
    Grapples with time in vain ;
      On to the main
Of dim forgetfulness for ever rolling,
    Earth's bubbles burst ;
Time o'er the wreck of ages sternly tolling
    The last accurst.

    The world is waxing old,
      Heaven dull and cold ;
    Nought lacketh here a close
      Save human woes.
    Yet they too have an end,—
      Death is man's friend :
Doomed for a while, his heart must go on breaking
    Day after day,
But light, love, life,—all,—all at last forsaking,
    Clay claspeth clay !

SONGS.

SONGS.

XXXIV.

O WAE BE TO THE ORDERS.

O WAE be to the orders that marched my luve awa',
And wae be to the cruel cause that gars my tears doun fa',
O wae be to the bluidy wars in Hie Germanie,
For they hae ta'n my luve, and left a broken heart to me.

The drums beat in the mornin' afore the scriech o' day,
And the wee wee fifes piped loud and shrill, while yet the morn was grey;
The bonnie flags were a' unfurled, a gallant sight to see,
But waes me for my sodger lad that marched to Germanie.

O, lang, lang is the travel to the bonnie Pier o' Leith,
O dreich it is to gang on foot wi' the snaw-drift in the teeth!
And O, the cauld wind froze the tear that gathered in my ee,
When I gade there to see my luve embark for Germanie!

I looked ower the braid blue sea, sae long as could be seen,
Ae wee bit sail upon the ship that my sodger lad was in;
But the wind was blawin' sair and snell, and the ship sail'd speedilie,
And the waves and cruel wars hae twinn'd my winsome luve frae me.

I never think o' dancin', and I downa try to sing,
But a' the day I spier what news kind neibour bodies bring;
I sometimes knit a stocking, if knittin' it may be,
Syne for every loop that I cast on, I am sure to let doun three.

My father says I'm in a pet, my mither jeers at me,
And bans me for a dautit wean, in dorts for aye to be;
But little weet they o' the cause that drumles sae my ee:
O they hae nae winsome luve like mine in the wars o' Ger-
    manie!

XXXV.

WEARIE'S WELL.

In a saft simmer gloamin',
  In yon dowie dell,
It was there we twa first met
  By Wearie's cauld well.
We sat on the brume bank
  And looked in the burn,
But sidelang we looked on
  Ilk ither in turn.

The corn-craik was chirming
  His sad eerie cry,
And the wee stars were dreaming
  Their path through the sky;
The burn babbled freely
  Its love to ilk flower,
But we heard and we saw nought
  In that blessed hour.

We heard and we saw nought
  Above or around;
We felt that our love lived,
  And loathed idle sound.
I gazed on your sweet face
  Till tears filled my ee,
And they drapt on your wee loof,—
  A warld's wealth to me.

Now the winter snaw's fa'ing
  On bare holm and lea ;
And the cauld wind is strippin'
  Ilk leaf aff the tree.
But the snaw fa's not faster,
  Nor leaf disna part
Sae sune frae the bough, as
  Faith fades in your heart.

Ye've waled out anither
  Your bridegroom to be ;
But can his heart luve sae
  As mine luvit thee ?
Ye'll get biggings and mailins,
  And monie braw claes ;
But they a' winna buy back
  The peace o' past days.
Fareweel, and for ever,
  My first luve and last,
May thy joys be to come,—
  Mine live in the past.
In sorrow and sadness,
  This hour fa's on me ;
But light, as thy luve, may
  It fleet over thee !

XXXVI.

SONG OF THE DANISH SEA-KING.

Our bark is on the waters deep, our bright blade's in our hand,
Our birthright is the ocean vast—we scorn the girdled land;
And the hollow wind is our music brave, and none can bolder be
Than the hoarse-tongued tempest raving o'er a proud and swelling sea!

Our bark is dancing on the waves, its tall masts quivering bend
Before the gale, which hails us now with the hollo of a friend;
And its prow is sheering merrily the upcurled billow's foam,
While our hearts, with throbbing gladness, cheer old Ocean as our home!

Our eagle-wings of might we stretch before the gallant wind,
And we leave the tame and sluggish earth a dim mean speck behind;
We shoot into the untracked deep, as earth-freed spirits soar,
Like stars of fire through boundless space—through realms without a shore!

Lords of this wide-spread wilderness of waters, we bound free,
The haughty elements alone dispute our sovereignty;
No landmark doth our freedom let, for no law of man can mete
The sky which arches o'er our head—the waves which kiss our feet!

The warrior of the land may back the wild horse, in his
    pride ;
But a fiercer steed we dauntless breast—the untamed ocean
    tide ;
And a nobler tilt our bark careers, as it quells the saucy
    wave,
While the Herald storm peals o'er the deep the glories of
    the brave.

Hurrah! hurrah! the wind is up—it bloweth fresh and free,
And every cord, instinct with life, pipes loud its fearless
    glee ;
Big swell the bosomed sails with joy, and they madly kiss
    the spray,
As proudly, through the foaming surge, the Sea-King bears
    away !

XXXVII.

THE CAVALIER'S SONG.

A STEED ! a steed of matchlesse speed,
  A sword of metal keene !
All else to noble heartes is drosse,
  All else on earth is meane.
The neighyinge of the war-horse prowde,
  The rowlinge of the drum,
The clangor of the trumpet lowde,
  Be soundes from heaven that come ;
And O ! the thundering presse of knightes
  Whenas their war cryes swell,
May tole from heaven an angel brighte,
  And rouse a fiend from hell.

Then mounte ! then mounte, brave gallants, all,
   And don your helmes amaine :
Deathe's couriers, Fame and Honour, call
   Us to the field againe.
No shrewish teares shall fill our eye
   When the sword-hilt's in our hand,—
Heart whole we'll part, and no whit sighe
   For the fayrest of the land !
Let piping swaine, and craven wight,
   Thus weepe and puling crye,
Our business is like men to fight,
   And hero-like to die !

XXXVIII.

THE MERRY GALLANT.

The Merry Gallant girds his sword,
   And dons his helm in mickle glee !
He leaves behind his lady love
For tented fields and deeds which prove
   Stout hardiment and constancy.

When round him rings the din of arms,—
   The notes of high-born chivalry,
He thinks not of his bird in bower,
And scorns to own Love's tyrant power
   Amid the combats of the Free.

Yet in the midnight watch, I trow,
   When cresset lights all feebly burn,
Will hermit Fancy sometimes roam
With eager travel back to home,
   Where smiles and tears await—return.

"Away! away!" he boldly sings,
  "Be thrown those thoughts which cling to me;
That mournful look and glistering eye—
That quivering lip and broken sigh;—
  Why crowd each shrine of memory?

"O, that to-morrow's dawn would rise
  To light me on my path of glory,
Where I may pluck from niggard fame
Her bravest laurels—and the name
  That long shall live in minstrel story!

"Then, when my thirst for fame is dead,
  Soft love may claim his wonted due;
But now, when levelled lances gleam,
And chargers snort, and banners stream,
  To lady's love a long adieu!"

XXXIX.

THE KNIGHT'S SONG.

ENDEARING! endearing!
  Why so endearing
Are those dark lustrous eyes,
  Through their silk fringes peering?
They love me! they love me!
  Deeply, sincerely;
And more than aught else on earth,
  I love them dearly.

Endearing! endearing!
  Why so endearing
Glows the glad sunny smile
  On thy soft cheek appearing?

It brightens! it brightens!
  As I am nearing;
And 'tis thus that thy fond smile
  Is ever endearing.

Endearing! endearing!
  Why so endearing
Is that lute-breathing voice
  Which my rapt soul is hearing?
'Tis singing, 'tis singing
  Thy deep love for me,
And my faithful heart echoes
  Devotion to thee.

Endearing! endearing!
  Why so endearing
At each Passage of Arms
  Is the herald's bold cheering?
'Tis then thou art kneeling
  With pure hands to heaven,
And each prayer of thy heart
  For my good lance is given.

Endearing! endearing!
  Why so endearing
Is the fillet of silk
  That my right arm is wearing?
Once it veiled the bright bosom
  That beats but for me;
Now it circles the arm that
  Wins glory for thee!

XL.

THE TROOPER'S DITTY.

Boot, boot into the stirrup, lads,
    And hand once more on rein ;
Up, up into the saddle, lads,
    A-field we ride again :
One cheer, one cheer for dame or dear,
    No leisure now to sigh,
God bless them all—we have their prayers,
    And they our hearts—" Good-bye !"
Off, off we ride, in reckless pride,
    As gallant troopers may,
Who have old scores to settle, and
    Long slashing swords to pay.

The trumpet calls—" trot out, trot out,"—
    We cheer the stirring sound ;
Swords forth, my lads—through smoke and dust
    We thunder o'er the ground.
Tramp, tramp, we go through sulphury clouds,
    That blind us while we sing,—
Woe worth the knave who follows not
    The banner of the King ;
But luck befall each trooper tall,
    That cleaves to saddle-tree,
Whose long sword carves on rebel sconce,
    The rights of Majesty.

Spur on, my lads ; the trumpet sounds
    Its last and stern command—
" A charge ! a charge !"—an ocean burst
    Upon a stormy strand.
Ha ! ha ! how thickly on our casques
    Their pop-guns rattle shot ;

Spur on, my lads, we'll give it them
   As sharply as we've got.
Now for it :—now, bend to the work—
   Their lines begin to shake ;
Now, through and through them—bloody lanes
   Our flashing sabres make !

" Cut one—cut two—first point," and then
   We'll parry as we may ;
On, on the knaves, and give them steel
   In bellyfuls to-day.
Hurrah ! hurrah ! for Church and State,
   For Country and for Crown,
We slash away, and right and left
   Hew rogues and rebels down.
Another cheer ! the field is clear,
   The day is all our own ;
Done like our sires,—done like the swords
   God gives to guard the Throne !

XLI.

HE IS GONE! HE IS GONE!

HE is gone ! he is gone !
   Like the leaf from the tree ;
Or the down that is blown
   By the wind o'er the lea.
He is fled, the light-hearted !
Yet a tear must have started
To his eye, when he parted
   From love-stricken me !

He is fled ! he is fled !
   Like a gallant so free,

Plumed cap on his head,
   And sharp sword by his knee ;
While his gay feathers fluttered,
Surely something he muttered,
He at least must have uttered
   A farewell to me !

He's away ! he's away
   To far lands o'er the sea,—
And long is the day
   Ere home he can be ;
But where'er his steed prances,
Amid thronging lances,
Sure he'll think of the glances
   That love stole from me !

He is gone ! he is gone !
   Like the leaf from the tree ;
But his heart is of stone
   If it ne'er dream of me !
For I dream of him ever :
His buff-coat and beaver,
And long-sword, O, never
   Are absent from me !

XLII.

THE FORESTER'S CAROL.

Lusty Hearts ! to the wood, to the merry green wood,
   While the dew with strung pearls loads each blade,
And the first blush of dawn brightly streams o'er the lawn,
   Like the smile of a rosy-cheeked maid.

Our horns with wild music ring glad through each shaw,
   And our broad arrows rattle amain ;

For the stout bows we draw, to the green woods give law,
   And the Might is the Right once again!

Mark yon herds, as they brattle and brush down the glade;
   Pick the fat, let the lean rascals go,
Under favor 'tis meet that we tall men should eat,—
   Nock a shaft and strike down that proud doe!

Well delivered, parfay! convulsive she leaps,—
   One bound more,—then she drops on her side;
Our steel hath bit smart the life-strings of her heart,
   And cold now lies the green forest's pride.

Heave her up, and away!—should any base churl
   Dare to ask why we range in this wood,
There's a keen arrow yare, in each broad belt to spare,
   That will answer the knave in his blood!

Then forward my Hearts! like the bold reckless breeze
   Our life shall whirl on in mad glee;
The long bows we bend, to the world's latter end,
   Shall be borne by the hands of the Free!

XLIII.

MAY MORN SONG.

The grass is wet with shining dews,
   Their silver bells hang on each tree,
While opening flower and bursting bud
   Breathe incense forth unceasingly;
The mavis pipes in greenwood shaw,
   The throstle glads the spreading thorn,
And cheerily the blythesome lark
   Salutes the rosy face of morn.

MAY MORN SONG.

       'Tis early prime ;
          And hark ! hark ! hark !
       His merry chime
          Chirrups the lark :
  Chirrup ! chirrup ! he heralds in
  The jolly sun with matin hymn.

Come, come, my love ! and May-dews shake
  In pailfuls from each drooping bough ;
They'll give fresh lustre to the bloom,
  That breaks upon thy young cheek now.
O'er hill and dale, o'er waste and wood,
  Aurora's smiles are streaming free ;
With earth it seems brave holyday,
  In heaven it looks high jubilee.
       And it is right,
          For mark, love, mark !
       How bathed in light
          Chirrups the lark :
  Chirrup ! chirrup ! he upward flies,
  Like holy thoughts to cloudless skies.

They lack all heart who cannot feel
  The voice of heaven within them thrill,
In summer morn when mounting high
  This merry minstrel sings his fill.
Now let us seek yon bosky dell
  Where brightest wild-flowers choose to be,
And where its clear stream murmurs on,
  Meet type of our love's purity ;
       No witness there,
          And o'er us hark !
       High in the air
          Chirrups the larks :
  Chirrup ! chirrup ! away soars he,
  Bearing to heaven my vows to thee !

XLIV.

THE BLOOM HATH FLED THY CHEEK, MARY.

THE bloom hath fled thy cheek, Mary,
　As spring's rath blossoms die,
And sadness hath o'ershadowed quite
　Thy once bright eye;
But, look on me, the prints of grief
　Still deeper lie.
　　　　Farewell!

Thy lips are pale and mute, Mary,
　Thy step is sad and slow,
The morn of gladness hath gone by
　Thou erst didst know;
I, too, am changed like thee, and weep
　For very woe.
　　　　Farewell!

It seems as 'twere but yesterday
　We were the happiest twain,
When murmured sighs and joyous tears,
　Dropping like rain,
Discoursed my love and told how loved
　I was again.
　　　　Farewell!

'Twas not in cold and measured phrase
　We gave our passion name;
Scorning such tedious eloquence,
　Our heart's fond flame
And long imprisoned feelings fast
　In deep sobs came.
　　　　Farewell!

Would that our love had been the love
   That merest worldlings know,
When passion's draught to our doomed lips
   Turns utter woe,
And our poor dream of happiness
   Vanishes so!
      Farewell!

But in the wreck of all our hopes,
   There's yet some touch of bliss,
Since fate robs not our wretchedness
   Of this last kiss:
Despair, and love, and madness, meet
   In this, in this.
      Farewell!

XLV.

IN THE QUIET AND SOLEMN NIGHT.

In the quiet and solemn night,
When the moon is silvery bright,
Then the screech owl's eerie cry
Mocks the beauties of the sky:
   Tu whit, tu whoo,
   Its wild halloo
Doth read a drowsy homily.

From yon old castle's chimneys tall,
The bat on leathern sail doth fall
In wanton-wise to skim the earth,
And flout the mouse that gave it birth.
   Tu whit, tu whoo,
   That wild haloo
Hath marred the little monster's mirth.

Fond lovers seek the dewy vale,
That swimmeth in the moonshine pale;
But maids! beware, when in your ear
The screech-owl screams so loud and clear:
    Tu whit, tu whoo,
    Its wild halloo
Doth speak of danger lurking near.

It bids beware of murmured sigh,
Of air-spun oath and wistful eye;
Of star that winks to conscious flower
Through the roof of leaf-clad bower:
    Tu whit, tu whoo,
    That wild halloo
Bids startled virtue own its power!

XLVI.

THE VOICE OF LOVE.

When shadows o'er the landscape creep,
And twinkling stars pale vigils keep;
When flower-cups all with dew-drops gleam,
And moonshine floweth like a stream;
    Then is the hour
That hearts which love no longer dream,—
    Then is the hour
That the voice of love is a spell of power!

When shamefaced moonbeams kiss the lake,
And amorous leaves sweet music wake;
When slumber steals o'er every eye,
And Dian's self shines drowsily;

Then is the hour
That hearts which love with rapture sigh,—
　　Then is the hour
That the voice of love is a spell of power !

When surly mastiffs stint their howl,
And swathed in moonshine nods the owl ;
When cottage-hearths are glimmering low,
And warder cocks forget to crow ;
　　Then is the hour
That hearts feel passion's overflow,—
　　Then is the hour
That the voice of love is a spell of power !

When stilly night seems earth's vast grave,
Nor murmur comes from wood or wave ;
When land and sea, in wedlock bound
By silence, sleep in bliss profound ;
　　Then is the hour
That hearts like living well-springs sound,—
　　Then is the hour
That the voice of love is a spell of power !

XLVII.

AWAY ! AWAY ! O, DO NOT SAY.

Away ! away ! O, do not say
　He can prove false to me :
Let me believe but this brief day
　In his fidelity ;
Tell me, that rivers backward flow,
That unsunned snows like fire-brands glow,
　I may believe that lay,

But never can believe that he
  Is false and fled away.

Ill acted part ! ill acted part !
  I knew his noble mind,
He could not break a trusting heart,
  Nor leave his love behind ;
Tell me yon sun will cease to rise,
Or stars at night to gem the skies,
  I may believe such lay ;
But never can believe that he
  Is false and fled away.

Can it be so ? O, surely no !
  Must I perforce believe
That he I loved and trusted so,
  Vowed only to deceive ?
Heap coals of fire on this lone head,
Or in pure pity strike me dead,—
  'Twere kindness, on the day
That tells me one I loved so well,
  Is false,—is fled away !

XLVIII.

O, AGONY! KEEN AGONY.

O, AGONY ! keen agony,
For trusting heart, to find
That vows believed, were vows conceived
As light as summer wind.

O, agony ! fierce agony,
For loving heart to brook,
In one brief hour the withering power
Of unimpassioned look.

O, agony! deep agony,
For heart that's proud and high,
To learn of fate how desolate
It may be ere it die.

O, agony! sharp agony,
To find how loath to part
With the fickleness and faithlessness
That break a trusting heart!

XLIX.

THE SERENADE.

WAKE, lady, wake!
Dear heart, awake
From slumbers light;
For 'neath thy bower, at this still hour,
In harness bright,
Lingers thine own true paramour,
And chosen knight!
Wake, lady, wake!

Wake, lady, wake!
For thy loved sake,
Each trembling star
Smiles from on high with its clear eye,
While nobler far
Yon silvery shield lights earth and sky;
How good they are!
Wake, lady, wake!

Rise, lady, rise!
Not star-filled skies
I worship now,
A fairer shrine I trust is mine
For loyal vow:

O that the living stars would shine
    That light thy brow !
    Rise, lady, rise !

    Rise, lady, rise,
    Ere war's rude cries
    Fright land and sea !
To-morrow's light sees mail-sheathed knight,
    Even hapless me,
Careering through the bloody fight
    Afar from thee !
    Rise, lady, rise !

    Mute, lady, mute ?
    I have no lute,
    Nor rebeck small
To soothe thine ear with lay sincere,
    Or Madrigal ;
With helm on head and hand on spear,
    On thee I call !
    Mute, lady, mute !

    Mute, lady, mute
    To love's fond suit ?
    I'll not complain,
Since underneath thy balmy breath
    I may remain
One brief hour more ere I seek death
    On battle plain !
    Mute, lady, mute !

    Sleep, lady, sleep !
    While watch I keep
    Till dawn of day :
But o'er the wold now morning cold
    Shines icy grey ;

While the plain gleams with steel and gold,
  And chargers neigh !
  Sleep, lady, sleep !

  Sleep, lady, sleep !
  Nor wake to weep
  For heart-struck me :
These trumpets knell my last farewell
  To love and thee !
When next they sound, 'twill be to tell
  I died for thee !
  Sleep, lady, sleep !

L.

COULD LOVE IMPART.

  Could love impart,
  By nicest art,
To speechless rocks a tongue,—
  Their theme would be,
  Beloved, of thee,—
Thy beauty, all their song.

  And, clerklike, then,
  With sweet amen,
Would echo from each hollow
  Reply all day ;
  While gentle fay,
With merry whoop, would follow.

  Had roses sense,
  On no pretence
Would they their buds unroll ;

For, could they speak,
'Twas from thy cheek
Their daintiest blush they stole.

Had lilies eyes,
With glad surprise
They'd own themselves outdone,
When thy pure brow
And neck of snow
Gleamed in the morning sun.

Could shining brooks,
By amorous looks,
Be taught a voice so rare,
Then, every sound
That murmured round
Would whisper, "Thou art fair!"

Could winds be fraught
With pensive thought
At midnight's solemn hour,
Then every wood,
In gleeful mood,
Would own thy beauty's power!

And, could the sky
Behold thine eye,
So filled with love and light,
In jealous haste,
Thou soon wert placed
To star, the cope of Night!

LI.

THE PARTING.

Oh ! is it thus we part,
And thus we say farewell,
As if in neither heart
Affection e'er did dwell ?
And is it thus we sunder
Without a sigh or tear,
As if it were a wonder
We e'er held other dear ?

We part upon the spot,
With cold and clouded brow,
Where first it was our lot
To breathe love's fondest vow !
The vow both then did tender
Within this hallowed shade*—
These vows we now surrender,
Heart-bankrupts both are made !

Thy hand is cold as mine,
As lustreless thine eye ;
Thy bosom gives no sign
That it could ever sigh !
Well, well ! adieu's soon spoken,
'Tis but a parting phrase,
Yet said, I fear, heart-broken
We'll live our after days !

Thine eye no tear will shed ;
Mine is as proudly dry ;

---

* Within this MOONLIT GLADE.—*MS. copy.*

But many an aching head
Is ours before we die !
From pride we both can borrow—
To part we both may dare—
But the heart-break of to-morrow,
Nor you nor I can bear !

LII.

LOVE'S DIET.

Tell me, fair maid, tell me truly,
  How should infant Love be fed ;
If with dewdrops, shed so newly
  On the bright green clover blade ;
Or, with roses plucked in July,
  And with honey liquored ?
    O, no ! O, no !
    Let roses blow,
And dew-stars to green blade cling :
    Other fare,
    More light and rare,
Befits that gentlest Nursling.

Feed him with the sigh that rushes
  'Twixt sweet lips, whose muteness speaks
With the eloquence that flushes
  All a heart's wealth o'er soft cheeks ;
Feed him with a world of blushes,
  And the glance that shuns, yet seeks :
    For 'tis with food,
    So light and good,
That the Spirit child is fed ;
    And with the tear
    Of joyous fear
That the small Elf's liquored.

LIII.

THE MIDNIGHT WIND.

Mournfully ! O, mournfully
  This midnight wind doth sigh,
Like some sweet plaintive melody
  Of ages long gone by :
It speaks a tale of other years—
  Of hopes that bloomed to die—
Of sunny smiles that set in tears,
  And loves that mouldering lie !

Mournfully ! O, mournfully
  This midnight wind doth moan ;
It stirs some chord of memory
  In each dull heavy tone :
The voices of the much-loved dead
  Seem floating thereupon—
All, all my fond heart cherished
  Ere death had made it lone.

Mournfully ! O, mournfully
  This midnight wind doth swell,
With its quaint pensive minstrelsy
  Hope's passionate farewell
To the dreamy joys of early years,
  Ere yet grief's canker fell
On the heart's bloom—ay ! well may tears
  Start at that parting knell !

POSTHUMOUS PIECES.

POSTHUMOUS PIECES.

LIV.

THE WAITHMAN'S WAIL.*

> The waithman goode of Silverwoode,
>   That bowman stout and hende,
> In donjon gloom abydes his doome;
>   God dele him getil ende.
>
> It breakes trew herte to see him sterte,
>   Whenas the small birdes sing;
> And then to hear his sighynges drere
>   Whenas his fetters ryng.
>
> Of bowe and shafte he bin bereft,
>   And eke of bugil horne;
> A goodlye wighte, by craftie slyghte,
>   Alake! is overborne.
>   —Old Ballad.

My heart is sick! my heart is sick!
  And sad as heart can be;
It pineth for the forest brook,
  And for the forest tree;
It pineth for all gladsome things
  That haunt the woodlands free.

O Silverwood, sweet Silverwood,
  Thy leaves be large and long;

---

* Waithman—hunter.

And there, God wot, in summer eve,
   To list the small bird's song,
Were med'cine to the heart that breaks,
   Like mine, in prison strong.

The sun, in idle wantonness,
   Shines in this dungeon cold,
But his bright glance, through Silverwood,
   I never shall behold!
I ne'er shall see each broad leaf gleam
   Like banner-flag of gold.

It pains me, this o'ermastering light,
   Fast flooding from the sky,
That streams through these black prison bars
   In sheerest mockery,
Recalling thoughts, by green woods bred,
   To mad me ere I die.

Dear western wind, now blowing soft
   Upon my faded cheek,
Thy angel whisperings seem even now
   Of Silverwood to speak;
Of streams and bowers that make man's heart
   As very woman's weak.

Soft western wind, with music fraught,
   Of all to heart most dear;
Of birds that sing in greenest glade,
   Of streams that run so clear;
Why pour thy sweetness o'er the heart
   That wastes in dungeon drear?

The sunshine's for the jocund heart,
   The breeze is for the free;
They be for those who bend stout bow
   Beneath the greenwood tree.
Sun ne'er should shine, breeze never blow,
   For fettered slave like me.

I hear the hawk's scream in the wood,
    The brayings of gaunt hound,
The sharp sough of the feathered shaft,
    The bugle's thrilling sound ;
I hear them ; and, oh God, these limbs
    With Spanish irons bound !

Strike these foul fetters from my wrist,
    These shackles from my knee,
Set this foot 'gainst an earthfast stone,
    This back 'gainst broad oak tree ;
Give but one span of earth for fight,
    And I once more am free !

A single hand, a single brand,
    Against uncounted foes ;
A heart that's withered like a leaf,
    In brooding o'er its woes
Are surely not such deadly odds
    For stout men to oppose.

But no ; bound here midst rotting straw,
    Within this noisome cell,
They joy to see a proud heart break,
    And ring its own sad knell ;
They joy to hear me, Silverwood,
    Bid thee and life farewell.

So let it be ; sweet Silverwood,
    On daylight's latest beam,
My spirit seeks again thy glades
    Revisits flower and stream ;
And fleets through thee, unchanged in love,
    In this my dying dream.

LV.

THE TROUBADOUR'S LAMENT.

It was a gallant troubadour,
  A child of sword and song,
That loved a gentle paramour,
  And loved her leal and long;
He woo'd her as a knight should woo,
  And laying lance in rest,
In listed fields, her colours flew
  O'er many a haughty crest.
He loved her as a bard should do,
  And taking harp in hand,
In sweetest lays, that lady's praise
  He poured o'er many a land:
    But all in vain,
    His noblest strain
  Awoke no kind return;
    That lady proud
    Smiled on the crowd,
  But his true love did spurn.

It was a tristful troubadour,
  Heart-broken by disdain,
That then to France and belle amour
  Bequeathed this mournful strain,
As riding on the yellow sand
  With many a knightly feere,
He smote his harp with feeblest hand,
  To sing with feebler cheer:
Adieu, proud love! adieu, fair land!
  Where heathen banners float,
This broken heart can act its part,
  Can die, and be forgot.
    Alas! too late;
    It was its fate

   To learn, with saddest pain,
    It loved one
    Who scorned to own
   Her heart could love again.

Fair France, farewell! my latest breath
 Shall still be spent for thee,
While meeting strife, I court my death
 In distant Galilee.
My soul is bound up with the glaive
 That glitters at my thigh,
And fixed upon the banner brave
 Now flashing to the sky.
A last adieu I well may waive
 To her I loved so well;
She does not care what doom I bear,
 Yet, heartless maid, farewell!
   No bridal sheet
   For me is meet,
  I seek the soldier's bier,
   Who, for his God,
   Sleeps on the sod,
  Unstained by woman's tear.

LVI.

WHEN I BENEATH THE COLD RED EARTH AM SLEEPING.

When I beneath the cold red earth am sleeping,
  Life's fever o'er,
Will there for me be any bright eye weeping
  That I'm no more?
Will there be any heart still memory keeping
  Of heretofore?

When the great winds through leafless forests rushing,
    Like full hearts break,
When the swollen streams, o'er crag and gully gushing,
    Sad music make;
Will there be one whose heart despair is crushing
    Mourn for my sake?

When the bright sun upon that spot is shining
    With purest ray,
And the small flowers their buds and blossoms twining,
    Burst through that clay;
Will there be one still on that spot repining
    Lost hopes all day?

When the night shadows, with the ample sweeping
    Of her dark pall;
The world and all its manifold creation sleeping,
    The great and small—
Will there be one, even at that dread hour, weeping
    For me—for all?

When no star twinkles with its eye of glory,
    On that low mound;
And wintry storms have with their ruins hoary
    Its loneness crowned;
Will there be then one versed in misery's story
    Pacing it round?

It may be so,—but this is selfish sorrow
    To ask such meed,—
A weakness and a wickedness to borrow
    From hearts that bleed,
The wailings of to-day, for what to-morrow
    Shall never need.

Lay me then gently in my narrow dwelling,
    Thou gentle heart;

And though thy bosom should with grief be swelling,
    Let no tear start;
It were in vain,—for Time hath long been knelling—
    Sad one, depart!

LVII.

SPIRITS OF LIGHT!—SPIRITS OF SHADE!

Spirits of Light! Spirits of Shade!
Hark to the voice of your love-craz'd maid,
Who singeth all night so merrily,
Under the cope of the huge elm tree.
The snow may fall, and the bitter wind blow,
But still with love must her heart overflow.

The great elm tree is leafy and high,
And its topmost branch wanders far up in the sky;
It is clothed with leaves from top to toe;
For it loveth to hear the wild winds blow,—
The winds that travel so fast and free,
Over the land, and over the sea,
Singing of marvels continuously.
The moon of these leaves is shining ever,
And they dance like the waves of a gleaming river.
But, oft in the night,
When her smile shines bright,
With the cold, cold dew they shiver.
Oh, woe is me, for the suffering tree,
And the little green leaves that shiver and dream
  In the icy moonbeam.
    Oh, woe is me!

I would I were clad with leaves so green,
And grew like this elm, a fair forest queen;

Could shoot up ten fingers like branches tall,
Till the cold—cold dews would on me fall ;
For to shiver is sweet when winds blow keen,
Or hoar frost powders the dreary scene.
And oh ! I would like that my flesh could creep
With cold, as it was wont to do ;
And that my heart, like a flower went to sleep,
When Winter his icy trumpet blew,
And shook o'er the wolds and moorland fells,
His crisping beard of bright icicles,
While his breath, as it swept adown the strath,
Smote with death the burn as it brawled on its path,
Stilled its tongue, and laid it forth
In a lily-white smock from the freezing north.
    But woe, deep woe,
    It is not so.

Spirits of Light ! Spirits of Shade !
Hearken once more to your love-stricken maid,
For, oh, she is sad as sad may be,
Pining all night underneath this tree,
Yet lacking thy goodly company.
She is left self-alone,
While the old forests groan,
As they hear, down rushing from the skies,
The embattled squadrons of the air,
Pealing o'er ridgy hills their cries
Of battle, and of fierce despair.
Through sunless valleys, deep and drear,
Hark, to their trumpets' brassy blare,
The tramp of steed, and crash of spear !
Nearer yet the strife sweeps on,
And I am left thus self-alone,
With never a guardian spirit near,
To couch for me a generous lance,
When the storm fiends madly prance
On their steeds of cloud and flame,

To work a gentle maiden shame,
    Oh, misery !
I die ; and yet I scorn to blame
    Inconstancy.
All in this old wood,
They may shed my blood,
But false to my true love
    I never can be.

Peace, breaking heart ! it is not so,
For sweetly I hear your voices flow—
All your sad soft voices flow
Like the murmurs of the ocean,
Kissed by Zephyrs into motion ;
And when shells have found a tongue
To sing, as they were wont to sing,
When this noble world was young ;
And the sea formed love's bright ring,
And hearts found hearts in every thing.
Now the trees find apt replying,
To your music, with a sighing
That doth witch the owl to sleep ;
And, waving their great arms to and fro,
They feel ye walk, and their heads they bow
In adoration deep.
And I, with very joy could now,
Like weakest infant weep,
That hath its humour, and doth go
With joy-wrung tears to sleep.

And now all the leaves that are sere and dry,
Noiselessly fall, like stars from the sky ;
They are showering down on either hand,
A brown, brown burden upon the land.
And thus it will be with the love-stricken maid,
That loveth the Spirits of Light and Shade,

And whose thoughts commune with the spirits that write
The blue book of heaven with words of light.
And who bend down in love for her,
　From their stately domes on high,
To teach her each bright character
　That gleameth in her eye,
When the solemn night unrols
The vast map of the world of souls.
Oh, ecstacy ! rapt ecstacy !
For a poor maiden of earth like me ;
　To have and hold
The spirits who shine like molten gold,
　Eternally.

Beautiful Spirits ! flee me not ;
For this is the hour, and this is the spot,
Where we were wont of old to spell
The language of the star-filled sky ;
And walk through heaven's own citadel,
With stately step and upcast eye,
And brows, on which were deeply wrought,
The fadeless prints of glorious thought.

Ye melt fast away in the dewy chill
O' the moonbeam, but yield to a maiden's will ;
Take, ere ye vanish, this guerdon fair,
A long lock of her sun-bright hair ;
It was shorn from temples that throbbed with pain,
As the fearful thought wandered through the brain.
That never again, as in days of yore,
It might be her hap to gather lore
From the dropping richness of liquid tones,
That fall from the lips of spiritual ones.
Scorn not my gift—Oh, it is fair,
As, streaming, it follows your course high in air ;
And here is a brave and flaunting thing :—

A jolly green garland, braided well
With roses wild, and foxglove bell—
With sage, and rue, and eglantine—
With ivy leaf and holly green.
Three times it was dipped in a faery spring,
And three times spread forth in a faery ring,
When the dews fell thick and the moon was full;
And three times it clipped a dead man's skull—
And three times it lay pillowed under this cheek,
And lips that would, but could not speak,
Where its bloom was preserved, by tears freshly shed,
From a bursting heart's fond fountain head.
Take these gifts, then, ere ye go,
Or my heart will break with its weight of woe,
    Oh, misery!
To love, and yet to be slighted so,
    Sad misery.

Spirits of Light! Spirits of Shade!
Once more thus prays your love-stricken maid:
Dig out, and spread in the white moonshine,
A goodly couch for these limbs of mine;
Fast by the roots of this stately tree,
And three fathoms deep that couch must be.
And lightly strew o'er her the withered leaf;
Meet shroud for maiden mild 'twill prove;
And as it falls it will lull her grief,
With gentlest rustlings, breathing love.
Then choose a turf that is wondrous light,
And lap it softly o'er this breast;
And charge the dew-drops, large and bright,
On its green grass for ever to rest.
So that, like a queen, clad in gems, she may lie,
    Right holily,
With hands crossed in prayer, gazing up to the sky,
    Tranquilly,
        Eternally.

LVIII.

THE CRUSADER'S FAREWELL.

The banners rustle in the breeze,
   The angry trumpets swell;
They call me, lady, from thy arms,
   They bid me sigh farewell!

They call me to a heathen land,
   To quell a heathen foe;
To leave love's blandishments, and court
   Rude dangers, strife, and wo.

Yet deem not, lady, though afar
   It be my hap to roam,
That this right loyal heart can stray
   From love, from thee, and home.

No! in the tumult of the fight,
   Midst Salem's chivalrie,
The thought that arms this hand with death
   Shall be the thought of thee.

LIX.

THE MIDNIGHT LAMP.

Thou pale and sickly lamp,
   Now glimmering like the glow-worm of the swamp,
Shine on, I pray thee, for another hour,
And shed thy wan and feeble lustre o'er
This precious volume of forgotten lore
   My eyes devour.

Shine on, I pray thee, but some little while
Soon will the morning's ruddy smile
Peep through the casement, like a well-known guest,
And give thee needful rest.

Even now the grey owl seeks his nest ;
And in the farm-yards, lusty cocks begin
To flap their wings, and, with a rousing din,
Cheer on the lagging morn.
Right soon the careful churle will go
To view his ripening corn ;
And up, and up, in a merry row,
A thousand many-voiced birds will spring,
And in one general chorus sing
Their matins to the skies.

Then live some little while, poor sickening light,
And glad my aching eyes ;
Thou wilt not die until the morrow bright
Has seen thy exequies.
Thou wilt not quit me like a thankless one,
Who, when grief closes with the fainting heart,
Doth shape his leave.
I pray thee tarry, then. Alas ! thou'rt gone.
Pity it is that in this mood we part.

LX.

COME DOWN, YE SPIRITS.

Come down, ye Spirits ! in your might, come down !
Come down, ye Spirits of this midnight hour ;
Come down in all your dim sublimity
And majesty of terror ! How I joy
To meet you in your own dark territories,

And hold mysterious converse in a tongue
That hath quite perished among the sons
Of fallen man! Ye Spirits that do roam
With unconfined footsteps o'er the paths
Of measureless eternity;—ye who skim
The bosomed cloud, or pace with hasty step
The earth's green surface, and its every spot,
Though ne'er so lone, deserted, and profound;
Repeople with strange sounds and voices sweet,
Which circle round, even when all else is still,
And breed in vulgar breasts a nameless dread
And awe inexplicable; which bids the flesh
To creep, as if its every fibre were
A many-footed and a living thing,
Come down! come down!

 I hear ye come! I hear your sounding wings
Beat the impassive air with mighty strokes,
And in the flickering moonshine I can see
Your shadowy limbs, descending like a mist
Of fleecy whiteness, on the slumbering earth.
And now I hear the mingled harmonies
Of all your voices, fill the vaulted sky.
Ye call upon me—and my soul is glad
To meet you on your pilgrimage, and join
Its feeble echoes to your mighty song.

LXI.

DING DONG!

Ding dong! ding dong!
The church bells chime
At early prime—
A solemn stave—
Ding dong! ding dong!
 O'er the lovers' grave.

Ding dong ! ding dong !
The slow sounds weep,
And cadence keep
With the wail of woe—
Ding dong ! ding dong !
  O'er the grave below.

Ding dong ! ding dong !
Strew garlands round
The holy ground,
Where twin hearts sleep.
Ding dong ! ding dong !
  And two friends weep.

Ding dong ! ding dong !
The church bells play
At close of day,
With hollow tone.
Ding dong ! ding dong !
They ever moan.

Ding dong ! ding dong !
Cold death hath laid
In earthly bed
Two hearts alone.
Ding dong ! ding dong !
  And made them one.

Ding dong ! ding dong !
The church bells loom
Above the tomb
Where true loves meet.
Ding dong ! ding dong !
  How sad and sweet !

LXII.

CLERKE RICHARD AND MAID MARGARET.

> A man must nedes love maugre his hed,
> He may not fleen it though he should be ded.
> —CHAUCER.

THERE were two lovers who loved each other
For many years, till hate did start,
And yet they never quite could smother
The former love that warmed their heart ;
And both did love, and both did hate,
Till both fulfilled the will of fate.

Years after, and the maid did marry
One that her heart had ne'er approved,
Nor longer could Clerke Richard tarry
Where he had lost all that he loved.
To foreign lands he reckless went
To nourish love—hate—discontent.

A word—an idle word of folly,
Had spilled their love when it was young,
And hatred, grief, and melancholy,
In either heart as idly sprung ;
And yet they loved—and hate did wane,
And much they wished to meet again.

Of Richard still is Margaret dreaming ;
His image lingered in her breast ;
And oft at midnight, to her seeming,
Her former lover stood confest ;
And shedding on her bosom tears,
The bitter wrecks of happier years.

Where'er he went, by land or ocean,
Still Richard sees dame Margaret there;
And every throb and kind emotion
His bosom knew were felt for her.
And never new love hath he cherished;
The power to love with first love perished.

Homeward is Clerke Richard sailing,
An altered man from him of old,
His hate had changed to bitter wailing,
And love resumed its wonted hold
Upon his heart, which yearned to see
The haunts and loves of infancy.

He knew her faithless, nathless, ever;
He loved her, though no more his own;
Nor could he proudly now dissever
The chain that round his heart was thrown.
He loved her without hope, yet true,
And sought her but to say adieu.

For even in parting there is pleasure,
A bitter joy that wrings the soul;
And there is grief surpassing measure
That will not bide nor brook control;
And yet a formal fond-leave taking
Is wished for by a heart nigh breaking.

Oh, there is something in the feeling,
And trembling falter of the hand,
And something in the tear down stealing,
And voice so broken and so bland,
And something in the word farewell
That worketh like a powerful spell!

These lovers met, and never parted;
They met as lovers wont to do
Who meet when both are broken-hearted,
To breathe a last and long adieu.

Pale Margaret wept.   Clerke Richard sighed ;
And, folded in each other's arms, they died.

Yes, they did die ere word was spoken ;
Surprise, grief-love had chained their tongue ;
And now that hatred was ywroken,
A wondrous joy in them had sprung.
And then despair froze either heart,
Which lived to meet—but died to part.

Clerke Richard, he was buried low
In fair Linlithgow ; and his love
Was laid beside him there ; and lo,
A bonnie tree did grow above
Their double grave, and it doth flourish
Green o'er the spot where love did perish.

LXIII.

LORD ARCHIBALD.

A BALLAD.

O SAFTLIE, saftlie laie him doun, and hap upo' his heid
The cauld reid erd ful lichtlie feris, this is a knichtlie rede ;
And pight a carvit croce of stane abune quhare he dois lye,
Syne it was for the halie rude Lord Archibald did die.

Its saftlie, saftlie have thay layd Lord Archibald in graif,
And its dowie, dowie owre his bouk thair plumis and banneris waif ;
And its lichtlie, lichtlie doe thay hap the red erth on his heid ;
And waefil was ilk knichtly fere to luik upon the deid.

Thay layd him doun wi' sighe and sab, and they layd him
 doun wi' tearis;
And nou abune the Olyve wuddis the ice-cauld mune apperis;
Quhyl thai muntit on thayr stedis amayne a sorrowand cum-
 panie,
And be the munelicht forthy thai begin a lang jornie.

Awa thai rade, away thai rade, and the wynd souchit eerie by,
And quhiskit aff ilk heavie tere quhilk gatherit in thair eye;
For weil thay luvit Lord Archibald as knichtis suld luve
 thair feris;
But littil thai affect Syr Hew, quha now thair fealtie bearis.

Its thai have spurrit, and egre spurrit, and thair stedes ar al
 a fome,
And nevir a word frae anie lip of thir silent knichtis hes
 come;
And still they spurrit and pukit on, til a lonesum lodge they
 wan,
Then voydit thae thair saddilis al, and til the yett thay ran.

Nae licht is schinand in the lodge, and nae portir keepis the
 dore;
Nae warder strade, wi lustie spere, that dreirie lodge before;
Nae harp is heard inurth the hall, and nae sang frae ladie
 braive,
But al was quiet as Ermites houff, and stylliche as the grave.

Swith pacit thai in be twa and twa, ilk wi his outdrawn
 swerd,
And thai gang throu vaultit passages, albeit nae sound thay
 heard,
Bot and it was the heavy clamp quhilk thair fit rang on the
 flore,
Til that thay stude, ilk knicht of them, fornentes the grit
 hall dore.

Now enter thou, the bauld Syr Hew, for treason do we feare;
Now entir first, as Captaine thou, of your brithern knichtis sae dier ;
For syne the gude Lord Archibald was laid aneth the stane,
Our manlyke courage has yfled, and al our hertis have gane.

The dark Syr Hew gade on before, and ane yreful man was he ;
"Oh, schame upon your manheidis al, and dishonour on ye be ;
"Quhat fleyis ye sua that nane may daur to threuw this chalmer lok ;"
Then wi' his iron gauntlet he that aiken dore has broke.

"Come in, Syr Hew ; come in, Syr Hew ;" a voice cryit fra within ;
"Come in, Syr Hew, my buirdly bairn, quhilk are sua wicht and grim,
"But nevir nane sal entir here bot an yoursel alane ;
"Now welcum blythe to dark Syr Hew in this puir lodge of stane."

Ilk knicht did hear the lonsum voyce, but the speiker nane did see,
And dark Syr Hew waxit deadlie pale, quhyl the mist cam owre his ee.
"Now turn wi' me, my merrie men al, to hald us on our way,
"For in this ugsum lodge this nicht nae pilgrimer may stay."
"Come back, Syr Hew, my knicht of grace, and come hither my trusty fere ;
"For thou hast wan a gudely fee, though nae lerges ye mote spere :
"Oh, three woundis were on your britheris face, and three abune his knee,
"But the deepest wound was throu his hert, and that was gi'en be thee."

Ilk ane has heard the lonesum voyce, for it was schil and hie;
Ilk ane has heard its eerie skreich as it gaed souning by;
Yet mervailous dul that lodge dois seem, and bot anie bruit or din;
Nae liand wicht dois herbour here but an that voyce within.

And everie knicht has turnit him round to leave that hauntit ha',
And muntit on his swelterand stede, and pricket richt sune awa';
And quhan this gallant cumpanye auld Askelon had nearit,
The wan mune had gane fra the lift, and the grai daylight apperit.

Then did they count thair numberis, and thay countit wyse and true,
And everilk ane was thair convenit bot and the dark Syr Hew;
But in the press his horse was kythit wi' ane saddil toom and bare;
Och and alace, its maister sure liggis in som lanelie lair.

Back hae thay ridden league and myl, but nevir Syr Hew thai see;
Back hae thay ridden league and myl til quhare that lodge suld be;
Och and alace, nae lodge is thair, nouthir of stane nor wud,
But quhair it was lay the dark Syr Hew amid thick clotterit blude.

His lyre was wan, his teeth were clenchit, and his eyne did open stare,
And wonderouslie lyke stiffened cordis stude up his coal-black hair,
And his hand was glewit until the haft of his swerd sue scharp and trew,
Bot the blade was broke, and on the grund it lay in pieces two.

He streiket was upon the garse, and it was red of blee,
Wi' the drappyng of the ruddie blude that trinklit doun his knee;
And his brunie bricht was dintit sair, and heart in pieces ten,
O nevir was a knicht sae hackit by armis of mortal men.

Thay sayit to raise him, bot alace, thai culd not muve a limm;
But heavie as the lead he lay, that Captaine dark and brym;
And his eye was luik, and fierslie fell, and his hand was rased a lite,
Albeit no lyf was in the corps of that cauld paly knighte.

Then did thay leave him on that spot to rot and fal away,
And thay put na stane upon his heid, and on his corps nae clay,
For thay had lerit in ferly wise that hindernicht I rede,
That dark Syr Hew, by felon means, did make his brither bleed.

LXIV.

AND HAVE I GAZED?

And have I gazed on this bright form
While it was fast decaying?
And have I looked on these pale lips
While ghastly death and woman's love
Thereon with smiles were playing?
And do I see that lustrous eye
Now quenched in hopeless night?
And was that feebly-murmured sigh
Thy spirit's heavenward flight?

A moment since that eye was bright,
A moment since it beamed on me,

And now that lovely orb of light
Is fixed on dull vacuity;
That bosom throbb'd, that cheek was warm,
And in that round and polish'd arm
The thin blue veins were filled with life;
Now motionless and pale they lie;
Sad beauteous wrecks of that stern strife
In which a soul escaped on high!
Can I forget thy sad sweet smile,
Thy last, thy long impassioned look?
Can I forget the last farewell
It then so fondly took?
Oh no—methinks thy lips still seem
That smile of deepest love to beam,
And these eyes that now calmly sleep
Beneath their half-closed thin transparent covers,
Have all the lustre in their slumber deep
They had in life, and proud dominion keep
With light and sunshine over hearts and lovers.
Vain thought! Imagination's hollow trick
To wean the heart from brooding o'er its sorrow,
Away! Death's blighting dews have fallen thick
On that dear maiden's pale and bloodless cheek.
She smiled to-day; some gentle words did speak,
But not one smile nor syllable will break
The silence of to-morrow!

Feast, feast mine eyes on happiness forelore,
Banquet on loveliness that hath not died,
A beauty slumbers there as heretofore,
A soul made to be deified.
What though the rose, like coward base, hath fled
From this cold cheek; the lily still is there;
And mark how its pure white is softly spread,
Where not one vagrant rose shall dare
Again to blossom on this maiden's cheek,
Or its bright innocence with shame to streak.

LXV.

SHE IS NOT DEAD.

She is not dead—oh! do not say she's dead.
Good friends, she lives! what though the rose hath fled
From her sweet face, doth not the lily there
As beautiful a form and 'semblance bear?
Good friends, I say she lives! her beauty lives!
And death destroys all loveliness of hue;
And were she dead, that lustre life but gives,
From her, methinks, would have evanished too.

Good friends, join with me—do but give me space
To feast upon the beauties of this face.
She lives in death, she triumphs in the tomb,
And, like a grave's flower, springs in fresher bloom
The nearer it is planted to the dead!
Raise, raise a little more her drooping head;
Her bosom heaves not—'tis, like marble, white,
And, like it, cold. But mark how exquisite
And finely fashioned is this pale stiff arm
Which sleeps upon it; touch it, it will not harm.
No, not one finger moves; they're locked in sleep,
And very cold withal; pray do not weep,
Else I would weep too, that I could not break
Her pleasant slumbers for your pity's sake.

Good friends, I pray withdraw that veil once more,
And say, is she not lovely as before;
Hath not this brow, this cheek, this neck, this arm,
And this fair body all some goodly charm
Hovering around them, though the soul is gone
On some far pilgrimage from this bright one?
Men say this maiden loved me—simple me,
Even from the cradle and sweet infancy,
Till we had learned speech to speak our loves
As others do, by streams and shaded groves;

But that is false in part, for never word
Of love from either lip by us was heard ;
The tongue is false and cogging, but the eye,
The vanishing rosy smile, speak faithfully.
Yes, Love beneath these cold lids did repair
As to a crystal palace, there to blend
His essence with the lights they did defend ;
And when they op'd their portals, what a light
Poured from the worlds they hid ! Two bright
All-radiant worlds—two stars of living fire,
Having joint sway and majesty entire
Within their fair domains and beauteous spheres,
And gemmed with diamonds like to dropping tears,
And Love was there enshrined, and laughed through,
The pensive glories of these eyes so blue.

LXVI.

SWEET EARLSBURN, BLYTHE EARLSBURN.

Sweet Earlsburn, blythe Earlsburn,
 Mine own, my native stream,
My heart grows young again, while thus
 On thy green banks I dream.
Yes, dream ! in sooth I can no more,
 For as thy murmurs roll,
They wake the ancient melodies
 That stirred my infant soul.

I've told thee, one by one, the thoughts ;
 Strange shapeless forms were they,
That hung around me fearfully
 In childhood's dreamy day.

And still thy mystic music spake
    Dimly articulate,
Yielding meet answer to the dreams
    That shadowed forth my fate.

I've wept by thee a sorrowing child;
    I've sported, mad with glee,
And still thou wert the only one
    That seemed to care for me;
For in whatever mood I came
    To wander by thy brim,
Thy murmurs were most musical,
    Soul-soothing as a hymn.

I've wandered far in other lands,
    And mixed with stranger men,
But still my heart untravelled sought
    Repose within thy glen.
The pictures of my memory
    Were fresh as they were limned,
Nor change of scene, nor lapse of years,
    Their lustre ever dimmed.

LXVII.

BEGONE, BEGONE THOU TRUANT TEAR.

BEGONE, begone thou truant tear
    That trembles on my cheek,
And far away be borne the sigh
    That more than words can speak.

And cease, my merry harp, to wake
    The song of former days,
And perish all the minstrel lyre
    That framed these happy lays.

She loves me not who woke these strains,
    Then, wherefore should they be ?
True, she doth smile as she was wont,
    But doth she smile on me ?

Her neck with kindly arch ne'er bends
    When listing to my song,
Nor does her passion-moving lips
    The trembling notes prolong.

Time was, indeed, when she would hang
    Enamoured on my theme ;
But ah, that happy time hath fled,
    And vanished like a dream.

Peace, thou proud heart, and prate no more,
    Thy sun of joy hath set,
And dark and starless is the sky
    The troubadour has met.

LXVIII.

O BABBLE NOT TO ME, GRAY EILD.

Oh babble not to me, Gray Eild,
    Of days and years mis-spent,
Unless thou can'st again restore
    Youth's scenes of merriment.

Can'st thou recal to me the heart
    That bounded sorrow-free,
Or wake to life the lovely one
    Who stole that heart from me ?

Can'st thou by magic art compel
   The shrouded dead to rise,
And all the friends of early years
   Again to glad my eyes ?

Can'st thou renew Hope flattering dream
   That promised joys in store,
Or bid me taste again those few,
   Alas ! that are no more ?

Then babble not to me, Gray Eild,
   Of days and years mis-spent,
Unless thou can'st again restore
   Youth's dreams of sweet content.

LXIX.

SONNET—THE PATRIOT'S DEATH.

His eye did lose its lustre for a space,
And a bright colour mantled o'er his face ;
His lips did tremulous move, as if to speak,
But no words came. On his brow did break
The heavy and cold dew of coming death ;
And thick and difficult hath grown his breath.
A moment's space, it was no more, for soon
Calmness and sunshine did again illume
His stern-resolved features, and a glow
Of deep but bridled wrath sat on his brow ;
But it frowned not, nor did his piercing eye
Speak aught that wronged his proud heart's privacy.
Fear did not there abide, nor yet did rage
Gleam in its fire. Far nobler moods assuage
Its potent brilliance and restrain its ire ;

It nothing knew but the brave patriot's fire,
Who slaketh life to grasp at liberty,
And dies rejoicing that he has lived free,
Well knowing that his death to other men
Will be a gathering call—a watchword, when
The brave on freedom look in after times.

LXX.

SONNET—PALE DAUGHTER OF THE NIGHT.

Oh thou most beautiful and meek-eyed virgin,
Pale daughter of the night, how tempest tost
And wildered in these thickening clouds thou art,
Yet smiling ever with so sweet a face
Of love around thee, that in truth, methinks,
Even at these clouds thou canst not take offence,
Knowing thy glory and majestic form
Cannot be sullied ; and the innocent,
Even like to thee, with undiminished beam,
Burst through the clouds of envious calumny
To shame the tongues, and give the lie to thoughts
Having no saintlike charity ! Oh, yes, like thee,
Thus shine on darkness with forgiving look,
For Innocence and Mercy are twin-born !

LXXI.

SONNET—THE HAND'S WILD GRASP.

The hand's wild grasp, the dark flash of the eye,
Like the troubled gleam of a winter's sky,
The bosom's bitter throb, the half-choked sigh,
When the parting hour is hurrying nigh,
   Are known but to those who love.
Sad is that fateful hour, and pale the cheek,
And fain the tongue would, but it cannot speak,
   And the cold lips will not move.

Oh, could the eyes find tears kind hope hath sprung,
And could the lips but syllable a sound,
Albeit to wail, the heart with passion wrung
Would to its prisoned feeling thus give vent ;
But in an icy circle they are bound,
And when that breaks, the heart's last chord is rent !

LXXII.

SONNET—SILVERY HAIRS.

Ha ! on my brow, what straggling silvery hairs
Be ye who curl and mingle in the throng
Of a more youthful race ? Beshrew my heart,
Ye have a frosty aspect right severe,
And come to babble nonsense of the times
That once have been, and of the days that speed
With noiseless pinions o'er me—of the grave
That hungers for me, and impatiently

Awaits my coming. Softly now, fair sirs,
Emblems of frail mortality; in sooth,
Are ye the fruits of time, or those chance weeds
That sorrow's sullen flood hath left to mock
The broken heart that it hath desolated,
And killed each bud of hope that blossomed there?

LXXIII.

LADY MARGARET.

I lay within the chamber lone
  Where the Lady Margaret died;
And wildly there the midnight wind
  Like hapless spirit sighed.

I mused upon that peerless One,
  So beautiful of blee;
And marvelled much of her sad death's
  Time-hallowed mystery:
For, as a rainbow-tinted cloud,
  Smote by a gentle wind,
Sails o'er the deep, slow paced and proud,
  Yet leaves no trace behind;
Nor can conjecture index true
  Where one bright shadow lay,
Till all has melted from the view,
  In nothingness away;
So did that lady vanish quite,
  In her sad latter day!

It is a hundred years agone
  Since living limb did rest
Within that chamber's chilling gloom,
  And rose a living guest!

But many a brave a stately corpse
   Of lord and lady tall,
Have here lain cold and motionless
   Ere their proud funeral :
For no sound or sight, however strange,
   Can lifeless flesh appal.
But ancient crones have noted well
   Of each corpse that lay there,
That writhen was each ghastly limb,
The eyelid opened wide, and grim
   Each cold dead eye did glare.

It is a hundred years agone,
   Even on this very night,
Since, in this unsunned room, and lone,
   Reposed that lady bright—
A miracle of loveliness—
   A very beam of light.
Blythe dawns the morn—her bridal morn,
   And merry minstrels play ;
The brisk bridegroom, and all his kin,
Came trooping with a joyous din,
   In seemliest array.
The bridegroom came, but ah ! the bride
   Was missing and away !
And of that gentle lady's fate
   None wot of till this day !
And, since that night, all tenantless
   Of life hath been her room ;
Till even I did madly break
   Upon its sacred gloom.

It was a dull and eerie night
   Of wind and bitter sleet,
When first that tomb-like chamber rung
   With the echoes of my feet ;
And on its narrow casements hard
   The hail and rain did beat,

While through each crazed and time-worn chink,
  The hollow wind did moan,
As if a hundred harps were strung
  Within that chamber lone,
And every minstrel there had been
  Some disembodied one!

But it is a lofty chamber,
  And passing rich withal
When on its gilded mouldings huge
  The quivering moonbeams fall.
And, ever and anon, in sooth,
  Even on that stormy night,
Would some pale tempest-shattered ray
Through the dim windows find its way—
  A very thread of light—
To glimmer on the needlecraft
  And curious tapestry
Which moulder on the walls,—brave scrolls
  Of dim antiquitye,
Embodying many a quaint device
  Of love and chivalrye.

Oh! it is a lofty chamber,
  But dull it is to see,
In the dead pause of the deep midnight,
  When the faggots dying be,
And nought but embers red
  Throw round a dubious gleam,
Like the indistinct forthshadowings
  Of a sad and unquiet dream.
Then suddenly to wake from sleep,
  To gaze round that dim room
We're sure to feel as one whose pulse
  Again beats in the tomb,
Swelling with idle life and strength
  Within its stifling gloom.

'Twas even so that I awoke
  (Sure awake I could not be),
Though with the life-likeness of waking truths
  Were all things clothed to me.
'Twas in terror I awoke
  Within that chamber dim;
The sweat drop burst on my cold brow,
  Dull horror numbed each limb.
In agony my temples beat,
  Life only throbbed there;
And creeping cold, like living things,
  Stood up each clammy hair.
It seemed as if a spell from hell
  Were drugg'd deep with the air;
Yet wherefore should I fear,
  To me was all unknown;
For that chamber was, as heretofore,
  Dim, desolate, and lone.
And I heard the angry winter's wind
  Still shrilly whistling by;
I heard it stir the leafless trees,
  And heard their faint reply.
While the ticking clock, right audibly,
  Did note time's passing sigh,
And, like some dusky banner broad,
  Loud flapping in the breeze,
The faded arras on the walls
  Sung its own exiquies.

Then, then, methought I heard a foot,
  It sounded soft and still;
And slowly then it died away,
  Like echo on the hill,
Or like the far faint murmuring
  Of a lone hermit rill.
Again that footstep sounded near,
  Again it died away;

And then I heard it gliding past
   The couch on which I lay !
I raised my head, and wildly gazed
   Into the glimmering gloom ;
But nothing save the embers red,
That on the spacious hearth were spread,
   I saw within that room.
And all was dusky round,
   Save where these embers shed
A pale and sickly gleam of light
   On the Lady Margaret's bed.
On the couch where I did lye
   That sickly light did shine
With one bright flash, when, as a voice
   Did cry—"**Revenge is mine** !"
Another answered straight,
   And said, "**The hour is come** !"
I listened—but these voices twain
   For evermore were dumb.
But again the still soft foot
   Came creeping stealthy on ;
And then, Oh God ! mine ear upcaught
   A deep and stifled groan.
It echoed through the lofty room
   So loud, so clear, and shrill,
Methinks even to my dying-day
   I'll hear that echo still.
Again that deep and smothered groan—
   That rattle in the throat—
That awful sob of struggling life—
   On my strained ear-strings smote.
In desperate fear I madly strove
   To start from that witch'd bed,
But on my breast there seem'd up-piled
   A mountain weight of lead.
And when I strove to speak aloud,
   To dissipate that spell,

I shuddered at the shapeless sounds
    That from mine own lips fell.
'Twas then, full filled with fear, I shut
    Mine eyes t' escape the gaze
Of that dim chamber's arras'd walls,
    With their tales of other days,
Lest ghastly shapes should start from them
    To sport in horrid glee
Before my tortured sight—dark scenes
    Of their life's tragedy,
And like exulting fiends proclaim
How black man's heart can be.

But visionless scant space I lay
    With throbbing downshut lid,
When o'er my brow and cheek, dear Lord !
    A clammy coldness slid.
O'er brow and cheek I felt it slide ;
    And, like a frozen rill,
The blood waxed thick within my veins,
    Grew pulseless, and stood still.
O'er brow and cheek I felt it slide,
    So clammy and so cold,
Like the touch of one whose lifeless limbs
    In winding-sheet are rolled.
Straight upward did I look, and then
    From the thick obscurity—
Oh, horrible ! there downward gleamed
    Two glittering eyes on me.
From the ceiling of that lofty room
    These glittering eyes did stare ;
They rested on me, under them,
    With a fixed and fearful glare.
Oh, never human eyes did flash
    So wild and strange a light,
As these twin eyes straight downward poured
    On that unhappy night.

Their beams shot down like lances long,
   Unutterably bright.
And still these glittering living lights
   Did steadfast gaze on me;
And each fibre of my heart shrunk up
   Beneath their sorcery.
Still, still they gleam—their searching glance
   Has pierced into my brain.
I feel the stream of fire pass through,
   I feel its cureless pain!

One moment seemed to pass, and then
   My vision waxed more clear
And livelier to my spell-fraught sight,
   These blazing eyes appear.
As with unholy light they lit
   A pallid cheek and brow,
And quivered on a lip as cold
   And blenched as driven snow.
And I did gaze on that pale brow,
   And on that lovesome cheek;
I watched those cold part-opened lips,
   Methought that they would speak
But motionless, and void of life
   As monumental stone,
Was every feature, save those eyes,
   That evermore out shone
With a fearful lustre, that to life
   On earth, is never known.
That face was all a deadly white,
   Yet beautiful to see;
And indistinctly floated down
   Its body's symmetry,
In ample folds and wimples quain
   Of gorgeous drapery.
And gleaming forth, like spots of
   On a sad coloured field,

A small white hand on either side
    Was partially revealed.
O'er me a deeper horror,
    A marvellous rush of light—
Long-perished memories returned
    Upon that dreadful night.
I heard the voice of other times,
    The tale of other years,
Re-acted were their direst crimes,
    Re-shed their bitterest tears!

LXXIV.

CRUXTOUN CASTLE.

The reader will find a brief, but instructive, account of this relic of Baronial times—which, at different periods, has been written Cruxtoun, Crocstoun, and Crookston—in a work entitled, "Views in Renfrewshire," by Philip A. Ramsay, one of the Poet's earliest and truest friends. Of the objects of antiquity remaining in Renfrewshire, Cruxtoun Castle, according to Mr. Ramsay, is, in point of interest, second only to the Abbey of Paisley. "The ruins of this castle," he observes, "occupy the summit of a wooded slope, overhanging the south bank of the White Cart, about three miles south-east from Paisley, and close to the spot where that river receives the waters of a stream called the Levern. The scenery in this neighbourhood is rich and varied, and although the eminence on which the Castle stands is but gentle, it is so commanding that our great Novelist has made Queen Mary remark, that "from thence you may see a prospect wide as from the peaks of Schehallion." To Cruxtoun Castle, then the property of Darnley, Mary's husband, tradition tells us, the royal bride was conducted, soon after the celebration of their nuptials at Edinburgh."

Thou grey and antique tower,
Receive a wanderer of the lonely night,
Whose moodful sprite
Rejoices at this witching time to brood
Amid thy shattered strength's dim solitude!

It is a fear-fraught hour—
A death-like stillness reigns around,
Save the wood-skirted river's eerie sound,
And the faint rustling of the trees that shower
Their brown leaves on the stream,
Mournfully gleaming in the moon's pale beam :
O ! I could dwell for ever and for ever
In such a place as this, with such a night !
When, o'er thy waters and thy waving woods
The moon-beams sympathetically quiver,
And no ungentle thing on thee intrudes,
And every voice is dumb, and every object bright !

Forgive, old Cruxtoun, if, with step unholy,
Unwittingly a pilgrim should profane
The regal quiet, the august repose,
Which o'er thy desolated summit reign—
When the fair moon's abroad, at evening's close—
Or interrupt that touching melancholy—
Image of fallen grandeur—softly thrown
O'er every crumbling and moss-bedded stone,
And broken arch, and pointed turret hoar,
Which speak a tale of times that are no more ;
Of triumphs they have seen,
When Minstrel-craft, in praise of Scotland's Queen,
Woke all the magic of the harp and song,
And the rich, varied, and fantastic lore
Of those romantic days was carped, I ween,
Amidst the pillared pomp of lofty hall,
By many a jewelled throng
Of smiling dames and soldier barons bold ;
When the loud cheer of generous wassail rolled
From the high deis to where the warder strode,
Proudly, along the battlemented wall,
Beneath his polished armour's ponderous load ;
Who paused to hear, and carolled back again,
With martial glee, the jocund vesper strain :

Thou wilt forgive ! Mine is no peering eye,
That seeks, with glance malign, the suffering part,
Thereby, with hollow show of sympathy,
To smite again the poor world-wounded heart:
No—thy misfortunes win from him a sigh
Whose soul towers, like thyself, o'er each lewd passer-by.

Relique of earlier days,
Yes, dear thou art to me !—
And beauteous, marvellously,
The moon-light strays
Where banners glorious floated on thy walls—
Clipping their ivied honours with its thread
Of half-angelic light :
And though o'er thee Time's wasting dews have shed
Their all-consuming blight,
Maternal moon-light falls
On and around thee full of tenderness,
Yielding thy shattered frame pure love's divine caress.

Ah me ! thy joy of youthful lustyhood
Is gone, old Cruxtoun ! Ever, ever gone !
Here hast thou stood
In nakedness and sorrow, roofless, lone,
For many a weary year—and to the storm
Hast bared thy wasted form—
Braving destruction, in the attitude
Of reckless desolation. Like to one
Who in this world no longer may rejoice,
Who watching by Hope's grave
With stern delight, impatient is to brave
The worst of coming ills—So, Cruxtoun ! thou
Rear'st to the tempest thy undaunted brow ;
When Heaven's red coursers flash athwart the sky—
Startling the guilty as they thunder by—
Then raiseth thou a wild, unearthly hymn,
Like death-desiring bard whose star hath long been dim !

Neglected though thou art,
Sad remnant of old Scotland's worthier days,
When independence had its chivalrie,
There still is left one heart
To mourn for thee !
And though, alas ! thy venerable form
Must bide the buffet of each vagrant storm,
One spirit yet is left to linger here
And pay the tribute of a silent tear ;
Who in his memory registers the dints
That Time hath graved upon thy sorrowing brow ;
Who of thy woods loves the Autumnal tints,
Whose voice—perforce indignant—mingles now
In all thy lamentations—with the tone,
Not of these paltry times, but of brave years long gone.

Nor is't the moonshine clear,
Leeming on tower, and tree, and silent stream,
Nor hawthorn blossoms which in Spring appear,
Most prodigal of perfume—nor the sweets
Of wood-flowers, peeping up at the blue sky ;
Nor the mild aspect of blue hills which greet
The eager vision—blessed albeit they seem,
Each with its charm particular—To my eye,
Old Cruxtoun has an interest all its own—
From many a cherished, intersociate thought—
From feelings multitudinous—well known
To souls in whom the patriot fire hath wrought
Sublime remembrance of their country's fame :
Radiant thou art in the ethereal flame—
The lustrous splendour—which those feelings shed
O'er many a scene of this my father-land !
Thou, grey magician, with thy potent wand,
Evok'st the shades of the illustrious dead !
The mists dissolve—up rise the slumbering years—
On come the knightly riders cap-a-pie—
The herald calls—hark, to the clash of spears !
To Beauty's Queen each hero bends the knee ;

Dreams of the Past, how exquisite ye be—
Offspring of heavenly faith and rare antiquity!

Light feet have trod
The soft, green, flowering sod
That girdles thy baronial strength, and traced,
All gracefully, the labyrinthine dance;
Young hearts discoursed with many a passionate glance,
While rose and fell the Minstrel's thrilling strain—
(Who, in this iron age, might sing in vain—
His largesse coarse neglect, and mickle pain!)
Waste are thy chambers tenantless, which long
Echoed the notes of gleeful minstrelsie—
Notes once the prelude to a tale of wrong,
Of Royalty and love.—Beneath yon tree—
Now bare and blasted—so our annals tell—
The martyr Queen, ere that her fortunes knew
A darker shade than cast her favourite yew,
Loved Darnley passing well—
Loved him with tender woman's generous love,
And bade farewell awhile to courtly state
And pageantry for yon o'ershadowing grove—
For the lone river's banks where small birds sing—
Their little hearts with summer joys elate—
Where tall broom blossoms, flowers profusely spring;
There he, the most exalted of the land,
Pressed, with the grace of youth, a Sovereign's peerless hand.

And she did die!—
Die as a traitor—in the brazen gaze
Of her—a kinswoman and enemy—
O well may such an act my soul amaze!
My country, at that hour, where slept thy sword?
Where was the high and chivalrous accord,
To fling the avenging banner of our land,
Like sheeted flame, forth to the winds of heaven?

O shame among the nations—thus to brook
The damning stain to thy escutcheon given !
How could thy sons upon their mothers look,
Degenerate Scotland ! heedless of the wail
Of thy lorn Queen, in her captivity !
Unmov'd wert thou by all her bitter bale—
Untouch'd by thought that she had governed thee—
Hard was each heart and cold each powerful hand—
No harnessed steed rushed panting to the fight ;
O listless fell the lance when Mary laid
Her head upon the block—and high in soul,
Which lacked not then thy frugal sympathy,
Died—in her widowed beauty, penitent—
Whilst thou, by foul red-handed faction rent,
Wert falsest recreant to sweet majesty !

'Tis past—she rests—the scaffold hath been swept,
The headsman's guilty axe to rust consigned—
But, Cruxtoun, while thine aged towers remain,
And thy green umbrage wooes the evening wind—
By noblest natures shall her woes be wept,
Who shone the glory of thy festal day :
Whilst aught is left by these thy ruins grey,
They will arouse remembrance of the stain
Queen Mary's doom hath left on History's pag
Remembrance laden with reproach and pain,
To those who make, like me, this pilgrimage !

LXXV.

ROLAND AND ROSABELLE.

A TOMB by skilful hands is raised,
   Close to a sainted shrine,
And there is laid a stalwart Knight,
   The last of all his line.

Beside that noble monument,
    A Squire doth silent stand,
Leaning in pensive wise upon
    The cross-hilt of his brand.

Around him peals the harmony
    Of friars at even-song,
He notes them not, as passing by
    The hymning brothers throng:
And he hath watched the monument
    Three weary nights and days,
And ever on the marble cold
    Is fixed his steadfast gaze.

" I pray thee, wakeful Squire, unfold"—
    Proud Rosabella said—
" The story of the warrior bold,
    Who in this tomb is laid?"
" A champion of the Cross was he"—
    The Squire made low reply—
" And on the shore of Galilee,
    In battle did he die,

" He bound me by a solemn vow,
    His body to convey
Where lived his love—there rests it now,
    Until the judgment-day:
And by his stone of record here,
    In loyalty I stand,
Until I greet his leman dear—
    The Lady of the Land!"

" Fair stranger, I would learn of thee
    The gentle warrior's name,
Who fighting fell at Galilee
    And won a deathless name?"

The Squire hath fixed an eye of light
  Full on the Lady tall—
" Men called," he said, " that hapless Knight
  Sir Roland of the Hall !

" His foot was foremost in the fray,
  And last to leave the field—
A braver arm in danger's day
  Ne'er shivered lance on shield !"
" In death, what said he of his love—
  Thou faithful soldier tell ?"
" Meekly he prayed to Him above
  For perjured Rosabelle."

" Thy task is done—my course is run—
  (O fast her tears did fall !)
I am indeed a perjured one—
  Dear Roland of the Hall !"
Even as the marble cold and pale,
  Waxed Rosabella's cheek ;
The faithful Squire resumed travail—
  The Lady's heart did break !

LXXVI.

SONG.

How I envy the ring that encircles thy finger !—
  Dear daughter of beauty how happy were I
If, by some sweet spell, like that ring, I might linger
  At ease in the light of thy heart-thrilling eye !

I would joy in the music thy light pulse is making,
  I would press the soft cheek where the rose-buds unfold—

I would rest on the brow where pure thought's ever waking,
  And lovingly glide through thy tresses of gold.

On the ripe smiling lip which young Cupid is steeping
  In dews of love's day dawn, I'd tenderly play—
And when in thy innocence, sweet, thou wert sleeping,
  I'd watch thee, and bless thee, and guard thee for aye !

LXXVII.

FOR BLITHER FIELDS AND BRAVER BOWERS.

For blither fields and braver bowers
  The little bird, in Spring,
Quits its old tree and wintry hold,
  With wanton mates to sing ;
And yet a while that wintry home
  To branch and twig may cling;
But wayward blast, or truant boy,
  May rend it soon away,
And scatter to the heedless winds
  The toil of many a day—
And where, when Winter comes, shall then
  The bird its poor head lay ?

The moss, the down, the twisted grass,
  The slender wands that bound
The dear warm nest, are parted now,
  Or scattered far around—
Belike the woodman's axe hath felled
  The old tree to the ground !
And now keen Winter's wreathing snows
  O'er frozen Nature lie—

The sun forgets to warm the earth,
    Forgets to light the sky ;
I fear me lest the wandering bird
    May, houseless, shivering, die !

Forgive me, Helen—thou art free
    To keep, or quit, the nest
I built for thee, and sheltered in
    The foliage of my breast,
And fenced so well none other might
    Be harbour'd there as guest.
Flee if thou wilt—if other love
    Thy fickle heart enfold,
Thou'rt free to rove where fancy waves
    Her wand of fairy gold—
But Helen, ere thou canst return,
    This bosom will be cold !

LXXVIII.

HOPE AND LOVE.

THROUGH life on journeying, by its thorny paths,
Or pleasant ways—its rank green hemlock wastes,
Or roseate bowers—in utter loneliness,
Or 'mid the din of busy multitudes—
Two babes of beauty linger near us still—
Twin Cherubim—that leave us not until
We've passed the threshold of that crowded inn
Which borders on Eternity ! One doth point,
With gleaming eye and finger tremulous,
To clefts in azure, where the sunbeams slumber
On couch of vermeil dye and amethyst,
Bordered with flowers that never know decay ;

Where living fountains, cool and argentine,
Trill on in measured cadence, night and morn :
The other, with an eye of sweet regard,
And voice the spirit of pure melody,
Sheds o'er the darkest track some ray of gladness—
To elevate the heart, and nerve the soul,
With unslacked sinews, vigorously to brave
The perils of the unattempted road :
Love, gentle Love—one fellow-pilgrim is—
The other Hope—dear, never-dying Hope !—
And they to churle, as well as keysour yield
The tender ministering of faithful friends !

LXXIX.

SONGE OF THE SCHIPPE.

WHEN surly windes and grewsome cloudes
    Are tilting in the skye,
And every little star's abed,
    That glimmered cheerilie—
O then 'tis meet for mariners
    To steer righte carefulie !
For mermaides sing the schippman's dirge,
    Where ocean weddes the skye—
A blessing on our gude schippe as lustilie she sailes,
O what can match our gude schippe when blest with favouring gales !

Blythely to the tall top-mast,
    Up springs the sailor boy—
Could he but hail a distant port,
    How he would leap with joy !

By bending yard and rope he swings—
    A fair-haired child of glee—
But oh ! a cruel sawcie wave
    Hath swept him in the sea !
There's sadness in the gude schippe that breasts the waters wild,
Though safe ourselves we'll think with tears of our poor ocean-child !

    Our main-mast now is clean cut downe,
        The tackle torn away—
    And thundering o'er the stout schippe's side,
        The seas make fearful play !
    Yet cheerlie cheerlie on we go,
        Though fierce the tempest raves,
    We know the hand unseen that guides
        The schippe o'er stormie waves !
We'll all still stand by the old schippe as should a trusty crew,
For He who rules the wasting waves may some port bring to view !

    Our gude schippe is a shapely schippe—
        A shapely and a stronge—
    Our hearts sang to our noble schippe,
        As she careered along !
    And fear ye not my sturdy mates
        Though sayles and masts be riven—
    We know, while drifting o'er the deep,
        Above there's still a haven !
Though sorely we're benighted upon the weltering foam,
The sun may rise upon the morn and guide us to a home !

LXXX.

HE STOOD ALONE.

He stood alone in an unpitying crowd—
His mates fell from him, as the grub worms drop
From the green stalk that once had nourished them,
But now is withered and all rottenness
Because it gave such shelter. Pleasure's train—
The light-winged tribes that seek the sunshine only—
No more endeavoured from his eye to win
The smile of approbation. Grief and Care
Stalked forth upon the theatre of his heart,
In many a gloomy and mishapen guise,
Till of the glories of his earlier self
The world, his base and hollow auditory,
Left but a ghastly phantom. As a tree,
A goodly tree—that stricken is and wasted,
By elemental conflicts—falls at last,
Even in the fulness of its branching honours,
Prostrate before the storm—yet majestic
In its huge downfal, so, at last, fell he!

LXXXI.

CUPID'S BANISHMENTE.

What recke I now of comely dame?
  What care I now for fair pucelle?
Unscorchde I meet their glance of flame,
  Unmovede I mark their bosoms swel,
  For Love and I have sayde farewel!

Go, prattlynge fool !—go, wanton wilde !
   Seke thy fond mother this to tel—
That loveliest maydes on me have smyled,
   And that I stoutly did rebel,
   And bade thee and thy arts farewel !

With me thy tyrant reigne is o'er,
   Thou hear'st thy latest warninge knel ;
Speed, waywarde urchin, from my doore,—
   My hert to thee gives no handsel,
   For thou and I have sworne farewel !

So trimme thy bow, and fleche thy shafte,
   And peer where sillie gallants dwel,
On them essaye thy archer crafte,
   No more on me thy bolte schal tel—
   False Love and I have sunge farewel !

LXXXII.

THE SHIP OF THE DESERT.

"Onward, my Camel !— On, though slow ;
   Halt not upon these fatal sands !
Onward my constant Camel go—
The fierce Simoom hath ceased to blow,
   We soon shall tread green Syria's lands !

"Droop not my faithful Camel ! Now
   The hospitable well is near !
Though sick at heart, and worn in brow,
I grieve the most to think that thou
   And I may part, kind comrade, here !

"O'er the dull waste a swelling mound—
   A verdant paradise—I see;
The princely date-palms there abound,
And springs that make it sacred ground
   To pilgrims like to thee and me!"

The patient Camel's filmy eye,
   All lustreless, is fixed in death!
Beneath the sun of Araby
The desert wanderer ceased to sigh,
   Exhausted on its burning path.

Then rose upon the Wilderness
   The solitary Driver's cry:
Thoughts of his home upon him press,
As, in his utter loneliness,
   He sees his burden-bearer die.

Hope gives no echo to his call—
   Ne'er from his comrade will he sever!
The red sky is his funeral pall;
A prayer—a moan—'tis over, all—
   Camel and lord now rest for ever!

A three hour's journey from the spring
   Loved of the panting Caravan—
Within a little sandy ring—
The Camel's bones lie whitening,
   With thine, old, unlamented man!

LXXXIII.

THE POET'S WISH.

O would that in some wild and winding glen
   Where human footstep ne'er did penetrate,

And from the haunts of base and selfish men
   Remote, in dreamy loneness situate,
I had my dwelling : and within my ken
   Nature desporting in fantastic form—
     Asleep in green repose, and thundering in the storm !

Then mine should be a life of deep delight,—
   Rare undulations of ecstatic musing ;
Thoughts calm, yet ever-varying, stream bedight
   With flowers immortal of quick Fancy's choosing—
And like unto the ray of tremulous light,
   Blent by the pale moon with the entranced water,
     I'd wed thee, Solitude, dear Nature's first-born daughter !

LXXXIV.

ISABELLE.

A SERENADE.

Hark ! sweet Isabelle, hark to my lute,
   As softly it plaineth o'er
The story of one to whose lowly suit
   Thy heart shall beat no more !
List to its tender plaints, my love,
Sad as the accents of saints, my love
   Who mortal sin deplore !

Awake from your slumber, Isabelle, wake,
   'Tis sorrow that tunes these strings ;
A last farewell would the minstrel take
   Of her whose beauty he sings :
The moon seems to weep on her way, my love,
And, shrouded in clouds, seems to say, my love,
   No hope with the morning springs !

Deep on the breeze peals the hollow sound
   Of the dreary convent bell;
Its walls, ere a few short hours wheel round,
   Will girdle my Isabelle!
They'll take thee away from these arms, love,
And bury thy blossoming charms, love,
   Where midnight requiems swell.

At the high altar I see thee kneel,
   With pallid and awe-struck face;
I see the veil those looks conceal
   That shone with surpassing grace—
The shade will prey on thy bloom, my love,
While I shall wend to the tomb, my love,
   And leave of my name no trace.

We lov'd and we grew, we grew and we lov'd,
   Twin flowers in a dewy vale;
The churchman's cold hand hath one removed,
   The other will soon wax pale:
O fast will be its decline, my love,
As this dying note of mine, my love,
   Lost in the evening gale!

LXXXV.

WHAT IS THIS WORLD TO ME?

WHAT is this world to me?
A harp sans melodie;
A dream of vain idlesse,
A thought of bitterness,
That grieves the aching brain,
And gnaws the heart in twain!

My spirit pines allwaie,
Like captive shut from day ;
Or like a sillie flower,
Estranged from sun and shower—
Which, withering, soon must die,
In love-lorne privacie.

No joye my hearte doth finde,
With those they calle my kinde ;
O dull it is and sad,
To see how men waxe bad :
As Autumn leaves decay,
So verteue fades away !

LXXXVI.

TO A LADY'S BONNET.

Invidious shade ! why thus presume,
O'er face so fair to cast thy gloom ;
And hide from the enamoured sight,
Those lips so sweet, and eyes so bright ?
Why veil those blushes of the cheek,
Which purity of soul bespeak ?
Why shroud that brow in hermit cell,
On which high thoughts serenely dwell ?
Why chain severe the clustering hair,
That whilome shed a radiance rare—
A golden mist—o'er neck and brow,
Like sunset over drifted snow ?

O kindly shade, for ever be
Between me and love's witchery !—
For ever be to Ellen's eyes,
Like grateful cloud in summer skies,

Mellowing the fervour of the day :
For should they dart another ray
Of their enchanting light on me,
Farewell the proud boast—I am free !

LXXXVII.

THE WANDERER.

No FACE I look upon doth greet me
   With smile that generous welcome lends ;
No ready hand, with cheerful glow,
   Is now stretched out, all glad, to meet me :
A chill distrust on every brow,
   Assures me I have here no friends !

I miss the music of home voices,
   The rushing of the mountain flood,
My country's birds that blithely sung
   In woodlands where green May rejoices,
Discoursing love when life was young,
   And mirthful ever was my mood.

The breezes soft that fan my cheek,
   The bower that shades the sun from me,
The sky that spans this Southern shore,
   Do all a different language speak
From breeze and bower I loved of yore,
   And sky that spans my own countree.

They bring not health to exiled men—
   They light not up the home-bent eye ;
No, piece-meal wastes the way-worn frame
   That longs to tread its native glen—
That trembles when it hears the name
   Of that land where its fathers lie !

The sun which shines seems not the sun
  That rose upon my native fields ;
Majestic rolls he on his way,
  A cloudless course hath he to run—
But beams he with the kindly ray
  He to our Northern landscape yields ?

The moon that trembles in these skies,
  Like to an argent mirror sheen—
Ruling with mistless splendour here—
  Does she above the mountains rise,
And smile upon the waters clear,
  As in my days of youth I've seen ?

O beautiful and peerless light,
  That thou should'st seem unlovely now,
That thou should'st fail to wake anew
  Those looks of heartfelt pure delight,
Which youthful Fancy upward threw,
  While gazing on thy cold, pale brow !

But this is not a kindred land,
  Nor this the old familiar stream ;
And these are not the friends of youth—
  O heartless, loveless, seems this strand—
Its people lack the kindly ruth,
  The soother of life's turbid dream !

Away regret ! Here must I die,
  Remote from all my soul held dear—
My grave, upon an alien shore,
  Will ne'er attract the passer-by
The lonely sleeper to deplore—
  No flower will grace the stranger's bier !

Winds of the melancholy night,
  Begin your solemn dirge and bland !

The giant clouds are gathering fast,
    The fearful moon withdraws her light—
In mournful visions of the past,
    Again I'll seek my native land!

LXXXVIII.

SONG.

I look on thee once more,—
    I gaze on thee and sigh,
To think how soon some hearts run o'er
    With love, and then run dry.

I need not marvel long
    That love in thee expires,
For shallowest streams have loudest song,
    Most smoke the weakest fires.

I deemed thee once sincere,—
    Once thought thy breast must be
A fountain gushing through the year
    With living love for me!

For so it was with mine,
    The well-springs of my soul
Were opened up, and streamed to thine,
    As their appointed goal.

And now they wander on,
    O'er barren sands unblest,
Since falsehood placed its seal upon
    Thy fair, but frozen, breast!

LXXXIX.

THE HUNTER'S WELL.

Life of this wilderness,
  Pure gushing stream,
Dear to the Summer
  Is thy murmuring!
Note of the song-bird,
  Warbling on high,
Ne'er with my spirit made
  Such harmony
As do thy deep waters,
  O'er rock, leaf, and flower,
Bubbling and babbling
  The long sunny hour!

Tongue of this desert-spot,
  Spelling sweet tones,
To the mute listeners—
  Old mossy stones;
Who ranged these stones near
  Thy silver rim,
Guarding the temple
  Where rises thy hymn?
Some thirst-stricken Hunter—
  Swarth priest of the wood,
Around thee hath strewn them,
  In fond gratitude.

Orb of the green waste,
  Open and clear,
Friend of the Hunter,
  Loved of the deer;
Brilliantly breaking
  Beneath the blue sky,

Gladdening the leaflets
  That tremulous sigh;
Star of my wandering,
  Symbol of love,
Lead me to dream of
  The Fountain above!

XC.

IT DEEPLY WOUNDS THE TRUSTING HEART.

It deeply wounds the trusting heart
  That ever throbs to good,
To know that by a perverse art
  It still is misconstrued:

And thus the beauties of the field,
  The glories of the sky,
To lofty natures often yield
  Sole solace ere they die.

The things that harmless couch on earth,
  Or pierce the blue of heaven,
Have mystic reasons in their birth
  Why they should be sin-shriven.

The secrets of the human breast
  No human eye may scan;
With Him alone those secrets rest
  Who made and judgeth man.

Nor lightly should we estimate
  The Hand which rules it so,
Nor idly seek to penetrate
  What angels may not know.

Enough that with a righteous will,
   In this disjointed scene,
The upright one, through good and ill,
   Will be as he hath been.

And should a ribald multitude
   Repay with hate his love,
He still can smile : man's ways are viewed
   By Him who rules above.

XCI.

THE ETTIN O' SILLARWOOD.

"O, SILLARWOOD! sweet Sillarwood,
   Gin Sillarwood were mine,
I'd big a bouir in Sillarwood
   And theik it ower wi' thyme ;
At ilka door, and ilka bore,
   The red, red rose, wud shine !"

It's up and sang the bonnie bird,
   Upon her milk-white hand—
" I wudna lig in Sillarwood,
   For all a gude Earl's land ;
I wudna sing in Sillarwood,
   Tho' gowden glist ilk wand !

" The wild boar rakes in Sillarwood,
   The buck drives thro' the shaw,
And simmer woos the Southern wind
   Thro' Sillarwood to blaw.
" Thro' Sillarwood, sweet Sillarwood,
   The deer hounds run so free ;
But the hunter stark of Sillarwood
   An Ettin lang is he !"

"O, Sillarwood! sweet Sillarwood,"
    Fair Marjorie did sing,
"On the tallest tree in Sillarwood,
    That Ettin lang will hing!"

The Southern wind it blaws fu' saft,
    And Sillarwood is near;
Fair Marjorie's sang in Sillarwood,
    The stark hunter did hear.

He band his deer hounds in their leash,
    Set his bow against a tree,
And three blasts on his horn has brocht
    The wood elf to his knee.

"Gae bring to me a shapely weed,
    Of silver and of gold,
Gae bring to me as stark a steed,
    As ever stepped on mold;
For I maun ride frae Sillarwood
    This fair maid to behold!"

The wood elf twisted sun-beams red
    Into a shapely weed,
And the tallest birk in Sillarwood
    He hewed into a steed;
And shod it wi' the burning gold
    To glance like ony glede.

The Ettin shook his bridle reins
    And merrily they rung,
For four and twenty sillar bells
    On ilka side were hung.

The Ettin rade, and better rade,
    Some thretty miles and three,
A bugle horn hung at his breast,
    A lang sword at his knee;

"I wud I met," said the Ettin lang,
  "The maiden Marjorie!"

The Ettin rade and better rade
  Till he has reached her bouir,
And there he saw fair Marjorie
  As bricht as lily flouir.

"O Sillarwood!—Sweet Sillarwood!—
  Gin Sillarwood were mine,
The sleuthest hawk o' Sillarwood
  On dainty flesh wud dine!"

"Weel met, weel met," the Ettin said,
  "For ae kiss o' that hand,
I wud na grudge my kist o' gold
  And forty fees o' land!

"Weel met, weel met," the Ettin said,
  "For ae kiss o' that cheek,
I'll big a bower wi' precious stanes,
  The red gold sal it theik:

"Weel met, weel met," the Ettin said,
  "For ae kiss o' thy chin,
I'll welcome thee to Sillarwood
  And a' that grows therein!"

"If ye may leese me Sillarwood
  Wi' a' that grows therein,
Ye're free to kiss my cheek," she said,
  "Ye're free to kiss my chin—
The Knicht that hechts me Sillarwood
  My maiden thocht sal win!

"My luve I've laid on Sillarwood—
  Its bonnie aiken tree—
And gin that I hae Sillarwood
  I'll link alang wi' thee!"

Then on she put her green mantel
    Weel furred wi' minivere :
Then on she put her velvet shoon,
    The silver shining clear.

She proudly vaulted on the black—
    He bounded on the bay—
The stateliest pair that ever took
    To Sillarwood their way !

'It's up and sang the gentil bird
    On Marjorie's fair hand—
" I wudna wend to Sillarwood
    For a' its timbered land—
Nor wud I lig in Sillarwood
    Tho' gowden glist ilk wand !

" The Hunters chace thro' Sillarwood
    The playfu' herte and rae ;
Nae maiden that socht Sillarwood
    E'er back was seen to gae ! "

The Ettin leuch, the Ettin sang,
    He whistled merrilie,
" If sic a bird," he said, " were mine,
    I'd hing it on a tree."

" Were I the Lady Marjorie,
    Thou hunter fair but free,
My horse's head I'd turn about,
    And think nae mair o' thee ! "

It's on they rade, and better rade—
    They shimmered in the sun—
'Twas sick and sair grew Marjorie
    Lang e'er that ride was done !

Yet on they rade, and better rade,
    They neared the Cross o' stane—

The tall Knicht when he passed it by
   Felt cauld in every bane.

But on they rade, and better rade,
   It evir grew mair mirk,
O loud, loud nichered the bay steed
   As they passed Mary's Kirk !

" I'm wearie o' this eerie road,"
   Maid Marjorie did say—
" We canna weel get Sillarwood
   Afore the set o' day ! "

" It's no the sinkin' o' the sun
   That gloamins sae the ground,
The heicht it is o' Sillarwood
   That shadows a' around."

" Methocht, Sir Knicht, broad Sillarwood
   A pleasant bield wud be,
With nuts on ilka hazel bush,
   And birds on ilka tree—
But oh ! the dimness o' this wood
   Is terrible to me ! "

" The trees, ye see, seem wondrous big,
   The branches wondrous braid,
Then marvel nae if sad suld be
   The path we hae to tread ! "

Thick grew the air, thick grew the trees,
   Thick hung the leaves around,
And deeper did the Ettin's voice
   In the dread dimness sound—
" I think," said Maiden Marjorie,
   " I hear a horn and hound ! "

" Ye weel may hear the hound," he said,
   " Ye weel may hear the horn,
For I can hear the wild halloo
   That freichts the face o' Morn !

" The Hunters fell o' Sillarwood
   Hae packs full fifty-three :
They hunt all day, they hunt all nicht,
   They never bow an ee :

" The Hunters fell o' Sillarwood
   Hae steeds but blude or bane :
They bear fiert maidens to a weird
   Where mercy there is nane !

" And I the Laird o' Sillarwood
   Hae beds baith deep and wide,
(Of clay-cauld earth) whereon to streik
   A proud and dainty bride !

" Ho ! look beside yon bonny birk—
   The latest blink of day
Is gleamin' on a comely heap
   Of freshly dug red clay ;

" Richt cunning hands they were that digged
   Forenent the birken tree
Where every leaf that draps, frore maid,
   Will piece a shroud for thee—
It's they can lie on lily breast
   As they can lie on lea !

" And they will hap thy lily breist
   Till flesh fa's aff the bane—
Nor tell thy freres how Marjorie
   To Sillarwood hath gane !

"The bed is strewed, Maid Marjorie,
  Wi' bracken and wi' brier,
And ne'er will gray cock clarion wind
  For ane that slumbers here—
Ye wedded have the Ettin stark—
  He rules the Realms of Fear!"

XCII.

LIKE A WORN GRAY-HAIRED MARINER.

LIKE a worn gray-haired mariner whom the sea
Hath wrecked, then flung in mockery ashore,
To clamber some gaunt cliff, and list the roar
  Of wave pursuing wave unceasingly;
His native land, dear home, and toil-won store
  Inexorably severed from his sight;
His sole companions Hopelessness and Grief—
  Who feels his day will soon be mirkest night—
Who from its close alone expects relief—
  Praying life's sands, in pity, to descend
And rid him of life's burden,—So do I
Gaze on the world, and time fast surging by,
  Drifting away each hope with each tried friend—
Leaving behind a waste where desolate I may die.

XCIII.

CHOICE OF DEATH.

MIGHT I, without offending, choose
  The death that I would die,
I'd fall, as erst the Templar fell,
  Aneath a Syrian sky.

Upon a glorious plain of war,
  The banners floating fair,
My lance and fluttering pennoncel
  Should marshal heroes there!

Upon the solemn battle-eve,
  With prayer to be forgiven,
I'd arm me for a righteous fight,
  Imploring peace of Heaven!

High o'er the thunders of the charge
  Should wave my sable plume,
And where the day was lost or won,
  There should they place my tomb!

XCIV.

FRIENDSHIP AND LOVE.

Oft have I sighed for pleasure past,
  Oft wept for secret smarting—
But far the heaviest drop of all
That ever on my cheek did fall
  The tear was at our parting.

Why did our bosoms ever beat
  Harmonious with each other,
If truest sympathies of soul
Might broken be, perhaps the whole
  Concentred in another?

My fear it was when other scenes,
  With other tongues and faces,
Should greet thee, thou would'st haply be
Forgetful of our amity
  In old frequented places.

'Tis even so—the thrall of love,
   Past ties to thee seem common—
Well, hearts *must* yield to beauty rare,
And proud-souled friendship hardly dare
   Contest the prize with woman !

Old friend, adieu ! I blame thee not,
   Since fair guest fills thy bosom—
Thy smiling love may flattered be
Our bonds to know, and feel that she
   The pow'r had to unloose them !

Since thou surrenderest all for her,
   May she, with faith unshaken,
Place every thought on thee alone,
While he who Friendship's dream hath known,
   Must from that dream awaken !

---

xcv.

THE LAY OF GEOFFROI RUDEL.

With faltering step would I depart,
From home and friend that claimed my heart—
And the big tear would dim mine eye,
   Fixed on the scenes of early years,
   (Each spot some pleasure past endears)
And I would mingle with a sigh
The accents of the farewell lay—
But for my love that's far way !

Friends and dear native land, adieu !
In hope we part—no tears bedew
My cheek—no dark regrets alloy
   The buoyant feelings of the hour
   That leads me to my ladye's bower—

My breast throbs with a wondrous joy,
While every life-pulse seems to say—
"Haste to thy love that's far away!"

XCVI.

ENVIE.

Ane plante there is of the deidliest pouir
   Quhilk flourischis deeply in the hert;
Its lang rutis creip and fald outoure
   Ilka vive and breathen part:
Lustilie bourgenis the weid anon
Till hert hath rottit and lyf hath flown.

Blak is the sap of its baleful stem,
   Lyk funeral blicht its leavis do fal;
In its moisture is quenchit luve's pure flame,
   It drappis rust on inmost saul:
Lustilie bourgenis the weid anon,
Till hert hath rottit and lyf hath flown.

Evir it flourischis meikel and hie,
   Nae stay, nae hindraunce will it bruik;
In ae nicht sprynging up, a burdlie tree,
   Schedding its bale at ae single luik:
Lustilie bourgenis the weid anon,
Till hert hath rottit and lyf hath flown.

It canna be kythit to the gudely sun,
   It pynyth sae at his nobil sicht;
It shrinkyth quyte like a thing undone
   Quhan luikit on by the blessit licht:
In hert whence heevinlie luve hath gone
Thilke evil weid aye bourgenis on.

Fell Envie's th' plant of mortal pouir
   Quhilk flourischis grenelye in the hert—
Raining the slawe and poisonous shouir
   Quhilk cankereth the vertuous part :
Black Envie wherever its seed is sawin,
Fashion is a hert like the foul Fiend's awin !

XCVII.

LOVE'S TOKENS.

Love's herald is not speech—
   His fear-fraught tongue is mute—
His presence is bewrayed
   By blushes deep that shoot
Athwart the conscious brow,
   And mantle on the cheek,
Then fleet for tints of snow
   Which soft confusion speak ;
Thus red and white have place
By turns on true love's face.

Love vaunteth not his worth
   In gaudy, glozing phrase,
His home is not in breast
   Where thought of worlding stays ;
In modest loyaltie
   His fountain doth abide ;
In bosom greatly good
   The lucid pulses tide
That ebb and flow there ever,
Till soul and body sever.

Trust not the ready lip
  Whence flows the fulsome song—
True love aye gently hymns,
  False love chaunts loud and long.
Young Beauty, cherish well
  The bashful, anxious eye,
The lip that may not move,
  The breast that stills the sigh—
A recreant to thee
Their lord will never be!

XCVIII.

O SAY NOT PURE AFFECTIONS CHANGE!

O SAY not pure affections change
  When fixed they once have been,
Or that between two noble hearts
  Hate e'er can intervene!

Though coldness for a while may freeze
  The love-springs of the soul,
Though angry pride its sympathies
  May for a time control,

Yet such estrangement cannot last—
  A tone, a touch, a look,
Dissolves at once the icyness
  That crisp'd affection's brook:

Again they feel the genial glow
  Within the bosom burn,
And all their pent-up tenderness
  With tenfold force return!

XCIX.

THE ROSE AND THE FAIR LILYE.

The Earlsburn Glen is gay and green,
    The Earlsburn water cleir,
And blythely blume on Earlsburn bank
    The broom and eke the brier !

Twa Sisters gaed up Earlsburn glen—
    Twa maidens bricht o' blee—
The tane she was the Rose sae red,
    The tither the Fair Lilye !

" Ye mauna droop and dwyne, Sister "—
    Said Rose to fair Lilye—
" Yer heart ye mauna brek, Sister—
    For ane that's ower the sea :

" The vows we sillie maidens hear
    Frae wild and wilfu' man,
Are as the words the waves wash out
    When traced upon the san'!"

" I mauna think yer speech is sooth,"
    Saft answered the Lilye—
" I winna dout mine ain gude Knicht
    Tho' he's ayont the sea ! "

Then scornfully the Rose sae red
    Spake to the puir Lilye—
" The vows he feigned at thy bouir door,
    He plicht in mine to me !"

" I'll hame and spread the sheets, Sister,
    And deck my bed sae hie—
The bed sae wide made for a bride,
    For I think I sune sal die !

"Your wierd I sal na be, Sister,
    As mine I fear ye've bin—
Your luve I wil na cross, Sister,
    It were a mortal sin!"

Earlsburn Glen is green to see,
    Earlsburn water cleir—
Of the siller birk in Earlsburn Wood
    They framit the Maiden's bier!

There's a lonely dame in a gudély bouir,
    She nevir lifts an ee—
That dame was ance the Rose sae red,
    She is now a pale Lilye.

A Knicht aft looks frae his turret tall,
    Where the kirk-yaird grass grows green;
He wonne the weed and lost the flouir,
    And grief aye dims his een:

At noon of nicht, in the moonshine bricht,
    The warrior kneels in prayer—
He prays wi' his face to the auld kirk-yaird,
    And wishes he were there!

C.

LIKE MIST ON A MOUNTAIN TOP BROKEN AND GRAY.

Like mist on a mountain top broken and gray,
The dream of my early day fleeted away:
Now the evening of life, with its shadows, steals on,
And memory reposes on years that are gone!

Wild youth with strange fruitage of errors and tears—
A midday of bliss and a midnight of fears—
Though chequer'd, and sad, and mistaken you've been,
Still love I to muse on the hours we have seen!

With those long-vanished hours fair visions are flown,
And the soul of the minstrel sinks pensive and lone;
In vain would I ask of the future to bring
The verdure that gladden'd my life in its spring!

I think of the glen where the hazel-nut grew—
The pine-covered hill where the heather-bell blew—
The trout-burn which soothed with its murmuring sweet,
The wild flowers that gleamed on the red deer's retreat!

I look for the mates full of ardour and truth,
Whose joys, like my own, were the sunbeams of youth—
They passed e'er the morning of hope knew its close—
They left me to sleep where our fathers repose!

Where is now the wide hearth with the big faggot's blaze,
Where circled the legend and song of old days?
The legend's forgotten, the hearth is grown cold,
The home of my childhood to strangers is sold!

Like a pilgrim who speeds on a perilous way,
I pause, ere I part, oft again to survey
Those scenes ever dear to the friends I deplore,
Whose feast of young smiles I may never share more!

CI.

YOUNG LOVE.

It seems a dream the infant love
   That tamed my truant will,
But 'twas a dream of happiness,
   And I regret it still !

Its images are part of me,
   A very part of mind—
Feelings and fancies beautiful
   In purity combined !

Time's sunset lends a tenderer tinge
   To what those feelings were,
Like the cloud-mellow'd radiance
   Which evening landscapes bear :

They wedded are unto my soul,
   As light is blent with heat,
Or as the hallowed confluence
   Of air with odours sweet.

Though she, the spirit of that dream,
   Lacks of the loveliness
Young fancy robed her in, yet I
   May hardly love her less :

Even when as in my boyish time
   I nestled by her side,
Her ever gentle impulses
   Thorrow my being glide !

CII.

TO THE TEMPEST.

CHAUNT on, ye stormy voices, loud and shrill
Your wild tumultuous melody—strip
The forest of its clothing—leave it bare,
As a deserted and world-trampled foundling!
Lash on, ye rains, and pour your tide of might
Unceasingly and strong, and blench the Earth's
Green mantle with your floods : Suddenly swell
The brawling torrent in the sleep-locked night,
That it may deluge the subjacent plain,
And spread destruction where security
Had fondly built its faith, and knelt before
The altar of its refuge—Sweep ye down
Palace and mansion, hall and lofty tower,
And creeping shed, into one common grave!

Ye lightnings that are flashing fitfully—
(Heaven's messengers) askant the lurid sky,
Burst forth in one vast sheet of whelming fire—
Pass through the furnace the base lords of earth,
With subtile fury inextinguishable—
That, purified, they may again appear
As erst they were, free of soul-searing sin
And worldly-mindedness! For mailed they be,
Obdurate all, in selfish adamant,
So rivetted, that it would need a fire
Potential as the ever-burning pit,
To overcome and melt it, so that hearts
Might beat and spirits move to chords sublime,
Tuned by the hand of the Omnipotent,
As when man, from His Hands, in His beauty came!

CIII.

SONG.

If to thy heart I were as near
　　As thou art near to mine,
I'd hardly care though a' the year
Nae sun on earth suld shine, my dear,
　　Nae sun on earth suld shine!

Twin starnies are thy glancin' een—
　　A warld they'd licht and mair—
And gin that ye be my Christine,
Ae blink to me ye'll spare, my dear,
　　Ae blink to me ye'll spare!

My leesome May I've wooed too lang—
　　Aneath the trystin' tree,
I've sung till a' the plantin's rang,
Wi' lays o' love for thee, my dear,
　　Wi' lays o' love for thee.

The dew-draps glisten on the green,
　　The laverocks lilt on high,
We'll forth and doun the loan, Christine,
And kiss when nane is nigh, my dear,
　　And kiss when nane is nigh!

CIV.

AND HAE YE SEEN MY AIN TRUE LUVE?

" And hae ye seen my ain true luve
　　As ye cam thro' the fair?
Ae blink o' her's worth a' the goud
　　And gear that glistens there!"—

MY AIN TRUE LOVE.

" And how suld I ken your true luve
    Frae ither lasses braw
That trysted there, busked out like queens,
    Wi' pearlins, knots and a'?"

" Ye may ken her by her snaw-white skin,
    And by her waist sae sma;
Ye may ken her by her searchin' ee,
    And hair like glossy craw;
Ye may ken her by the hinnie mou,
    And by the rose-dyed cheek,
But best o' a' by smiles o' licht
    That luve's ain language speak!

" Ye may ken her by her fairy step—
    As she trips up the street,
The very pavement seems to shine
    Aneath her genty feet!
Ye may ken her by the jewell'd rings
    Upon her fingers sma',
Yet better by the dignity
    That she glides through them a'.

" And ye may ken her by the voice—
    The music o' her tongue—
Wha heard her speak incontinent
    Wad think an angel sung!
And such seems she to me, and mair
    That wale o' woman's charms—
It's bliss to press her dear wee mou
    And daut her in my arms!"

CV.

GOE CLEED WI' SMYLIS THE CHEEK.

Goe cleed wi' smylis the cheek,
　　Goe fill wi' licht the eye,—
O vain when sorrows seek
　　The fontis of bliss to drie !

Quhan Hope hath pyned away,
　　Quhan carke and care haif sprung,
Quhan hert hath faun a prey
　　To grief that hed nae tongue ;
O then it is nae tyme
　　To feinzie quhat we fele,
Or wi' ane merrie chime,
　　To droun the solemne peal
Quhilk ringis dreir and dul,
Quhan hert and eyne ar ful.

Nae joy is thair for me
　　In lyf againe to knowe—
Nae plesuir can I see
　　In its fals and fleetinge schew !—
Lyk wyld and fearful waste
　　Of wavis and bollen sand,
Apperis the path I've tracit
　　Inwith my natif land :
Fra it I must depairt,
And fra al quhilk hed mie hert.

Fareweil to kith and kin,
　　Fareweil to luve untrew,
Fareweil to burn and lin,
　　Fareweil to lift sua blew—

Fareweil to banck and brae,
  Fareweil to sang and glee—
Fareweil to pastyme gay,
  Quhilk ance delytit me—
Fareweil thou sunny strand,
Fareweil ance kinde Scotland !

Fresch flouris beare mie frend,
  Unto mie earlie graive,
Thair bid them nevir dwyne,
  But ower mie headstane waive ;
Perchance to sume they'll wake
  Remembrance o' mie dome—
And though fading, they maye make
  Less lonesum-lyk mie tombe—
Sins they will emblems be
Of thy luvinge sympathye.

Now fareweil day's dear licht—
  Now fareweil frend and fae—
Hail to the starrie nicht,
  Whair travailit saul maun gae !

CVI.

THE SPELL-BOUND KNIGHT.

LADY, dar'st thou seek the shore
Which ne'er woman's footstep bore ;—
Where beneath yon rugged steep,
Restless rolls the darksome deep ?

Dar'st thou, though thy blood run chill,
Thither speed at midnight still—
And when Horror rules the sky,
Raise for lover lost the cry ?

Dar'st thou at that ghastliest hour
Breathe the word of magic power—
Word that breaks the mermaid's spell,
Which false lover knows too well ?

When affrighted spectres rise
'Twixt pale floods and ebon skies,
Dar'st thou, reft of maiden fear,
Bid the Water-Witch appear ?

When upon the sallow tide
Pearly elfin boat does glide,
When the mystic oar is heard,
Like the wing of baleful bird—
Dar'st thou with a voice of might
Call upon thy spell-bound knight ?

When the shallop neareth land,
Dar'st thou, with thy snow-white hand,
Boldly on the warrior's breast
Place the Cross by Churchman blest ?—
When is done this work of peril,
Thou hast won proud Ulster's Earl !

CVII.

O THAT THIS WEARY WAR OF LIFE !

O THAT this weary war of life
 With me were o'er,
Its eager cry of wo and strife
 Heard never more !
I've fronted the red battle field
 Mine own dark day ;
I fain would fling the helmet, shield,
 And sword away.

I strive not now for victory—
    That wish hath fled ;
My prayer is now to numbered be
    Among the dead—
All that I loved, alas !—alas !
    Hath perished !

They tell me 'tis a glorious thing,
    This wearing war ;
They tell me joy crowns suffering
    And bosom scar.
Such a speech might never pass the lips
    That could unfold
How shrinketh heart when sorrow nips
    Affections old :
When they who cleaved to us are dust,
    Why live to moan ?
Better to meet a felon thrust
    Than strive alone—
Better than loveless palaces
    The churchyard stone !

CVIII.

THE POET'S DESTINY.

DARK is the soul of the Minstrel—
    Wayward the flash of his eye ;
The voice of the proud is against him,
    The rude sons of earth pass him by.

Low is the grave of the Minstrel—
    Ungraced by the chissel of art ;
Yet his name will be blazoned for ever
    On the best of all 'scutcheons—the heart !

Strong is the soul of the Minstrel—
   He rules in a realm of his own ;
His world is peopled by fancies
   The noblest that ever were known.

Light is the rest of the Minstrel,
   Though heavy his lot upon earth ;
From the sward that lies over his ashes
   Spring plants of a heavenly birth !

CIX.

I MET WI' HER I LUVED YESTREEN.

I MET wi' her I luved yestreen,
   I met her wi' a look o' sorrow ;
My leave I took o' her for aye,
   A weddit bride she'll be the morrow !

She durst na gie ae smile to me,
   Nor drap ae word o' kindly feelin',
Yet down her cheeks the bitter tears,
   In monie a pearly bead, were stealin'.

I could na my lost luve upbraid,
   Altho' my dearest hopes were blighted,
I could na say—" ye're fause to me !"—
   Tho' to anither she was plighted.

Like suthfast friens whom death divides,
   In Heaven to meet, we silent parted ;
Nae voice had we our griefs to speak,
   We felt sae lone and broken-hearted.

I'll hie me frae my native lan',
  Far frae thy blythesome banks o' Yarrow!
Wae's me, I canna bide to see
  My winsome luve anither's marrow!

I'll hie me to a distant lan',
  Wi' down-cast ee and life-sick bosom,
A wearie waste the warld's to me,
  Sin' I hae lost that bonnie blossom!

CX.

TO THE LADY OF MY HEART.

They oft have told me that deceit
  Lies hid in dimpled smiles,
But eyes so chaste and lips so sweet
  Conceal not wanton wiles!

I'll trust thee, lady!—To deceive,
  Or guileful tale to speak,
Was never fashioned I believe
  The beauty of thy cheek!

Yes, I will trust the azure eye
  That thrilled me with delight,
The loving load-star of a sky
  Which erst was darkest night.

Ever, dear maid, in weal or wo,
  In gladness and in sorrow,
Hand clasped in hand, we'll forward go,
  Both eventide and morrow!

CXI.

THE FAUSE LADYE.

"The water weets my toe," she said,
  "The water weets my knee;
Haud up, Sir Knicht, my horse's head,
  If you a true luve be!"

" I luved ye weel, and luved ye lang,
  Yet grace I failed to win;
Nae trust put I in ladye's troth
  Till water weets her chin! '

" Then water weets my waist, proud lord,
  The water weets my chin;
My achin' head spins round about,
  The burn maks sik a din—
Now, help thou me, thou fearsome Knicht,
  If grace ye hope to win!"

"I mercy hope to win, high dame,
  Yet hand I've nane to gie—
The trinklin' o' a gallant's blude
  Sae sair hath blindit me!"

"Oh! help!—Oh! help!—If man ye be
  Have on a woman ruth—
The waters gather round my head
  And gurgle in my mouth!"

"Turn round and round, fell Margaret,
  Turn round and look on me—
The pity that ye schawed yestreen
  I'll fairly schaw to thee!

"Thy girdle-knife was keen and bricht—
    The ribbons wondrous fine—
'Tween every knot o' them ye knit
    Of kisses I had nine!

"Fond Margaret! Fause Margaret!
    You kissed me cheek and chin—
Yet, when I slept, that girdle-knife
    You sheathed my heart's blude in!

"Fause Margaret! Lewde Margaret!
    The nicht ye bide wi' me—
The body, under trust, you slew,
    My spirit weds wi' thee!"

CXII.

MY AIN COUNTRIE.

Ye bonnie haughs and heather braes
Whare I hae daft youth's gladsome days,
A dream o' by-gane bliss ye be
That gars me sigh for my ain countrie!

Lang dwinin' in a fremit land
Doth feckless mak' baith heart and hand,
And starts the tear-drap to the ee
That aye was bricht in the auld countrie.

Tho' Carron Brig be gray and worn,
Where I and my forebears were born,
Yet dearer is its time-touched stone
Than the halls of pride I now look on.

As music to the lingerin' ear
Were Carron's waters croonin' clear ;
They call to me, where'er I roam,
The voices o' my long-lost home !

And gin I were a wee wee bird,
Adown to licht at Randie Ford,
In Kirk O' Muir I'd close mine ee,
And fald my wings in mine ain countrie !

CXIII.

TO A FRIEND AT PARTING.*

FAREWELL, my friend !—Perchance again
  I'll clasp thee to a faithful heart—
Farewell my friend !—We part in pain,
  Yet we must part !

Were this memento to declare
  All that the inward moods portray,
Dark boding grief were pictured there,
  And wild dismay !

For thee, my fancy paints a scene
  Of peace on life's remoter shore—
Thy wishes long fulfilled have been,
  Or even more :

And when success hath crowned thy toil,
  And hope hath raised thy heart to Heaven—
Thou well mayst love the generous soil
  Where love was given.

---

* The "Friend at Parting" was Mr. Robert Peacock, at present (July, 1848) resident, I believe, in Germany.—K.

For me, my friend, I fear there's nought,
  In dim futurity, of gladness;
That ever rises on my thought
  A dream of sadness:

Yet gazing upon guileless faces,
  Sunned by the light of laughing eyes,
I recreant were to own no traces
  Of social ties.

Even I may borrow from another
  The smile I fain would call my own,
Striving, with childish art, to smother
  The care unknown.

Farewell! Farewell!—All good attend thee—
  At home, abroad—on land, or sea—
That Heaven may evermore befriend thee,
  My prayer shall be!

Should a dark thought of him arise
  Whose parting hand thou must resign,
Let it go forth to stormy skies,
  Not tarnish thine:

Never may Melancholy's brood
  Disturb the fountain of thy joy,
Nor dusky Passion's fitful mood
  Thy peace alloy!

"Up, anchor! up!"—The mariner
  Thus hymns to the inconstant wind—
Heave not one sigh, where'er you steer,
  For me behind!

CXIV.

I PLUCKED THE BERRY.

I'VE plucked the berry from the bush, the brown nut from the tree,
But heart of happy little bird ne'er broken was by me ;
I saw them in their curious nests, close couching, slyly peer,
With their wild eyes, like glittering beads, to note if harm were near :
I passed them by, and blessed them all ; I felt that it was good
To leave unmoved the creatures small whose home is in the wood.

And here, even now, above my head, a lusty rogue doth sing,
He pecks his swelling breast and neck, and trims his little wing,
He will not fly ; he knows full well, while chirping on that spray,
I would not harm him for a world, or interrupt his lay ;
Sing on, sing on, blythe bird! and fill my heart with summer gladness,
It has been aching many a day with measures full of sadness!

CXV.

SONG.

O LICHT, licht was maid Ellen's fit—
　It left nae print behind,
Until a belted Knicht she saw
　Adown the valley wind!

And winsome was maid Ellen's cheek,
   As is the rose on brier,
Till halted at her father's yett
   A lordly cavalier.

And merrie, merrie was her sang,
   Till he knelt at her bouir—
As lark's rejoicin' in the sun,
   Her princely paramour.

But dull, dull now is Ellen's eye,
   And wan, wan is her cheek,
And slow an' heavy is her fit
   That lonesum paths would seek :

And never sang does Ellen sing
   Amang the flowers sae bricht,
Since last she saw the dancin' plume
   Of that foresworne Knicht !

CXVI.

TO * * * *

I NEVER dreamed that lips so sweet,
   That eyes of such a heavenly hue,
Were framed for falsehood and deceit,
   Would prove, as they have proved—untrue.

Methought if love on earth e'er shone,
   'Twas in the temple of thine eyes,
And if truth's accents e'er were known,
   'Twas in the music of thy sighs.

Has then thy love been all a show,
  Thy plighted troth an acted part—
Did no affection ever glow
  In the chill region of that heart?

And could'st thou seem to me to cling
  Like tendril of the clasping vine,
Yet all prove vain imagining,
  Thy soul yield no response to mine?

It has been so—so let it be—
  Rejoice, thou false one, in thy guile,
Others, perhaps, may censure thee,
  I would not dim thy fickle smile.

Farewell!—In kindness I would part,
  As once I deemed in love we met—
Farewell!—This wrong'd and bleeding heart
  Can thee Forgive, but not Forget!

CXVII.

THE KNIGHT'S REQUIEM.

They have waked the knight so meikle of might,
  They have cased his corpse in oak;
There was not an eye that then was dry,
  There was not a tongue that spoke.
The stout and the true lay stretched in view,
  Pale and cold as the marble stone;
And the voice was still that like trumpet shrill,
  Had to glory led them on;
And the deadly hand whose battle brand
  Mowed down the reeling foe,
Was laid at rest on the manly breast,
  That never more mought glow.

THE KNIGHT'S REQUIEM.

With book, and bell, and waxen light,
   The mass for the dead is sung;
Thorough the night in the turret's height,
   The great church-bells are rung.
Oh wo! oh wo! for those that go
   From light of life away,
Whose limbs may rest with worms unblest,
   In the damp and silent clay!

With a heavy cheer they upraised his bier,
   Naker and drum did roll;
The trumpets blew a last adieu
   To the good knight's martial soul.
With measured tread thro' the aisle they sped,
   Bearing the dead knight on,
And before the shrine of St. James the divine,
   They covered his corpse with stone:
'Twas fearful to see the strong agony
   Of men who had seldom wept,
And to hear the deep groan of each mail-clad one,
   As the lid on the coffin swept.

With many a groan, they placed that stone
   O'er the heart of the good and brave,
And many a look the tall knights took
   Of their brother soldier's grave.
Where banners stream and corslets gleam
   In fields besprent with gore,
That brother's hand and shearing brand
   In the van should wave no more:
The clarions call on one and all
   To arm and fight amain,
Would never see, in chivalry,
   Their brother's make again!

With book, and bell, and waxen light,
   The mass for the dead is sung,
And thorough the night in the turret's height,
   The great church-bells are rung.

Oh wo ! oh wo ! for those that go
  From the light of life away,
Whose limbs may rest with worms unblest,
  In the damp and silent clay !

CXVIII.

THE ROCKY ISLET.

PERCHANCE, far out at sea, thou may'st have found
Some lean, bald cliff—a lonely patch of ground,
Alien amidst the waters :—some poor Isle
Where summer blooms were never known to smile,
Or trees to yield their verdure—yet, around
That barren spot, the dimpling surges throng,
Cheering it with their low and plaintive song,
And clasping the deserted cast-away
In a most strict embrace—and all along
Its margin, rendering freely its array
Of treasured shell and coral. Thus we may
Note love in faithful woman ; oft among
The rudest shocks of life's wide sea she shares
Man's lot, and more than half his burden bears
Around whose path are flowers, strewn by her tender cares.

CXIX.

TRUE WOMAN.

No QUAINT conceit of speech,
  No golden, minted phrase—
Dame Nature needs to teach
  To echo Woman's praise ;
Pure love and truth unite
To do thee, Woman, right !

She is the faithful mirror
   Of thoughts that brightest be—
Of feelings without error,
   Of matchless constancie ;
When art essays to render
   More glorious Heaven's bow—
To paint the virgin splendour
   Of fresh-fallen mountain snow—
New fancies will I find,
To laud true Woman's mind.

No words can lovelier make
   Virtue's all-lovely name,
No change can ever shake
   A woman's virtuous fame :
The moon is forth anew,
   Though envious clouds endeavour
To screen her from our view—
   More beautiful than ever :
So, through detraction's haze,
True Woman shines alwaies.

The many-tinted Rose,
   Of gardens is the queen,
The perfumed Violet knows
   No peer where she is seen—
The flower of woman-kind
Is aye a gentle mind.

CXX.

THE PAST AND THE FUTURE.

I've looked, and trusted, sighed, and loved my last!
The dream hath vanished, the hot fever's past
    That parched my youth!
Though cheerless was the matin of my years,
And dim life's dawning through a vale of tears,
    Yet Hope, in ruth,
With smile persuasive, evermore would say—
" Live on, live on!—Expect Joy's summer day "—
    Vain counsel, void of truth!

Yes, to the world I've clung with fond embrace,
And each succeeding day did more efface
    Its hollow joys,
And friends died out around me every where,
And I was left to the idle stare
    Of vagrant boys—
A land-mark on the ever-shifting tide
Of fashion, folly, impudence, and pride,
    And ribald noise.

Yes, I have lived, and lived until I knew
The world ne'er alters its ungrateful hue,
    And glance malign;
And though, at times, some chance-sown noble spirit
Its wilderness a season may inherit,
    In want and pine,
Yet these be weeded soon, and pass away,
All unbefriended, to their funeral clay!

Array thyself for flight, my soul, nor tarry—
Thou bird of glory ne'er wert doomed to marry
    A sphere so rude—

But to be mated with some hermit star,
O'er heaven's soft azure keeping watch afar,
   In pulchritude :
Uplift thy pinions, seek thy resting-place,
Where kindred spirits long for thy embrace—
   Dear brotherhood.

CXXI.

OH, TURN FROM ME THOSE RADIANT EYES!

Oh, turn from me those radiant eyes,
   With love's dark lightning beaming,
Or veil the power that in them lies
   To set the young heart dreaming !
Oh, dim their fire, or look no more,
   For sure 'tis wayward folly
To make a spirit, gay before,
   To droop with melancholy !

Ungen'rous victor ! not in vain
   Thy wild wish to subdue me—
To woo once more thy glance I'm fain,
   Even should that glance undo me :
What pity that thy lips of rose
   So fitted for heart healing,
Should not, with tenderest kisses, close
   The wounds thine eyes are dealing !

CXXII.

O THINK NAE MAIR O' ME, SWEET MAY.

O THINK nae mair o' me, sweet May,
    O think nae mair o' me !
I'm but a wearied ghaist, sweet May,
    That hath a weird to dree ;
That langs to leave a warld, sweet May,
    O' eerie dule and pain,
And pines to gang the gate, sweet May,
    That its first luve hath gane !

Although the form is here, sweet May,
    The spirit is na sae ;
It wanders to anither land—
    A far and lonely way.
My bower is near a ruined kirk,
    Hard by a grass-green grave,
Where, fed wi' tears, the gilliflowers
    Above a true heart wave !

Then think nae mair o' me, sweet May,
    If I had luve to gie,
It suld na need a glance but ane
    To bind me, dear, to thee.
But blossoms twa o' life's best flower
    This heart it canna bear—
It cast its leaves on Mary's grave,
    And it can bloom nae mair !

CXXIII.

THE LOVE-LORN KNIGHT AND THE DAMSEL PITILESS.

"Uplift the Gonfanons of war—exalt the ruddy Rood—
Arise ye winds and bear me on against the Paynim brood !
Farewell to forest-cinctured halls, farewell to song and glee,
For toilsome march and clash of swords in glorious Galilee !
And grace to thee, haught damoisel—I ask no parting tear—
Another love may greet thee when I'm laid upon my bier !

"My bark upon the foaming flood shall bound before the gale,
Like arrow in its flight, until the Holy Land we hail ;
Then firmly shall our anchors grasp the belt of Eastern land,
For planks will shrink and cordage rot ere we regain this strand ;
And welcome be the trumpet's sound, the war-steed's tramp and neigh,
And death, for Palestina's cause, in the battle's hot mellay !"

O never for that love-lorn youth did vessel cleave the seas !
The hand of death was on the lips that wooed the ocean breeze ;
They bare him to the damoisel, they laid him at her knee,
Though knight and pilgrim wept aloud—no tear dropt that ladye—
Three times she kissed the clay-cold brow of her unbidden guest,
Then took the vows at Mary's shrine, and there her ashes rest.

CXXIV.

LOVE IN WORLDLYNESSE.

The gentle heart, the truthful love,
   Have flemed this earth and fled to Heaven—
The noblest spirits earliest prove
Not Here below, but There above,
   Is Hope no shadow—Bliss no sweven !

There was a time, old Poets say,
   When the crazed world was in its nonage,
That they who loved were loved alwaye,
With faith transparent as the day,
   But this, meseems, was fiction's coinage.

We cannot mate here as we ought,
   With laws opposed to simple feeling ;
Professions are, like lute string, bought,
And worldly ties soon breed distraught,
   To end in cold congealing !

Forms we have worshipped oft become,
   If haply they affect our passion,
Though faultless, icy cold and dumb,
Because we are not rich, like some,
   Or proud—Such is this strange world's fashion !

Rapt Fancy lends to unchaste eyes
   Ideal beauty, and on faces
Where red rose blent with lily tries
For mastery, in wanton wise,
   Bestows enchanting graces :

Yet, as we gaze, the charms decay
   That promised long with these to linger ;
Of love's delight we're forced to say,
It melts like dreamer's wealth away,
   Which cheers the eye but mocks the finger !

And, therefore, move I calmly by
   The siren bosom softly heaving,
And mark, untouched, the tempter's sigh,
Or make response with tranquil eye—
   " Kind damsel, I am past deceiving !"

Long sued I as a man should do,
   With cheek high flushed by deep emotion—
My lady's love had no such hue,
Hard selfishness would still break through
   The glowing mask of her devotion !

No land had I—but I had health—
   No store was mine of costly raiment—
My lady glided off by stealth
To wed a lozel for his wealth—
   And this was Loyalty's repayment !

The language of the trusting heart,
   The soothfast fondness firm, but tender—
Are now to most a studied part,
A tongue assumed, a trick of art,
   Whereof no meaning can I render.

And hence I say that loyal love
   Hath flemed the Earth and fled to Heaven ;
And that not here, but there above,
Souls may love rightfully, and prove
   Hope is no shadow—Bliss no sweven !

CXXV.

A NIGHT VISION.

> Lucina shyning in silence of the nicht :
> The hevin being all full of starris bricht ;
> To bed I went, bot there I tuke no rest,
> With hevy thocht I was so sair oppressed,
> That sair I langit after dayis licht.
> Of fortoun I complainit hevely,
> That echo to me stude so contrarously ;
> And at the last, quhen I had turnyt oft
> For werines, on me ane slummer soft
> Came, with ane dreming and a fantesy.
> —*Dunbar.*

I HAD a vision in the depth of night—
A dream of glory—one long thrill of gladness—
A thing of strangest meaning and delight ;
And yet upon my heart there came such sadness,
And dim forebodings of my after years,
That I awoke in sorrow and in tears !

There stood revealed before me a bright maid,
Clad in a white silk tunic, which displayed
The beautiful proportions of her frame ;
And she did call upon me by my name—
And I did marvel at her voice, and shook
With terror, but right soon the smiling look
Of gentleness, that radiant maiden threw
From her large sparkling eyes of deepest blue,
Did reassure me. Breathless, I did gaze
Upon that lovely one, in fond amaze,
And marked her long white hair as it did flow,
With wanton dalliance, o'er the pillared snow
Of her swan-like neck ;—and then my eye grew dim
With an exceeding lustre, for the slim
And gauze-wove raiment of her bosom fair,
Was somewhat ruffled by the midnight air ;

And as it gently heaved, there sprung to view
Such glories underneath—such sisters two
Of rival loveliness! Oh, 'twere most vain
For fond conceit to fancy such again.
The robe she wore was broidered fetouslye
With flower and leaf of richest imagerye;
And threads of gold therein were entertwined
With quaintest needlecraft; and to my mind
It seemed, the waist of this most lovely one,
Was clipped within a broad and azure zone,
Studded with strange devices—One small hand
Waved gracefully a slender ivory wand,
And with the other, ever and anon,
She shook a harp, which, as the winds sighed past,
Gave a right pleasant and bewitching tone
To each wild vagrant blast.

      Meseems,
After this wondrous guise, that maiden sweet
Stood visible before me, while the beams
Of Dian pale, laughed round her little feet
With icy lustre, through the narrow pane;
And this discourse she held in merry vein;
Although methought 'twas counterfeited, and
The matter strange, that none might understand.

 She told me, that the moon was in her wane—
And life was tiding on, and that the world
Was waxen old—that nature grew unkind,
And men grew selfish quite, and sore bechurled—
That Honour was a bubble of the mind—
And Virtue was a nothing undefined—
And as for Woman, She, indeed, *could claim*
A title all her own—She *had* a name
And place in Time's long chronicles, DECEIT—
And Glory was a phantom—Death a cheat!

 She said I might remember her, for she
Had trifled with me in mine infancy;

And in those days, that now are long agone,
Has tended me, as if I were her own
And only offspring. When a very child,
She said, her soothing whispers oft beguiled
The achings of my heart—that in my youth,
She, too, had given me dreams of Honour, Truth,
Of Glory and of Greatness—and of Fame—
And the bright vision of a deathless name!
And she had turned my eye, with upward look,
To read the bravely star-enamelled book
Of the blue skies—and in the rolling spheres
To con strange lessons, penned in characters
Of most mysterious import—she had made
Life's thorny path to be all sown with flowers
Of diverse form and fragrance, of each shade
Of loveliness that glitters in the bowers
Of princely damoisels,—Nay, more, her hand
Had plucked the bright flowers of *another* land,
Belike of Faerye, and had woven them
Like to a chaplet, or gay diadem,
For *me* to wear in triumph—But that she
Had fostered me so long, she feared, I'd spoil
With very tenderness, nor ever be
Fit for this world's coarse drudgery and moil;
Did she not even now take leave of me,
And her protecting, loving arms uncoil
For ever and for ever,—and though late,
Now leave me to self-guidance, and to fate.

Then passed that glorious spirit, and the smile
She whilome wore fled from her beauteous cheek;
And paleness, and a troubled grief the while
Subdued her voice.—Methought I strove to speak
Some words of tender sympathy, and caught
Her small white trembling hand, but, she, distraught,
Turned her fair form away, and nearer drew
To where the clustering ivy leaves thick grew,

And shaded half the casement—There she stood,
Like a tall crystal column, in the flood
Of the fair moonshine, and right thoughtful-wise
She seemed to scan the aspect of the skies ;
Sudden a tremulous tear filled either eye,
Yet fell not on her cheek, but dubiously,
Like dew gems upon a flower, hung quivering there ;
And, like a love-crazed maiden, she half sang,
Half uttered mournful fancies in despair ;
And indistinctly in my ear there rung
Something of years to be,—of dark, dark years,
Laden with sorrow, madness, fury, tears—
Of days that had no sunshine—and of nights
Estranged from slumber—of harsh worldly slights—
Of cruel disappointments—of a hell
That gloweth in the bosom, fierce and fell,
Which may not be extinguished—of the pains
Of journeying through lone and trackless plains
Which have no limits—and of savage faces,
That showed no trait of pity !

    Then that maid
Stretched her long arms to heaven, and wept for shame ;
And as upon her soul dim bodements came,
Once more, in veriest sadness, thus she said :
" I may not cheer him more ! I may not breathe
Life in his wasting limbs, nor healthy fire
In his grief-sunken eye—I may not wreathe
Fresh flowers for *him* to gaze on, nor inspire
Delicious dreamings when the paly host
Of cares and troubles weigh his spirit down,
And hopes delayed, in worse despair are lost ;
Unaided, he may sink upon the path,
No hand of succour near, nor melting eye
To yield its pittance poor of sympathy ;
Already, too successful have I weaved
My tiny web of folly ; undeceived,

At length, he'll view his baseless fabric pass,
Like fleeting shadows o'er the brittle glass,
Leaving no substance there ; and he may curse,
With bitter malison, his too partial nurse,
And charge *her* with *his* sufferings!"

                     So wept
That maid, in seeming sorrow, till there fell
From her lips Grief's volume-word—Farewell!
And then, methought, she softly passed away,
As a thin mist of glory on a ray
Of purest moonshine ; or like starlet bright
Sailed onward through the ocean of the night!

   And then, meseems, I heard the wailing sound
Of a wind-harp afar, and voice of one
Who sung thereto a plaintive melody ;
And some words reached me, but the rest were drowned
In dimest distance, and the hollow moan
Of the night-breezes fitful sweeping by ;
Yet these stray words, erewhile on earth they fell,
Told Hope had pitying smiled before her last farewell.

   Then all grew dark and loveless, and afar
I saw the falling down of many a star,
As the moon paled in sorrow—And the roar
Of darkly tumbling floods I heard, that dashed
Through the deep fissures of the rifted rock—
While phantoms flitted by with ghastly mock,
And jeers malign—and demons on me glar'd
Looks of infernal meaning ; then in silence
Troop'd onwards to their doom !

                  Starting, I broke
Sleep's leaden bonds of sorrow, and awoke,
Wondering to find my eye-balls red with tears !
And my breast heaving with sepulchral fears.

CXXVI.

THIS IS NO SOLITUDE.

This is no Solitude ; These brown woods speak
   In tones most musical—this limpid river
   Chaunts a low song, to be forgotten never !—
These my beloved companions are so meek,
So soul-sustaining, I were crazed to seek
   Again the tumult, the o'erpowering hum,
   Which of the ever busy hiving city come—
Parting us from ourselves.—Still let us breathe
   The heavenly air of contemplation here ;
   And with old trees, grey stones, and runnels clear,
Claim kindred and hold converse. He that seeth
Upon this vesper spot no lovliness,
Nor hears therein a voice of tenderness,
Calling him friend, Nature in vain would bless !

CXXVII.

THE LONE THORN.

Beneath the scant shade of an aged thorn,
   Silvered with age, and mossy with decay,
I stood, and there bethought me of its morn
   Of verdant lustyhood, long passed away ;
Of its meridian vigour, now outworn
   By cankering years, and by the tempest's sway
Bared to the pitying glebe.—Companionless,
   Stands the gray thorn complaining to the wind—
Of all the old wood's leafy loveliness
   The sole memorial that lags behind ;
Its compeers perished in their youthfulness,
   Though round the earth their roots seem'd firmly twined :
How sad it is to be so anchored here
As to outlive one's mates, and die without a tear !

CXXVIII.

THE SLAYNE MENSTREL.

Ane harper there was—ane harper gude—
    Cam' harpin' at the gloamin fa'—
And he has won to the bonnie bield
    Quhilk callit is the Newtoun Ha'.

" Brume, brume on hil "—the harper sang—
    " And rose on brier are blythe to see—
I would I saw the brume sae lang,
    Quhilk cleidis the braes o' my ain countree ! "

" Out on ye, out, ye prydefu' loun,
    Wi' me ye winna lig the nicht—
Hie to some bordel in borrowe toun :
    Of harpand craft I haud but licht !

" Out on ye, out, ye menstrel lewde"—
    Sayd the crewel Laird o' the Newtoun Ha'—
" Ye'll nae bide here, by blessit Rude,
    Gif harpe or lyf ye reck ava' ! "

" I care na for mie lyf ane plack"—
    Quoth that auld harper sturdilie—
" But this gude harpe upon mie back
    Sal ne'er be fylit by ane lyk thee ! "

" Thou liest there, thou menstrel wicht ! "
    Outspak the Laird o' the Newtoun Ha'—
" For ye to death bedene art dicht,
    Haif at thee here and mend thy saw ! "

Alace, Alace, the harper gude
    Was borne back aganis the wa',
And wi' the best o' his auld hertis blude,
    They weetit hae the Newtoun Ha' !

Yet did he die wi' harpe in han',
    Maist lyk ane menstrel o' degree—
There was na ane in a' the land
    Might matche wi' him o' the North countree!

Erle Douglas chauncit to ryde therebye—
    Ane gallant gentleman was he—
Wi' four score o' weel harnessit men,
    To harrie in the South countree.

He haltit at the Newtoun Ha'—
    " Quhat novelles now, bauld Laird, hae ye? "
" It's I haif slayne a worthlesse wicht,
    Ane menstrel lewde, as you may see!"

" Now schaw to me the harper's heid,
    And schaw to me the harper's hand,
For sair I fear you've causeless spilt
    As gentil blude as in a' Scotland!"

" Kep then his heid, thou black Douglas"—
    Sayd boastfullie fase Newtoun Ha'—
" And kep his hand, thou black Douglas,
    His fingers slim his craft may schaw!"

The stout Erle vysit first the heid,
    Then neist he lukit on the hand—
" It's foul befa' ye, Newtoun Ha',
    Ye've slayne the pryde o' gude Scotland.

" Now stir ye, stir, my merrie men,
    The faggot licht, and bete the flame,
A fire sal rise o'er this buirdly bield,
    And its saulless Laird in the lowe we'll tame!"

The bleeze blew up, the bleeze clipt roun'
    The bonnie towers o' the Newtoun Ha',
And evir as armit men ran out,
    Black Douglas slewe them ane and a'.

    The bleeze it roarit and wantonit roun'
        The weel-pilet wawis o' the Newtoun Ha',
And ruif and rafter, bauk and beam,
        Aneath the bauld fyris doun did fa' !

Now waly for the crewel Laird—
        As he cam loupin' through the lowe,
Erle Douglas swappit aff his heid
        And swung it at his saddil bowe !

CXXIX.

THE MERMAIDEN.

" The nicht is mirk, and the wind blaws schill,
        And the white faem weets my bree,
And my mind misgi'es me, gay maiden,
        That the land we sall never see !"
Then up and spak' the mermaiden,
        And she spak' blythe and free,
" I never said to my bonnie bridegroom,
        That on land we sud weddit be.

" Oh ! I never said that ane erthlie priest
        Our bridal blessing should gi'e,
And I never said that a landwart bouir
        Should hauld my love and me."
" And whare is that priest, my bonnie maiden,
        If ane erthlie wicht is na he ?"
" Oh ! the wind will sough, and the sea will rair,
        When weddit we twa sall be ? "

" And whare is that bouir, my bonnie maiden,
        If on land it sud na be ? "
" Oh ! my blythe bouir is low," said the mermaiden,
    " In the bonnie green howes of the sea :

My gay bouir is biggit o' the gude ship's keels,
    And the banes o' the drowned at sea ;
The fisch are the deer that fill my parks,
    And the water waste my dourie.

" And my bouir is sklaitit wi' the big blue waves,
    And paved wi' the yellow sand,
And in my chaumers grow bonnie white flowers
    That never grew on land.
And have ye e'er seen, my bonnie bridegroom,
    A leman on earth that wud gi'e
Aiker for aiker o' the red plough'd land,
    As I'll gi'e to thee o' the sea ?

" The mune will rise in half ane hour,
    And the wee bright starns will schine ;
Then we'll sink to my bouir, 'neath the wan water
    Full fifty fathom and nine !"
A wild, wild skreich gi'ed the fey bridegroom,
    And a loud, loud lauch, the bride ;
For the mune raise up, and the twa sank down
    Under the silver'd tide.

CXXX.

SONG.

He courted me in parlour, and he courted me in ha',
He courted me by Bothwell banks, amang the flowers sae sma',
He courted me wi' pearlins, wi' ribbons, and wi' rings,
He courted me wi' laces, and wi' mony mair braw things ;
But O he courted best o' a' wi' his black blythesome ee,
Whilk wi' a gleam o' witcherie cuist glaumour over me.

We hied thegither to the Fair—I rade ahint my joe,
I fand his heart leap up and doun, while mine beat faint
    and low ;
He turn'd his rosy cheek about, and then, ere I could trow,
The widdifu' o' wickedness took arles o' my mou!
Syne, when I feigned to be sair fleyed, sae pawkily as he
Bann'd the auld mare for missing fit, and thrawin him ajee.

And aye he waled the loanings lang, till we drew near the
    town,
When I could hear the kimmers say—"There rides a come-
    lie loun!"
I turned wi' pride and keeked at him, but no as to be seen,
And thought how dowie I wad feel, gin he made love to Jean!
But soon the manly chiel, aff-hand, thus frankly said to me,
"Meg, either tak me to yourself, or set me fairly free!"

To Glasgow Green I link'd wi' him, to see the ferlies there,
He birled his penny wi' the best—what noble could do mair :
But ere ae fit he'd tak me hame, he cries—"Meg, tell me noo?
Gin ye will hae me, there's my lufe, I'll aye be leal an' true."
On sic an honest, loving heart, how could I draw a bar?
What could I do but tak Rab's hand, for better or for waur?

CXXXI.

THE LEAN LOVER.

I PACED, an easy rambler,
    Along the surf-washed shore—
And watched the noble freightage
    The swelling ocean bore.
I met a moody fellow
    Who thus discoursed his wo—
"Across the inconstant waters,
    Deceitful woman, go!

" I loved that beauteous lady—
   More truly wight ne'er loved—
I loved that high-born lady,
   My faith she long had proved :
Her troth to me she plighted
   With passion's amorous show—
Go o'er the inconstant waters,
   Ungrateful worldling, go !

" Be mine yon cliff-perched chapel
   Which beetles o'er the deep ;
There, like some way-worn palmer,
   I'll sit me down and weep.
I'll note upon the billows
   Her lessening sail of snow,
And waft across the waters—
   Go, fleeting fair one, go !"

He clambered to the chapel
   That toppled o'er the deep—
There, like a way-worn palmer,
   He laid him down to weep :
And still I heard his wailing
   Upon the strand below—
" Go o'er the inconstant waters,
   Go, faithless woman, go !"

CXXXII.

AFFECTEST THOU THE PLEASURES OF THE SHADE?

AFFECTEST thou the pleasures of the shade,
And pastoral customs of the olden time,
When gentle shepherd piped to gentle maid
On oaten reed, his quaint and antique rhyme ?

Then welcome to the green and mossy nook,
The forest dark and silver poppling brook,
And flowers in fragrant indolence that blossom
On the sequestered valley's sloping bosom—
Where in the leafy halls glad strains are pealing,
The woodland songsters' amorous thoughts revealing:
Look how the morning's eager kisses wake
The clouds that guard the Orient, blushing red—
Behold heaven's phantom-chasing Sovereign shake
The golden honours of his graceful head
Above that earth this day-dawn saw so fair !—
Now damsels lithe trip lightsomely away,
To bathe their clustered brows and bosoms bare
In virgin dews of budding, balmy May !

CXXXIII.

MUSIC.

Strange how the mystically mingled sound
Of voices rising from these rifted rocks
And unseen valleys—whence no organ ever
Thundered harmonious its stupendous notes,
Nor pointed arch, nor low-browed darksome aisle,
Rolled back their mighty music—seems to me
An ocean vast, divinely undulating,
Where, bathed in beauty, floats the enraptured soul:
Now borne on the translucent deep, it skirts
Some dazzling bank of amaranthine flowers,
Now on a couch of odours cast supine,
It pants beneath o'erpowering redolence :—
Buoyant anon on a rejoicing surge,
It heaves, on tides tumultuous, far aloft,
Until it verges on the cope of heaven,
Whence issued, in their unity of joy,
The anthems of the earth-creating Morn :

Yielding again to an entrancing slumber,
In sweet abandonment, it glideth on
To amber caves and emerald palaces,
Where the lost Seraphs—welcomed by the main—
Their lyres suspended in their time of sorrow,
Amid the deepening glories of the flood ;—
There the rude revels of the boisterous winds
The tranquillous waves afflict not, nor dispart
The passionate clasping of their azure arms!

CXXXIV.

THE SHIP-WRECKED LOVER.

THE Port-Reeve's maid has laid her down
    Upon a restless pillow,
But wakeful thought is wandering
    Ayont the ocean billow.
Her love's away—he's far away—
    A world of waves asunder—
Around him now the storm may burst
    With fearful peals of thunder !

But yet—the night wind's breath is faint,
    The night-beam entereth meekly ;
But when the moon's fair face is free,
    Strange she should shine so weakly !—
Yet guided by her waning beam
    His ship must swim securely—
Beneath so fair a sky as this
    He'll strike his haven surely !

There came a knocking to the door,
    That hour so lone and stilly ;
And something to the maiden said—
    " Arise for true love Willie !"

Another knock! another still—
  Three knocks were given clearly—
Then quickly rose the Port-Reeve's maid—
  Her seaman she loved dearly!

And first she saw a streak of light,
  Like moonshine cold and paly;
And then she heard a well-known step—
  The maiden's pulse beat gaily!
She saw a light, she heard a step,
  She marked a figure slender
Across the threshold pass like thought,
  And stand in her lone chamber.

It paced the chamber once and twice,
  It crossed it three times slowly—
But when she to her Maker prayed,
  It fled like sprite unholy.
The form the vanished shadow wore
  Was of her true love Willie—
O not a breath escaped the lips
  That pallid looked and chilly!

Long motionless the maiden stood,
  In wonder, fear, and sorrow—
A tale of wreck, a tale of wo
  Was told her on the morrow!
The ship of her returning hopes
  Had sunk beneath the billow—
The ocean-shell, the ocean-weed
  Were now her lover's pillow!

CXXXV.

HOLLO, MY FANCY.

Hollo, my Fancy! Thou art free—
Nor bolt nor shackle fetters thee!
Thy prison door is cleft in twain,
And Nature claims her child again;
Doff the base weeds of toil and strife,
And hail the world's returning life!

  Up and away! 'Tis Nature's voice
Bids thee hie fieldward and rejoice;
She calls thee from unhallowed mirth
To walk with beauty o'er the earth;
Proudly she calls thee forth, and now
Prints blandest kisses on thy brow;
On lip, on cheek, on bosom bare,
She pours the balmy morning air:
The fulness of a mother's breast
  Swells for thee in this gracious hour;
Up, Sluggard, up! from dreams unblest,
  And let thy heart its love outpour!
Up, Sluggard, up! all is awake
  With song and smile to welcome thee;
The flower its timid buds would break
  Wert thou but once abroad to see!
Teeming with love, earth, ocean, air
Are musical with grateful prayer;
Each measured sound, each glorious sight,
Personifies intense delight!
The breeze that crisps the summer seas,
Or softly plains through leafy trees,
Or, on the hill-side, stoops to chase
The wild kid in its giddy race—
The breeze that, like a lover's sigh,
Of mingled fear and ecstacy,

Plays amorous over brow and cheek,
Methinks it has a voice to speak
The joys of the awakening morn—
When, on exulting pinion borne,
The lark, sole monarch of the sky,
Pours from his throat rich melody.

Hollo, my Fancy! Fast a-field,
Aurora's face is just revealed:
Night's shadows yet have scanty sped
Midway up yonder mountain's head—
While in the valley far below,
The misty billows, ebbing, show
Where fairy isles in beauty glow;
Delicious spots of elfin green,
Emerging from a world unseen,
Of dreams and quaintest phantasies—
Spots that would the Faerye Queen
To a very tittle please!
Away the shadowy phantoms roll,
  Up-borne by the rising breeze,
Fluttering like some banner scroll;
  While, peering o'er the silent seas
Of yon far shore, thou may'st descry
The red glance of the Day-Star's eye!

Hollo, my Fancy! Let us trace
The breaking of the vestal dawn!
  Through dappled clouds, with stealthy pace,
It travels over mount and lawn.
Lacings of crimson and of gold,
Threaded and twined an hundred-fold,
Bar the far Orient, while the sea
Of molten brass appears to be.
And lo! upon that glancing tide
Vessels of snowy whiteness glide:
Some portward, self-impelled are steering,
Some in the distance disappearing;

And some, through mingled light and shade,
Like visions gleam—like visions fade.
Strange are these ocean mysteries !
No helmsman on the poop one sees,
No sailor nestled in the shrouds,
Singing to the passing clouds.
But let us leave old Neptune's show,
And to the dewy uplands go !
Now skyward, in a chequered crowd,
Rolls each rosy-edged cloud,
Flaunting in the upper air
Many a tabard rich and rare ;
And mantling as they onward rush,
Every hill top with a blush,
To dissolve, streak after streak,
Like rose tints on a maiden's cheek,
When, in wanton waggish folly,
The chord of love's sweet melancholy
Is rudely smitten, and the cheek
Tells tales the lip might never speak.

Hollo, my Fancy ! It is good
To seek soul-soothing solitude ;
To leave the city, and the mean,
Cold, abject things that crawl therein ;
Flee crowded streets and painted hall,
Where sin rules rampant over all ;
To roam where greenwoods thickest grow,
Where meadows spread and rivers flow,
Where mountains loom in mist, or lie
Clad in a sunshine livery ;
Wander through dingle and through dell,
Which the sweet primrose loveth well ;
And where, in every ivied cranny
Of mouldering crag, unseen by any,
Clouds of busy birds are dinning
Anthems that welcome day's beginning :

Or, like lusty shepherd groom,
Wade through seas of yellow broom ;
And, with foot elastic tread
On the shrinking flowret's head,
As it droops with dew-drops laden,
Like some tear-surcharged maiden :
Skip it, trip it deftly, till
Every flower-cup liquor spill,
And green earth grows bacchanal,
Freed from night's o'ershadowing pall ;
Or let us climb the steep, and know
How the mountain breezes blow.

Hither, brave Fancy ! Speed we on,
Like Judah's bard to Lebanon !
Every step we take, more nigh
Mounts the spirit to the sky.
Sounds of life are waxing low
As we high and higher go,
And a deeper silence given
For choice communing with heaven ;
On this eminence awhile
Rest we from our vigorous toil :
Forth our eyes, mind's scouts that be,
Cull fresh food for fantasy !
Like a map, beneath these skies,
Fair the summer landscape lies—
Sea, and sand, and brook, and tree,
Meadow broad, and sheltered lea,
Shade and sunshine intermarried,
All deliciously varied :
Goodly fields of bladed corn,
Pastures green, where neatherd's horn
Bloweth through the livelong day,
Many a rudely jocund lay :
There be rows of waving trees,
Hymning saintliest homilies

To the weary passer by,
Till his heart mount to his eye,
And his tingling feelings glow
With deep love for all below,
While his soul, in rapturous prayer,
Finds a temple everywhere.
See, each headland hath its tower,
Every nook its own love bower—
While, from every sheltered glen,
Peep the homes of rustic men ;
And apart, on hillock green,
Is the hamlet's chapel seen :
Mingled elms and yews surround
Its most peaceful burial ground ;
Like sentinels the old trees stand,
Guarding death's sleep-silent land.
Adown the dell a brawling burn,
With wimple manifold, doth spurn
The shining pebbles in its course,
Foaming like spur-fretted horse—
A mighty voice in puny form,
Miniature of blustering storm,
It rates each shelving crag and tree
That would abridge its liberty,
And roundly swears it will be free !
'Tis even so, for now along
The plain it sweeps with softened song ;
And there, in summer, morn and noon,
And eve, the village children wade,
Oft wondering if the streamlet's tune
Be by wave or pebble made ;
But, unresolved of doubt, they say
Thus it tunes its pipe alway.

Wood-ward, brave Fancy ! Over-head
The Sun is waxing fiery red ;
No cloud is floating on the sky
To interrupt his brilliancy,

Or mar the glory of his ray
While journeying on his lucid way.
But here, within this forest chase,
We'll wander for a fleeting space,
'Mid walks beneath whose clustering leaves
Bright noontides wane to sober eves;
And where, 'mong roots of timbers old,
Pale flowers are seen like virgins cold—
(Virgins fearful of the Sun,
Most beautiful to look upon)—
In some soft and mossy nook,
Where dwells the wanderer's eager look.

Until the Sun hath sunken down
Over the folly-haunting town,
And curious Stars are forth to peer
With frost-like brilliance, silvery clear,
From the silent firmament—
Here be our walk of sweet content.
Around is many a sturdy oak
Never scaithed by woodman's stroke;
Many a stalwart green-wood tree,
Loved of Waithman bold and free,
When the arrow at his side,
And the bow he bent with pride,
Gave the right to range at will,
And lift whate'er broad shaft might kill.
Here, belike famed Robin Hood,
Or other noble of the wood,
Clym of the Cleuch, or Adam Bell,—
Young Gandelyn that shot full well,—
Will Cloudeslie, and Little John,
Or Bertram, wight of blood and bone,
Plied there woodcraft, maugre law:
Raking through the greenwood shaw,
Bow in hand, and sword at knee,
They lived true thieves, and Waithman free.

In the twilight of this wood—
And, awe-breathing solitude—
Heathens of majestic mind,
Might a fitting temple find
Underneath some far spread oak,
Nature blindly to invoke.
What is groined arch to this
Mass of moveless leafiness ?
What are clustered pillars to
The gnarled trunk of silvery hue,
That, Titan-like, heaves its huge form
Through centuries of change and storm,
And stands as it were planted there,
Alike for shelter and for prayer ?

Hither, my jocund Fancy ! Turn,
And note how Heaven's pure watchfires burn
In yonder fields of deepest blue,
Investing space with glories new !
And hark how in the bosky dell
Warbles mate-robbed Philomel !
Every sound from that glade stealing
Sadness woos with kindred feeling—
The notes of a love-broken heart
Surpass the dull appeal of art ;
Here rest awhile, for every where,
  On lake, lawn, tower, and forest tree,
Falleth in floods the moonshine fair—
  How beautiful night's glories be !
No stir is heard upon the land,
  No murmur from the sea ;
The pulse of life seems at a stand
  As nature quaffeth, rapturously,
From yonder ambient worlds of light,
Deep draughts of passionate delight.

Hollo, my Fancy ! It is well
To ponder on the spheres above—

To bid each fount of feeling swell
Responsive to the glance of love.
See! trooping in a gladsome row,
How steadfastly these tapers glow;
And light up hill and darksome glen
To cheer the path of wand'ring men,
And eke of frolic elf and fay
That haunt the hollow hill, or play
By crystal brook, or gleaming lake,
Or dance until the green wood shake
To fits of choicest minstrelsie,
Under the cope of the witch elm-tree.

When all is hush around and above,
Then is the hour to carpe of love;
When not an eye but ours is waking,
Nor even the slightest leaflet shaking—
When, like a newly-captured bird,
The fluttering of the heart is heard;
When tears come to the eye unbidden,
And blushing cheeks are in bosom hidden!
While hand seeks softer hand, and there
Seems spell-bound by the amorous air—
When love, in very silence, finds
The tone that pleads, the pledge that binds.

Hollo, my Fancy! Whither bounding?
Go where rolling orbs are sounding
This dull nether world astounding
With celestial symphonies;
Inhale no more the soft replies
Which gurgling rills and fountains make,
  Nor feed upon the fervid sighs
Of winds that fan the reedy lake;
  Leave all terrestrial harmonies
That flow for pining minstrel's sake.

Skyward, adventurous Fancy! Dare
To cleave the ocean of the air;

Soaring on thy vane-like wings
Rise o'er earth and clod-like things.
Smite the rolling clouds that bar
Thy progress to those realms afar ;
Career it with the Sisters seven,
Pace it through the star-paved heaven ;
Snatch Orion's baldrick,—then,
Astride upon the Dragon, dare
To hunt the lazy-footed Bear
Around the pole and back again ;
Scourge him tightly, scourge him faster,
Let the savage know his master !
And, to close the mighty feat,
Light thy lamp of brave conceit
With some grim, red-bearded star,
(Sign of Famine, Fire, and War,)
And hang it on the young moon's horn
To show how poet thought is born.

CXXXVI.

LOVE'S POTENCIE.

If men were fashioned of the stone,
   Then might they never yield to love—
But fashioned as they are, they owne
   (On earth, as in the realme above,)
That Beauty, in perfection stil
Controls the thoughts, impels the wil.

And sure 'twere vaine to stemme the tide
   Of passion surging in the breast—
Since fierce ambition, stubborn pryde
   Have each the sovereigne power confest ;
Which rolleth on, despite al staie,
Sweeping ilk prudent shifte awaye.

What though the mayden that we love
    May fail to meet the troth we bear—
Nor once its generous warmth approve,
    Nor bate one jot of our despaire—
Doth not the blind dictator say—
" Thou foolish wichte pyne on alwaie !"

We cannot read the wondrous lawes
    That knit the soul to lovelinesse ;
We feel their influence, but their cause
    Remains a theme of mysticknesse—
We only know Love may not be
    O'ermastered by Wil's energie.

Nor would I wish to break the dream
    Of troubled joy ; that still is mine—
Albeit that the cheering gleam
    Of hope hath almost ceased to shine—
So long as Beauty light doth give,
My heart must feel, its love must live !

CXXXVII.

LIFE.

O LIFE ! what is thy quest ?—What owns this world
Of stalking shadows, fleeting phantasies,
Enjoyments substanceless—to wed the mind
To its still querulous, ever-faltering mate—
Or crib the pinion of the aspiring soul
(Upborne ever by the mystical)
To a poor nook of this sin-stricken earth,
Or sterile point of time ?—The Universe,
My spirit, is thy birth-right—and thy term
Of occupance, thou river, limitless—
Eternity !

CXXXVIII.

SUPERSTITION.

Dim power! by very indistinctness made
More potent, as the twilight's shade
Gives magnitude to objects mean;
Thou power, though deeply felt, unseen,
That with thy mystic, undefined,
And boundless presence, fills my mind
With unimaginable fears, and chills
My aching heart, and all its pulses stills
Into a silence deeper than the grave,
That erst throbbed quick and brave!
Wherefore, at dead of night, by some lone stream,
Dost thou, embodying its very sound
In thy own substance, seem
To speak of some lorn maiden, who hath found
Her bridal pillow deftly spread
Upon the tall reeds' rustling head,
And the long green sedges graceful sweep,
Where the otter and the wild drake sleep?
And wherefore, in the moonshine clear,
Doth her wan form appear
For ever gliding on the water's breast
As shadowy mist that hath no rest,
But wanders idly to and fro
Whithersoe'er the wavering winds may blow?

Thou mystic spirit tell,
Why in the hollow murmurs of that bell
Which load the passing wind,
Each deep full tone but echoes to my mind
The footfall of the dead—
The almost voiceless, nameless tread,
And restless stirring to and fro of those
To whom the grave itself can never yield repose,

But whose dark, guilty sprites
Wander and wail with glowworm lights
Within the circle of the yew tree's shade,
Until the gray cock flaps his wings,
And the dubious light of morn upsprings
O'er yonder hoar hills' dewy head?

And say, while seated under this grey arch
Where old Time oft in sooth
Hath whet his pitiless tooth,
And gnawed clean through
Its ivy and moss-velvet coat of greenest hue,
I watch the moon's swift march
Through paths of heavenly blue :
Methinks that there are eyes which gaze on me,
And jealous spirits breathing near, who be
Floating around me, or in pensive mood
Throned on some shatter'd column's ivied head,
Hymning a warning lay in solitude,
Making the silent loneness of the place
More chilly, deep, and dead,
And more befitting haunt for their aerial race?

Terribly lovely power ! I ask of thee,
Wherefore so lord it o'er my phantasye,
That in the forests moaning sound,
And in the cascade's far-off muttered noise,
And in the breeze of midnight, and the bound
And leap of ocean billows heard afar,
I still do deem these are
The whispering melodies of things that be
Immortal, viewless, formless—not of earth,
But heaven descended, and thus softly
At midnight mingling their wild mirth :
Or, when pale Dian loves to shroud
Her fair and glittering form, beneath the veil
Of watery mist or dusky fire-edged cloud,
And giant shadows sail

With stately march athwart the heaven's calm face;
Say then, why unto me is given
A clearer vision, so that I do see
Between the limits of the earth and heaven
A bright and marvellous race—
A goodly shining company—
Flaunting in garments of unsullied snow,
That ever and anon do come and go
From star to hill top, or green hollow glen,
And so back again?

Those visions strange, and portents dark and wild,
That in fond childhood had a painful pleasure,
Have not, by reason's voice, been quite exiled,
But still possess their relish in full measure;
And by a secret and consummate art
At certain times benumb my awe-struck heart—
Making it quail, but not with dastard fear,
But strange presentiment and awe severe,
With curious impertinence to pry
Behind the veil of dim futurity,
And that undying hope that we may still
Grasp at the purpose of the Eternal Will.

CXXXIX.

YE VERNAL HOURS!

Ye vernal hours, glad days that once have been!
When life was young, and hopes were budding seen!
When hearts were blythe, and eyes were glistening bright,
And each new morn awoke to new delight;
Ye happy days that softly passed away
In boyish frolic and fantastic play!

Why have ye fled? why left no more behind,
Ye sunbright relics of my earlier years,
Than that faint music which, the viewless wind
At midnight, to the lonely wanderer bears
From sighing woods, to melt him into tears?
The bridled stream by art may backwards flow,
Youth's fires, once spent, again shall never glow;
The flower-stalk broke, each blossom must decay,
And youth, once past, for aye hath past away!

CXL.

COME, THOU BRIGHT SPIRIT!

Come, thou bright spirit of the skies,
With witching harp or potent lyre,
And bid those magic notes arise
That kindle souls, and tip with fire
The prophet's lips. Begin the strain,
That like the trumpet's stirring sound
Makes the lone heart to bound
From death-like lethargy to life again,
Bracing the slackened nerve and limb,
And calling from the eye, all sunk and dim,
Unwonted fire and noble daring;
Or wake that soothing melody
That stills the tumults of the heart despairing,
With all its many murmurings small,
Of soft and liquid sounds that be
Like to the music of a water-fall,
Heard from the farthest depths of some green wood,
In quiet moon-lit night, that stills the mood
Of painful thought, and fills the soul
With pleasant musings, such as childhood knows
When basking on some greenwood shady knoll,
And weaving garlands with the drooping boughs.

Or dost thou sing of woman—of the eye
That pierces through the heart, and wrays
Its own fond secrets by a sympathy
That scorns slow words and idle phrase ?
Or of the lips that utter wondrous love,
And yet do scarcely move
Their ruby portals to emit a sound,
Or syllable a name, but round and round
Irradiate themselves with pensive smiles ?
Or of the bosom, stranger to the wiles
And thoughts of worthless worldlings, which doth swell
With soft emotion underneath its cover,
And speaks unto the keen-eyed conscious lover
Thoughts, feelings, sympathies, tongue ne'er could tell ?
Sing'st thou of arms—of glory in the field—
Where patriots meet in death's embrace,
To reap high honours where the clanging shield
And gleaming spear—the swayful ponderous mace,
And the shrill trumpet rings aloud its peal
Of martial music furious and strong ;
Where ardent souls together throng
And struggle in the press of griding steel,
And fearful shout and battle cry,
Herald the quivering spirit's sigh,
That leaves the strife in agony,
And as it fleets away, still throws
Its stern defiance on its conquering foes,
Shrieking in wrath, not fear ?

CXLI.

LAYS OF THE LANG BEIN RITTERS.

AMONG the ungarnered Poems left by the late Mr. Motherwell, I have found certain wild, romantic, and melancholy measures, fittingly enshrined in a story of Teutonic spirit and colouring, entitled "The Doomed Nine, or the Lang Bein Ritters." To publish the prose narrative lies not within the purpose of this selection—but the songs, which conveyed to us a very singular pleasure in days endeared to memory by the delights of friendship, may not inaptly form the concluding strains of a volume whose general aspect accords well (too well) with the Poet's cast of thought and premature departure.—K.

THE RITTERS RIDE FORTH.

"On the eastern bank of the noble Rhine stood a lofty tower, named the Ritterberg; and, in the pleasant simple days of which we speak, it was held by nine tall knights, men of huge stature and prodigious strength, whose principal amusement was knocking off the heads of the unfortunate serfs who inhabited the fruitful valleys circumjacent to their stronghold. They madly galloped over meadow and mountain, through firth and forest, blowing their large crooked hunting horns, and ever and anon uplifting their stormy voices in song."—MOTHERWELL.

> O, BEAUTIFUL valley,
> We scar not thy bosom;
> O bright gleaming lake, we
> Disturb not thy slumber;
> O tall hill, whose gray head
> Is weeping in heaven,
> We come not to pierce thro'
> Thy dim holy chambers—
> We see thee and love thee,
> And never will mar thee:—
> O beautiful valley,
> Bright lake, and tall mountain,
> The Ritters ride forth!

Churls scratch, with the base share,
The flower-girdled valley;
And sheer, with the sharp keel,
The dream-loving billow;
They pierce to the heart of
The grand giant mountain,
And fling on the fierce flame
His pale yellow life-strings.
We come to avenge thee,
To slay the destroyer.
O, beautiful valley,
Bright lake, and tall mountain,
The Ritters ride forth!

CXLII.

LAY OF THE BROKEN-HEARTED AND HOPE-BEREAVED MEN.

"Some of those who had been bereaved by these merciless marauders, and would not be comforted, then paced towards the hills, and looked back on the scenes of their youth. They sang with melancholy scorn and embittered passion, this querulous ditty, which later generations have remembered as the 'Lay of the Broken-hearted and Hope-bereaved men,' who went up to the hollowed mountain, where they shut themselves up in a cavern, building up its mouth strongly with huge stones; and there, in sunlessness and unavailing sorrow, these broken-hearted ones died."—MOTHERWELL.

THE rude and the reckless wind,
  ruthlessly strips
The leaf that last lingered on
  old forest tree;
The widowed branch wails for
  the love it has lost;
The parted leaf pines for
  Its glories foregone.
Now sereing, in sadness, and
  quite broken-hearted,

It mutters mild music, and
        swan-like on-fleeteth
A burden of melody,
        musing of death,
To some desert spot where,
        unknown and unnoted,
Its woes and its wanderings may
        both find a tomb,
Far far from the land where
        it grew in its gladness,
And hung from its brave branch,
        freshly and green,
Bathed in blythe dews and
        soft shimmering in sunshine,
From morn until even-tide,
        A beautiful joy!

CXLIII.

DREAM OF LIFE'S EARLY DAY, FAREWELL FOR EVER.

*"Others of the 'Broken-hearted and Hope-bereaved men,' as they went on their way, poured forth these melancholy measures."—*MOTHERWELL.

BRIGHT mornings! of beauty and bloom, that, in boyhood,
Gleamed gay with the visionings glorious of glad hope;
Dear days! that discoursed of delights never-dying,
And painted each pastime with tints of pure pleasure;
Bright days, when the heart leapt like kid o'er the mountain,
And gazed on the fair fields—one full fount of feeling—
When wood and when water, flower, blossom, and small leaf,
Were robed in a sunshine that seemed everlasting;
Ye were but a dream, and like dream have departed!
    O! Dream of Life's early day, farewell for ever.

As the pale cloud that circled in morning the hill top,
Flitteth, in fleecy wreathes, fast in the sun-blaze ;
Or, as the slim shadows steal silently over
The gray walls at noon-tide, so ghost-like ongliding,
And leave not a line for remembrance to linger on ;
So soon and so sadly have terribly perished
The joys we did muse of in youth's mildest morn ;
Time spreads o'er the brow soon his pale sheaf of sorrow,
And freezes each heart-fount that whilome gushed freely ;
  Oh ! Dream of Life's early day, farewell for ever.

The woods and the waters, the great winds of heaven,
Sound on and for ever their grand solemn symphonies ;
The moon gleams with gladness,—the wakeful stars wander,
With bright eyes of beauty that ever beam pleasure ;
The sun scatters golden fire—bright rays of glory—
Till proud glows the earth, graithed in harness from heaven ;
The fields flourish fragrant with summer flower blossoms ;
Time robs not the earth of its brightness and braveries,
But he strips the lorn heart of the loves that it lived by.
  Oh ! Dream of Life's early day, farewell for ever.

We have sought for the smiles that shed sunshine around us,
For the voices that mingled mind-music with ours ;
For hearts whose roots grew where the roots of our own grew,
While pulse sang to pulse the same lay of love-longing.
In the fair forest firth, on the wide waste of waters,
By brooks that gleam brightest, and banks that blush bravest,
On hill and in hollow, green holm, and broad meadow,
We have sought for these loved things, but never could find them,
We have shouted their names, and sad echoes made answer,
  Oh ! Dream of Life's early day, farewell for ever.

CXLIV.

THE RITTERS RIDE HOME.

As EAGLES return to their eyrie,
Gorged with the flesh of the young kid,
Even so we return from the battle—
The banquet of noble blood.
We are drunk with that ruddy wine ;
We are stained with its droppings all over ;
We have drunk till our full veins are bursting,
Till the vessel was drained to its dregs—
Till the tall flaggons fell from our hands,
That were wearied with ever uplifting them :
We have drunk till we no longer could find
The liquor divine of heroes.
   The Ritters ride home !

Ask where great glory is won ?
Enquire of the desolate land ;
Of the city that hath no life,
Of the bay that hath no white sail,
The land that is trenched with mad feet,
Which turned up the soil in despair ;
The city is silent and fireless,
And each threshold is crowded with dry bones ;
The bay glitters sheenly in sunlight,
No oar shivers now its clear mirror ;
The mast of the bark is not there,
Nor the shout of the mariner bold.
But the sea-maidens know of strange men,
Beclasped in strong plaits of iron :
They know of the pale-faced and silent,
Who sleep underneath the waves,
And never shall waken again
To stride o'er the beautiful dales,
The green and the flower-studded land.
   The Ritters ride home !

We have come from the strife of shields ;
From the bristling of mighty spears ;
From the smith-shop, where brynies were anvils,
And the hammers were long swords and axes.
We have come from the mounds of the dead,
Where hero forms lay like hewn forests ;
Where rivers run red in the sun,
And the ravens of heaven were made glad !
    The Ritters ride home !

The small ones of earth pass away,
As chaff they have drifted and gone.
When the angry winds rush from the North,
And sound their great trumpets of wrath,
The tempest-steeds rush forth to battle,
They plough up the earth in their course,
They hollow a grave for the dead,
As the share scoops a bed for the seed.
    The Ritters ride home !

Beautiful ! beautiful ! beautiful !
Is the home-coming of the War-faring ;
Of them who have swam on the ocean ;
Of fountains that spring from great hearts.
The sunshine of glory's around them ;
Their names are the burthen of songs ;
Their armour and banners become
The richest adornments of halls.
    The Ritters ride home !

Beautiful ! beautiful ! beautiful !
Sounds the home-coming of the War-faring ;
And their triumph-song echoes for ever
'Mid the vastness of gloomy Valhalla.
    The Ritters' last home !

CXLV.

LINES,

Written after a Visit to the Grave of my Friend, WILLIAM MOTHERWELL, *November, 1847.*

PLACE we a stone at his head and his feet;
Sprinkle his sward with the small flowers sweet;
Piously hallow the Poet's retreat!
      Ever approvingly,
      Ever most lovingly,
Turned he to nature, a worshipper meet.

Harm not the thorn which grows at his head;
Odorous honours its blossoms will shed,
Grateful to him, early summoned, who sped
      Hence, not unwillingly—
      For he felt thrillingly—
To rest his poor heart 'mong the low-lying dead.

Dearer to him than the deep Minster bell,
Winds of sad cadence, at midnight, will swell,
Vocal with sorrows he knoweth too well,
      Who, for the early day,
      Plaining this roundelay,
Might his own fate from a brother's foretell.

Worldly ones treading this terrace of graves,
Grudge not the minstrel the little he craves,
When o'er the snow-mound the winter-blast raves—
      Tears—which devotedly,
      Though all unnotedly,
Flow from their spring, in the soul's silent caves.

Dreamers of noble thoughts, raise him a shrine,
Graced with the beauty which lives in his line ;
Strew with pale flow'rets, when pensive moons shine,
  His grassy covering,
  Where spirits hovering,
Chaunt, for his requiem, music divine.

Not as a record he lacketh a stone !
Pay a light debt to the singer we've known—
Proof that our love for his name hath not flown
  With the frame perishing—
  That we are cherishing
Feelings akin to the lost Poet's own.

      WILLIAM KENNEDY.

RENFREWSHIRE

CHARACTERS AND SCENERY:

A Poem,

IN THREE HUNDRED AND SIXTY-FIVE CANTOS.

BY

ISAAC BROWN,

LATE MANUFACTURER IN THE PLUNKIN OF PAISLEY.

Paisley:

PRINTED FOR T. DICK, BOOKSELLER,
And to be had of all the Booksellers in the Flourishing Towns,
in the West of Scotland.

1824.

But the most pleasant of all outward pastimes is that of Areteus, deambulatio per amœna loca, to make a pretty progress, a merry journey now and then with some good companions, to visit friends, see cities, castles, towns.

> Visere sæpe amnes nitidos, per amænaque Tempe,
> Et placidas summis sectari in montibus auras.
> *Burton's Anatomy of Melancholy.*

What do you lack, Gentlemen, what do you lack? any fine fancies, figures, humours, characters, ideas, definitions of lords and ladies? waiting women, parasites, knights, captains, courtiers, lawyers? What do you lack?
Jonson's Magnetick Lady.

> As that small bush stands in my eye as large
> As yon far mountain, so the mind is filled
> Not as the object's great, but as 'tis near.
> *Shadow, a Tragedy.*

TO THE PUBLIC.

I AM requested, as trustee on the estate of Isaac Brown, the author, inventor, or manufacturer, of this superior article, now offered to the public, to say in what manner, and on what account it has been brought to sale.—Mr. Brown was a manufacturer of *Lappets, Sufflees,* and *Foundations,* or, as ordinary people would call him, a *Muslin Manufacturer,* in Orchard-street, commonly called Plunkin, in this Burgh. He had been, though otherwise a correct man, always very careless about his business. He was a remarkably friendly man, in his way, perhaps more so than he should have been for his own good. It was aye said of him, that as long as there was a friend to serve, he would not serve himself. For a short while he had been more inattentive than ever, both to the manufacture and sale of his goods. His warehouse was often, for days together, locked up, and he himself wandering about the country for no end; so that neither the weavers, nor the merchants from Glasgow, Renfrew, or London, who might be calling round, could gain admission thereto. I am informed, too, that, when in his warehouse, he spent much time in dozing in a corner by the fireside; and, when in these sleepy moods, he could not bear to be disturbed by any one whatsomever. What was worse, he was often very unmannerly to these merchants, if they happened to call when he was occupied with some of the sundry trifles he was in the way of spending his time with—such as, making pictures of his cronies, and rhymes for those of them that might be courting. A report runs, that he turned a great Glasgow merchant out of his warehouse, by the shoulders, for having made some remarks disagreeable to him, on his refusing to show him, (the said Glasgow merchant,) his goods, and, for which, he would have paid him cash down, because he was at the time examining an old worn-out farthing. But, though he was a very imprudent man, I cannot allow myself to think that he dared to do so dreadful a thing. Things could not go on long that way, and, accordingly, he, a short while ago, disappeared altogether, and left his creditors to look to themselves. They, and all of them, I may say, are very sensible, acute men, at their first meeting, appointed me as trustee, to manage the estate; and, in justice to myself, I may say, that I have managed it wholly to the mind and satisfaction of my employers, and shall be glad to be employed in any similar business, that may cast up, either in Paisley, Glasgow, Kilbarchan, Beith, or in any of the other trading towns in the vicinity. Testimonials of my character and fitness will be given, if required. But to return to Mr. Brown. On being appointed trustee I lost no time in taking an account of all the goods and property he had left behind him. There were a good many blankets of goods in the warehouse; and I had gone over most of them, when the young man, a nephew of my own, and a well-doing young man he is, who was assisting me, said he had come to a small blanket of goods, he could not lift from its great weight. I immediately supposed that it was a blanket of rich silk shawls, which Mr. Brown might have purchased, and which are much heavier than his own manufacture. I hastened to open the blanket, but what was my surprise, and also astonishment to find, in place of *Silk Shawls*, *Tippets*, or *Plaids*, a great mass of paper, written over, with a ticket on the top, having these words, "Renfrewshire Scenery and Characters, in 365 cantos, written during the year 1821." All this put me quite to a stand. Had the paper not been written on, I would have sold it to a dealer in the article, but every leaf and page had some writing upon it, so that I could not tell what to do with it. In case, however, there might have been any thing of the nature of bills or title deeds amongst it, I thought it my duty to peruse the whole. It cost me eight days to do this, working from 7 o'clock in the morning, till 8 o'clock at night; but, after all my labour, I found nothing of the kind I was in search of. I got my eye at one time on the expression, "twenty thousand pound," and concluded that I had made an important discovery for the creditors, but on looking more particularly, I found that Mr. Brown was merely telling the price of the brigs at Inchinnan. In this difficulty, I called a meeting of the creditors to receive instructions from them in the business. A good many of them reckoned that the paper in question, should be sold by the pound to the highest bidder; one gentleman, however, who told them he knew well about these matters, said, that *Rhymes*, like *Flounces* and *Trimmings*, took the market well just now : for that wholesale dealers in the article gave at the rate of five shillings per yard for them. The creditors, hereupon, directly resolved to print, and sell the whole *web*, if I may call it; but as that would be too much to offer at once to the public, they proposed that it should be sold in *pieces*, or cantos, as they are called. I can recommend it strongly to the public as an excellent article; the lines are all of a good length; for Mr. Brown was a fair dealing man; and the paper and print, as may be seen, are of the best quality. As I am not in the way of describing and ticketting such goods, I have, by permission of the creditors, put it into the hands of a very learned schoolmaster, a *sticket minister*, and a friend of my own, who, I am sure, will do it all justice. I should mention, in justice to Mr. Brown, that his estate has already produced nineteen shillings and nine-pence per pound, and that it is only the last three-pence, with the expenses, that is now wanted, to let every one have their own:—most of the creditors, perhaps, should be content with what they have got, for Mr. Brown was not very particular about the prices he paid for his yarn, &c., &c. Should there be a few hundred pounds over by this sale, after paying all, it will be safely deposited in the Union Bank here, to be paid to Mr. Brown, or his heirs, when they apply for it, and give me a proper discharge. It is supposed that Mr. Brown has gone to the Cape of Good-Hope.

N.B.—In perusing the public prints, I find that a number of gentlemen, in different parts of England, have unaccountably disappeared. As Mr. B. was in the way of visiting London, peradventure he may have gone off with them; being of a vagrant turn, and fond of strange companions. It would be a great ease to my mind, if, in their inquiries for their strayed friends, they would also spier after mine.

ANDREW WILSON.

Paisley, 2d Jan. 1824.

JUDICIOUS AND REFLECTING READER!

THOU wilt be lost in admiration that a person of my gravity, learning, and discretion, should undertake to illustrate, by the ornate flourishes of his cunning pen, the Works of one who hath disported himself in the idle frivolities of Verse-making; a labour altogether unmeet for a solid and sober understanding. But, before thou passest a hasty censure on my present labour, I pray thee hearken to a few of the weighty and sufficient reasons which commoved me, Cornelius Mac Dirdum, Ludimagister and Session Clerk, to enterprise the same; and which reasons, for thy satisfaction, and mine own exoneration, I shall here distinctly and compendiously deliver, set forth, and declare. And, in the first place, *Firstly*, Be it understood, that the worthy gentleman who hath put this Poem to the press, for behoof of the umquhyle Mr. Isaac Brown, his creditors, is mine esteemed friend and compotator, a very *Fides Achates*, with whom I have been familiarly acquainted from my youth upwards, and unto whom I owe a large debt of gratitude, for sundry special offices of kindness. *Secondly*, Numbers of the said creditors have, in contemplation of my so employing my abilities, in rendering saleable an article wherein they have something at stake, sent their children to my Seminary, wherein, with modesty be it said, I have conscientiously endeavoured to teach the first rudiments of humane letters; and for my pains in *bottoming* these tender juvenals in the pleasant avenues of knowledge, the parents, like good Christians, begrudged not the labourer his hire, but have honestly and liberally rewarded my diligent labour in the premises, with a fair and

Of the reasons which induced me to write notes for this Work.

and befitting Honorarium, for the which, I am right well content, satisfied, and withal truly grateful. *Thirdly*, The flighty and mercurial nature of Poesy requireth some ballast of substantial Prose to preserve it in *Equilibrio* otherwise it hath a tendency to degenerate into flat nonsense, or to rise up into stupend extravagance, yea, as one may say, into a sort of Lunatic exaltation fearful to behold. Moreover, it doth for the most part, only skim the superficies of things, letting fall a dark hint here, and a wide conjecture there; making all that it discourseth of to partake of a kind of hazy splendour, which dazzleth the eye, but giveth to the mind no distinct image wherewithal the judgment may be fed, and the understanding filled with profitable knowledge. *Fourthly*, I have observed that it is now the fashion to garnish all the trumpery Rhyme Books, put forth by the Ingenious of this generation, with copious notes; and though the purchaser of the books so commented on, may decry the fashion, as swelling its bulk, and adding to its price, yet, Fashion, in a sense, is omnipotent, and no wise man will but against it, if he hath any regard for the salvation of his skull. *Fifthly*, I have noted, that to endite comments on books of Poesy is noways derogatory to the dignity of a learned character: For Mr. Hobbes, called by way of periphrasis, the Philosopher of Malmerbury, did pen a bouncing epistle, pregnant with much matter, touching " Gondibert," the work of that worthy but noseless knight, Sir William Davenant; and another work, written by that learned gentleman, Michael Drayton, entituled " Poly Olbion," which intreateth of the Rivers of England, hath been deemed by a singularly gifted antiquarian, lawyer and scholar, namely, Mr. John Selden, as meet to be enriched with the profits of his searching wit, in the way of notemaking thereon. Wherefore, and for many more famous reasons here pretermitted for the sake of brevity, I, in whom centre the honourable and useful callings of Schoolmaster, Session Clerk, and Precentor, have been prevailed on to supply a running commentary, a sort of slight scholium or gloss upon the author's text, thereby making, if I may so speak, the sunshine of mine own intellect, to gladden and glorify the creations of another's fancy.

Having thus given thee, courteous reader, a candid statement of the reasons which wrought on my simple nature, to dip my oar in the water on this occasion, I shall now deliver, with a like candour, mine own sentiments touching the work itself, and its author, Mr. Isaac Brown, his qualities.

The work then, of which only a small portion is in the following pages, at present submitted to the public, hath been diligently perused and digested by me in the course of this and the preceding winter. Its contents are multifarious and strange, such as may be expected from an unconcocted judgment united to a vigorous and wilful fancy; not that I wish it to be inferred, that the author lacketh of judgment and understanding, when he willeth to put these forth, but only that, in the main, he is some deal corky-headed and extravagant; though in his gambolings, methinks, he often sheweth a set of sharp teeth, which bite shrewdly in an unguarded moment. In so far as I can dive into the author's intent, it appeareth to me that he wisheth to give a sort of poetical map, a description of the whole shire of Renfrew, at least of the principal portions thereof; which, either on account of their natural beauty—of the value of their products—of the history or traditions connected therewith—of the remarkable buildings erected therein, whether monuments of decayed grandeur, or evidences of present opulence and taste—of their manufactures—of the populous towns, and their suburban families—of the prosperous villages wherewithal the face of the country is presently dotted, as the bright colours of a comely maiden's cheek are livelierly contrasted by having a dusky visaged mole peeping forth from amidst its delicate rose buds and pale lilies—and in brief, of all things natural or artificial, which solicit the attention of an enlightened,

A Censure of the work and its Author

observant, and comprehensive mind. Added to which, he doth now and then sketch off the character of some notable personage, with no mean ability, after a playful and good-humoured vein, without any spice of malignity, either in his heart or his pen.

Some of his main arguments have been cautiously sifted, and nicely perpended in my mind, and, in conclusion, this much have I to say, that they, in my weak judgment, for the most part, are handled *Touching the Author's handling of his subject, and of his Style.* after a neat and judicious, pleasant and commendable fashion. And, albeit, I have no relish for, and do wholly disapprove of the travail of those Wits who clothe the offspring of their minds and feelings in the wanton and unseemly raiment of harlot poesy ; nathless, it must be confessed, that our author had chosen a stately and modest attire in the structure of his verse, such as was conceited of old, by that perfect and not to be paralelled gentleman, poet, and historian, Mr. Edmund Spenser, in his "Faerye Queene." And it is remarkable, that, while "building his lofty rhyme," after the model of that approved architect, our author hath eschewed any slavish imitation of his illustrious archetype, and escaped all tincture of that quaint phraseology, and thick sprinkling of obsolete and antique terms wherewith the pages of the chivalrous and romantic poet mentioned above, are, as with ivy, marvellously overgrown, and curiously interlaced. This, to the hasty and superficial reader, will be no mean recommendation ; for many affect the Oyster, who yet lack the craft to open its rough and indurate shell.

At the time I was impetrated by my respected friend, the Trustee, to pen learned annotations upon this work, I suggested to him, in divers conferences and sociable communings, which we had on the subject, in a quiet houff in St. Mirren's *Captain Crawford's to wit, 'Tis a quiet & sequestered spot,* Wynd, that the same ought to be announced as a "New Continuation of a late Continued but as yet Unfinished History of Renfrewshire." To this title the work would, with the battalia of notes, diversity of readings, emendations on the text, &c., with which I intended to fortify and ensconse it, in due time establish and vindicate its right ; and, moreover, spread a wide and salutary consternation among the unweildy and indolent pens, who have essayed, but failed to produce a pleasant and profitable history of the county. In furtherance of which idea, much precious time I consumed in picking out and assorting certain parcels of the large poem, so as it might be published in divisions of parish by parish : but, alas! I had got a Gordian knot to untye, and before I had taken the magnanimous resolution of cutting through every obstruction, and reducing the whole to the method and order I had devised, I received a peremptory letter from my friend, in these terms, "Dear Sir, I have to advise you, that the last dividend on the estate of Mr. Brown, is to be paid on the penult of March proximo, as you will see by an advertisement, in the Gazette of the 19th ultimo ; and as there will be a shortcoming of the funds, provided the proceeds of his poem are not forthcoming by that date, I have to request that you will not do any thing farther in your proposed alterations thereon, but just give a handful of it to the printer, to be wrought up as speedily as possible, for the market ; any part will do, but you had better begin with the top of the bale. I think there will be a brisk sale of it, for I have conferred with the Baron Club, and all the members have promised to take a copy. So I beg you will, on receipt, attend to this, and I remain," &c.

where the contemplative have it in their power to muse on the vain and shadowy picturings of Hope, and the brittleness of human joys, over a pipe and a glass of ale.

I am interrupted when about to imitate Alexander the Great.

Copy of a Letter from my very good friend, the Trustee, the contents whereof discomposed me much.

In consequence of the above order, I had to abandon all my purposed improvements, and take to the compilation of a few scanty notes, which had been more elaborate and worthy the attention of the public, but for the urgency of the occasion.

And now, courteous Reader, wishing thee much contentment, and wholesome digestion from the entertainment, which is set forth in the ensuing pages, in such guise as befitteth the circumstance of those who furnish it, I bid thee, heartily, Farewell.

RENFREWSHIRE SCENERY AND CHARACTERS.

A Poem.

CANTO FIRST.

1.

Oh yes, we have full many a varied scene,
Of rural grace, here in the *West countrie:*
Green undulating hills, soft glens between,
Where still the peasant loves his home to be,
Beside the brook that murmurs pleasantly :
Rich vales, where equally the graceful skill
Of Culture's hand, and Nature's gifts we see,
Where fresh'ning rivers, swell'd by many a rill,
Their winding channels, high as their green margins, fill.

2.

But none of all these scenes to me ere seems,
Than pastoral Inchinnan, half so sweet ;
Where, gliding through their vales, two sister streams,
After long devious wanderings, haste to meet,
And stay together in that calm retreat.
That scene holds o'er my heart, a pleasing spell ;
Still, as my lingering visits I repeat,
I love it more ; and yet I scarce can tell,
What dear associations this heart-pleasure swell.

3.

The church of simplest form, and hoary age,
The grassy church-yard, with its moss-grown stones,
And circling trees, that cast a soft umbrage,
And soothe the dead, with sighs and gentle moans ;

Warning the living loiterer, that postpones
His ghostly task, with truths most sage ; close by,
The neat snug manse, a cheerful sight—green lones,
Where Age right garrulous rests pleasantly,
And Youth, let loose from school, sports like the summer fly.

4.

A country manse improves a landscape much ;
It makes us think of many a blessing rare ;
Blessings for mind and mouth—we feel, we touch ;
An active leisure, and a pleasing care,
For *duties* done of love a double share,
Fat hens, fresh eggs, from out the gudewife's store,
Of meal, and malt, what the gudeman can spare,
From bridegroom's *superfines*, still valued more,
And augmentations, which make heritors feel sore.

5.

I say not, were it hard press'd upon me,
I would refuse a wealthy bishoprick;
Say were it steepy Durham's golden See,
For, in ambition, I'm not quite a stick,
But mine burn'd to the latest snuff of wick
Would be with any Scottish country manse—
My teeth are wat'ring for the tiends—I'll lick
My lips whene'er I get them :—Ah, no chance
Have I for this, no more than being king of France.

6.

The pious pastor, watchful o'er his flock,
Wooing, supporting, guiding them to heaven ;
Though infidels and wantons jeer and mock,
I deeply venerate. Whilst we are driven

With *goose-wings*, down the wind, such men are given,
To hail, arrest us in our course, and aid
To reef, bear up, and strive as those have striven
Who now ride safe in port, 'gainst currents, trade-
Winds—all by devilish passions, men and devils made.

7.

As old Polonius says, " where did I leave,"
'Twas 'bout Inchinnan, which I love so well ;
The monarchs of the A, B, C, 'twould grieve,
Were I my many truant tricks to tell,
When a poor school-slave, yielding to the spell,
With which the rural nymphs had bound me, chief
Those that love by Cart's blending streams to dwell
Description, at the best, is *low-relief;*
Go, then, and use your eyes, the walk's most sweet and
    brief.

8.

Go, without pausing, to the eastern bridge,
(For there are two, and stately structures both,)
And place yourself upon the very ridge ;
When there, to gaze for hours you'll not be loath :
When asked the petty dues,* Oh, be not wroth,
One penny sure is small for a fine view ;
And, O believe me, avarice is a moth
That eats our happiness even through and through,
And turns the heart to dust, which time cannot renew.

9.

These bridges were uprear'd some years ago,
And cost, I think, full twenty thousand pound ;
The old one, though not old, was builded so,
That, when it fell, it seem'd an earthy mound,

---

* A penny was exacted from foot passengers.

Or that the stones to powder had been ground;
Too late, alas, that 'twas a sandy pile,
Thin cas'd in ill-built stone, the public found:
'Twas waggish work to build in such a style,
But let us draw some morals from the tale, the while.

10.

And first of all, from hence we're clearly taught
That judgment must not rest on outward guise,
How oft the man that seems with virtues fraught,
When better known, we utterly despise.
By works a wise man each man round him tries,
Oft by some current deep life's path is cross'd,
To some true friend, *as bridge*, the pilgrim hies
He's half way o'er, just when he needs it most,
The bridge proves cas'd, and in the centre stream he's lost.

11.

The other morals which we meant to teach,
We must let rest to a more fitting time:
And now the proper point of view we reach,
And 'tis of summer day the cheerful prime;
Look every way, and say if even rhyme
Can tell the gladness which the heart now feels,
Can ring in unison with its full chime:
Ah, there are high and inward rapture-peals,
By nature wak'd, which rhyme, blank verse, nor prose reveals.

12.

What of the poor heart would become, were prose
The only outlet, when its tide swells high;
So pent, how desperate would be its throes!
Prose is a reptile that crawls heavily;

But eagle Poesy mounts to the sky.
Our earthly thoughts in drossy prose remain,
But all that have their fiery source on high,
Mount in the flame of poesy, to gain
Their sphere, the whilst their glory all men's eyes constrain.

13.

No quaint apologies I deign to make,
For these digressions ; to digress is *law*,
For *lawyers* oft do so—even for the sake
Of glorious liberty, I'd hum and haw,
And, peevishly, at stated rules cry, pshaw.
And, really, when in bondage with these rhymes,
To be the slave of *method*—that Bashaw—
Would be a punishment no common crimes
Should meet—'twould make still worse these very worst of times.

14.

Look o'er the northern ledge—a glorious view,
Wood, water, islets, lawns, and meadows green,
Round grassy knolls, brown hills, and mountains blue ;
Beneath a rushing, wide-spread stream is seen
To bear a double tribute to the queen,
Or king, if that's preferred, of Scottish rivers :
Clyde is the Thames of Scotland now, I ween,
Not from the water hourly it delivers,
But from the trading bustle which its current fevers.

15.

There, on that green lawn, rather to the right,*
New labours of the architect appear,
By old high trees, half hidden from the sight ;

---

* Renfield House, the residence of Campbell of Blythswood.

A noble pile—the castle of good cheer,
Whose sunny visag'd lord's known far and near
For generous living, and for generous deeds ;
"Live and let live," his motto—it is queer,
So rich and lavish, that he ne'er proceeds
Certain small things, to blot one in the *Red Book* reads.

16.

Still farther to the right, the place is seen,
Where great Argyle, playing the patriot's part,
Was seized. How has no monument yet been
Reared there ? Look to the left bank of the Cart.
In fancy do you see helm'd warriors, swart,
Tilting beside yon green hill—near that spot,
From battlements, the pride of Gothic art,
The banner of Knights Templars once did float.
Yon farther hills are trac'd by the Roman wall and moat.

17.

Look o'er the southern ledge—a goodly sight ;
The distant *Paisley-braes* the prospect bound,
The Mistilaw towers further on the right ;
A fleecy cloud its sunny peak floats round ;
But, nearer, see yon hill with tall spire crown'd,
Studded with many a mansion, school, and church,
Whilst round its base, a thronging town is wound ;
A town upon whose merits we would wish to touch,
'Bout which, so great they are, we cannot say too much.

18.

Paisley, it is y'clep'd ; of much renown,
Near and far known for many a wondrous deed ;
For *turning* kings, and wooden trenchers round ;

For weaving muslin webs of finest reed,
And schemes political that *must* succeed ;
For *wealthy* tradesmen, and for *deep* divines ;
Wise bailies ; *prudent* matrons, that take heed
To all their neighbours' *virtues*; chief, it shines
With writers *douce,* save when *Pap-in* their wit refines.

19.

Pap-in ! thou beveridge of the gods—Pap-in !
That giv'st a soul to him who may have none,
In every club thou swellest every skin
Like Arab bottles. Whatso'er the sun
Can do for earth, by thee, for us, is done.
Beneath thy sway life is both warm and bright ;
Like *Docks* and *Dandy-lions,* Wit and Fun,
Spread forth their beauties to thy genial light ;
Wise saws, like haws and hips, thick clustering to the sight.

20.

This town is noted too, for *rhyming* men,
Whose fame, o'er all the country wide, has spread,
It has, of living songsters, nine or ten,
And many more have been, alas, now dead ;
When Milton is forgot they will be read.
There I myself, endeavour to reside,
Though almost starv'd ; my ample *sign* is spread
In *Plunkin,* which runs off the Causeyside,
Where those, that lie in wait for monied merchants, bide.

21.

This merchant-catching is a cruel trade ;
That 'tis a crime the *council* must decree.
Some say, that our prosperity would fade,

If merchants were not caught thus craftily,
Oh, 'tis a sight worth ten miles' walk to see,
Behind their *webs*, these spiders lurking sly,
And peering forth, lest any prey may be,
And darting on the unsuspecting fly—
Sucking its blood, till as a whistle it is dry.

22.

Ye muslin regions! climes where *Corks* have thriven,
Where sign-boards, in their glory, flourish still,
Should from your *flow'ry* paradise be driven,
And pack'd, with baggage, o'er the *three-mile hill*,
We innocents, of manufacturing skill,
Worse than a fall of prices it would be;
Rather than in that thorny desert till,
Call'd "Glasgow city," from its growthless tree,
I'd dangle like the bell, which on its branch we see.

23.

'Tis luxury beyond compare, all day,
About the Causeyside, from door to door,
With hands in breeches' pocket, warm, to stray,
And tell and hear queer stories o'er and o'er,
And into all our neighbour's business bore;
And then, O rare, the penny club at night,
Where, socially, we hum-drum, smoke, and snore,
Dreaming of times—we have the second sight—
When merchant swarms appear, with purses long and bright.

24.

Fine muslins, and fine woman we have both:
The former always takes the market well;
But how the merchants should continue loath
To take the latter too, I cannot tell.

Had I the management, I would not sell
The one, unless the other too was taken.
One damsel fair, with every thousand ell,
Is not too much, or I am much mistaken.
It breaks my heart to see our maidens thus forsaken.

25.

Look to the eastern border of the town,
And there you see a darkly towering fane,
The "Abbey Church," 'tis call'd, now half thrown down:
I wish I saw it proudly rear'd again.
The blot of vandalism, the name must stain
Of those who strew'd in dust its saintly choir.
The knavish rascals let the nave remain,
But not the transepts, with their lofty spire.
Some say, its labell'd bell is now in Durham shire.

26.

The dust, the golden dust of royalty,
Is held within its consecrated bound;
Parents of kings too—Walter and Margery—
Have long since there a place of slumber found.
Where such repose, a glory hovers round;
And many more, of various titled name,
Enrich, with noble dust, the sacred ground.
Death beats the *leveller* at his favourite game;
To him the monarch, noble, peasant, are the same.

27.

The *sounding aisle* you've seen; like other people,
Who visit our New Town and Burgh, no doubt,
You've sought that aisle, and climb'd the High Church
    steeple.

In that dim aisle of echoes, round about,
From wall and groin'd roof, unseen spirits shout,
Answering to him who calls : But when is sung,
By some sweet choral band, a hymn devout,
 Ah, then is heard full many a seraph tongue :
For mortal sounds, back raptured strains of heaven are flung.

28.

Thanks to the D. D. who, so piously,
Bemoan'd, *wip'd off* the deep disgrace, which time
And hands profane, had laid on *Queen Blear-eye* ;
Both eyes with moss were blear'd, and dust and slime,
Her noble cheeks and robes, did sore begrime ;
But now, in seemly state, both clean and neat,
Upon her stone couch does she safe recline
Within this aisle, as waiting to repeat
Some holy sister's strain, in echoings lingering sweet.

29.

Oh, wherefore in this bustling age was cast
My woful lot, in which man's wretched life
Is like the quickened mails, that run too fast,
Holding with time a vain and jading strife.
With a most reckless sweep, the pruning knife
Lops every graceful bough from life's fair tree :
'Tis only where the *golden fruit* is rife,
 That the relentless hand may sparing be ;
Thus paring life to shapeless, bare *utility*.

30.

The *golden age* is past—'tis no such thing ;
At least the age for thirsting after gold ;
For golden dreams, and costly off'erings
To Mammon, God of wealth, so called of old.

All goes for yellow-metal. I'll uphold
That if you bid for *Noses* a fair price,
Soon by the gross you'll find these to be sold,
And, if in quality you're not so nice,
Behold, you've made the age quite noseless in a trice.

31.

Bottles are labell'd, telling what's within,
So are the dead, and why not living men ?
With name and place, the label might begin,
Next—age, and rank, and birth, both where and when.
The temperament, the *principles*, and then
The lowest sum that can be taken for *these*,
The label, in nine cases out of ten,
Would be the porter's charge, "just what you please,"
To hold our *principles* does nothing else but teaze.

32.

These calculating times are not for me ;
I should have lived three hundred years ago,
And spent my easy days in errantry,
As monk, or knight, to care a mortal foe.
I'd like to fight, indeed, but so and so ;
With fiery dragons, and with giants grim
When others fought, I might have cried—bravo !
With age, these monster's eyes would have been dim,
Ere to molest their peace, *my* heart had been in trim.

33.

More in my element I would have been,
Wandering, at pleasure, all the country round,
A peaceful brother, Monk, or Capuchin,
Whilst in each house, a kindly host I found ;

Or loitering in the shady cloister's bound;
Or sunning myself on bank, where wild-thyme grows;
In that calm sphere, each stilly sight and sound
Would have called forth my genius for repose;
Kind cherishing each high propensity—to doze.

34.

To nod, to doze, to slumber, to sleep sound,
These form, of human happiness, the scale;
For walking bliss has never yet been found;
At least, if found, it very soon turns stale:
The *grains of paradise*, they mix with ale,
In drowsy bliss, the willing senses steep,
Whilst *care* makes still our slumberings to fail.
To eat, to walk is but to *sow*—*to reap*
Life's richest harvest—is, in corner warm, *to sleep*.

35.

I hope the good old times will yet come back,
The jovial times of nuns and monks, and masses.
I think, I'm gifted with the sacred knack
Of playing *Abbot*—riding upon asses,
In which this town each other town surpasses.
The *Abbot of Paisley*, then, I ought to be:
With many a holy tax I'd bless all classes:
The *Paisley bank-notes* would belong to me,
For pictur'd on each one the Abbot's self you see.

36.

Quickly, the *New Town* shall demolish'd be,
And with the stones rebuilt the *garden wall*;
Within, I'll plant each goodly flower and tree,
From the low snow-drop to the poplar tall;

Mazes I'll form, and arbours, fountains, all
That minister to ease, and soft delight ;
The mill and mulcturer ground to powder small,
I'll rear a neat refectory on the site,
Where lunch and waterfalls will soothe my care-worn sprite.

37.

Oh, Smith, thou son legitimate of song,
First cousin of the vocal sisters nine,
Thou far too modest, worthy man, I long
To see thee, whilst we kneel at Mary's shrine,
Leading my choir-men, chaunting airs divine,
Delating, warming, ravishing each heart,
With those rich, mellow, gushing tones of thine :
Fortune will *play* thee, then, a truer part—
St. *Peter's* men, to bob for purses, know the art.

38.

St. Peter and St. Andrew, Andrew———
(Association joins these by her spell,)
Andrew ! thou man of genius, queer and knacky,
What hast thou done with our good High Church bell ?
What malice 'gainst it in *thy* breast could dwell ?
Thou tun'd it with a vengeance—took it down,
Then hung it up, to ring its *funeral knell ;*
Thou didst not cease till all its tones had flown ;
Till what was once its pride, disgraces now the town.

39.

It's ghost will haunt thee, thou hard-hearted one ;
It's broken tones will grate still in thine ear :
With such a thing how thought ye to make fun ;
I'm sure, in conscience' pangs, 'twill cost thee dear.

Such bell we'll never get, again, I fear,
It's solemn, lengthy, deep, sonorous tones,
Which did each *Paisley man's* heart good to hear,
Fill'd, with their tide, the houses, streets, and lones,
And fuller swell'd, till even they thrill'd the very stones.

40.

They floated wide, o'er hill and plain around,
In the still morning, and the stiller eve ;
Rousing the hind to toil, from sleep profound,
And calling him again these toils to leave.
The far-off peasant, now, will sadly grieve,
Missing those sacred sounds on Sabbath morn ;
Whilst, scarce the bosom of the air they heave,
The wild bee drowns them with his tiny horn,
But still, again, they're caught, through the hush'd distance borne.

41.

Andrew ! thou man of double-*attic* bliss,
Thy thin frame perch'd in *Paton's attics* high,
Thy spirits in *those* of Happiness, I wis :
Beneath, the clouds of Care may meet thine eye,
But ne'er can reach thee, in the middle sky.
Smiling enthusiast ! every new moon brings
Thee some new fancy, whilst confusedly lie
Discarded whims, snuff boxes, coins, base-strings,
Bells, music, varnish'd sticks, and all such oddish things.

42.

Singing of Andrews, and of a genius too,
Shall I not, Andrew Lindsay, sing of thee,
And of thy good bow-hand ? so bold and true ;
Neil Gow's might be more fine, but not more free.

Each heel was winged—each eye and heart were glee,
Even with the tuning flourish of thy bow,
The reel struck up, and each had made congee,
What crossing, skipping, swinging to and fro—
High cutting, shuffling, whirling—such we'll see no moe.

43.

Good humour'd, virtuous man ! Nature on thee,
Above mere fiddling, has bestow'd a mind :
Thou art a *scholar* of no mean degree ;
A linguist, though from infancy stone blind.
I see the son-taught mother, meekly kind,
Reading to thee on Greek or Hebrew page :
And Oh, it grieves me, Andrew, now to find
Thee press'd at once, by poverty and age.
Shall *Paisley town* neglect her minstrel and her sage ?

END OF CANTO FIRST.

NOTES.

Stanza 3.

THE Church of Inchinnan is truly of "simplest form and hoary age." Tradition, which never stickles at a trifle, says it was built in 1110.* A very gentle eminence rises from the brink of the Black Cart, and, on this eminence, the Church stands. A few old trees throw their sad and solemn shadows upon the church, the green hillocks of the dead and the still waters, imparting to this secluded spot, a tranquil loveliness to be felt, not described. Many of the tomb-stones appear to be of remote antiquity; and, on a few, there may still be seen, sculptured, the cross peculiar to the order of Military Friars, to whom the Church at one time belonged. And no doubt under these faded monuments repose the ashes of many a stout and valiant Red-cross knight, who hath confronted the horrors of Paynim war, and done his devoir to advance the glory of Christian chivalry, on the distant shores of Palestine or Egypt. If, to be curious about the choice of a place of sepulture, were a comfort to one's spirit, after it hath laid aside the garments of its mortality, methinks, there are few places that could be more affected than this, as a depository for decaying bones, it is so lone and pleasant withal. And I would make bold to opine, that here the most fretful and malicious ghost, that ever begrudged the living their enjoyments, and had the most lively inclinations to mar them, what, between the murmur of the waters, and the music of the trees, would be so fascinated as

---

* Statistical Account of Scotland, art. Inchinnan, Vol. III., p. 534.

never to dream of wandering beyond the narrow girth of its grave, or of revisiting its former haunts, and mingling again in the affairs of men, to prosecute its wonted avocations, like the restless apothecary, Christopher Monig,* or those two pestilent knaves, the Cobler of Breslaw, and the Alderman of Pentsch in Silesia.†

Stanza 5.

"Say, were it steepy Durham's golden see." The author alludes to the lofty situation of Durham Cathedral, and the amplitude of its revenues.

Stanza 6.

Mr. Brown, in his many voyages in the pleasant æstuary of the Clyde, and the lochs circumjacent, picked up much maritime knowledge, which circumstance accounts for the multitude of nautical phrases occurring in this stanza. I believe the term *Goose-wings,* is used to describe the peculiar appearance which the fore and main-sail of a schooner-rigged vessel assume when it is running before the wind, these sails being then spread to opposite sides : And of a verity, for I have seen the spectacle myself, the ship doth then look like unto a prodigious goose in full flight.

Stanza 14.

"Clyde is the Thames of Scotland," &c. We hear that the enterprizing Glasgow merchants have sagely resolved to construct East and West India Docks at the Broomielaw ! When this takes place, Greenock and Port-Glasgow's occupation will be gone. But the ancient Burgh of Renfrew, determined not to be outdone in Utopian projects, and in

---

* Satan's Invisible World Discovered.
† More's Antidote to Atheism, Book III., Cap. 8, 9.

honest rivalship of St. Mungo's City, had resolved, as we are creditably informed, to deepen the Pudzeoch, and run long moles into the Clyde, and to form such stupendous docks for shipping of every possible size and tonnage, as will make the Broomielaw, and all its conceited improvements, when brought into competition, appear as insignificant as duck puddles and midden dubs.

It is perhaps not generally known that Renfrew, at one time, had no less than sixty Whalers.*

Stanza 15.

We are much at a lose to comprehend to what Mr. Brown alludes in the two concluding lines of this stanza ; perhaps it may be to some very trifling government pension enjoyed by the gentleman's sisters, at least we can think of nothing else.

Stanza 16.

A little way to the east of Inchinnan bridge, and in a field on the north side of the road to Renfrew, a large stone is shewn, as marking the spot where Argyle was apprehended. This stone has evidently been used for the purposes of the ferry, which at one time was here. The top of it is hollow, where probably an iron ring has once been fixed, and the middle part of the stone is worn, as if with the friction of cables winding about it.† The last continuator of Crawfurd's History of Renfrewshire, in a note, hath noticed what he

---

* Mr. MacDirdum's patriotism makes him swerve a small jot from the truth. His *whalers* turn out to be salmon cobles. Speaking of Renfrew, Bishop Lesly says : " Municipes rei piscatoriæ ita operam dant, ut in eo sœpe videre licet sexaginta piscatorias naves toto vere æstateque piscatione occupatus "—The Burgh now can only muster half a dozen salmon boats, with one or two sand punts.
Printer's Devil.

† The curious Reader will find further mention made of this Stone in the "Historiola Beati Mireni" subjoined to these Notes.

conceives to be a topographical error in calling the place, where Argyle was taken, a ford of the Inchinnan. But this wise gentleman is himself mistaken, for, from the point where the two Carts are united to that of their efflux into the Clyde, the united stream assumes the common appellation of the water of Inchinnan ; and the ford and the ferry were always called the ford and ferry of Inchinnan, till Mr. Robertson, who has the admirable knack of discovering errors, where in fact none exist, and of unaccountably overlooking gross mistakes when they really occur, found a new name for them.*

The accounts of Argyle's seizure all vary in some minute particulars. That given by Woodrow is perhaps the most correct, and it is the one followed by Fox. Captain Creichton says, that " Argyle was found alone, a mile above *Greenknock* "at the *waterside*, endeavouring to get into a little boat, and "grappling with the owner thereof, (a poor *weaver*.) It "seems he wanted presence of mind, to engage the man with " a piece of money to set him over on the other side."† But as Creichton professes only to give memoirs of himself, and not a history of the times, it will be as well to adhere to the account which the Marquis has given of this transaction as related by Woodrow :—

"The way of my taking was, in short, when our friends "had run so far, that to follow and rally them would never "do, I was past a possibility of getting to Argyleshire. I "attempted to hide, but I fell from one difficulty into an- "other, till two militia-men fell upon me, after I had laid "by my sword, to pass for a countryman. I answered their

---

* " On these lands (Kirkland) near to the Bridge of Inchinnan, there is a grey stone still fondly visited by those who admire the ill-fated Argyle, who perished on the scaffold in the reign of James II. He was taken at this spot endeavouring to escape by a ford where the bridge is now built. Laing and Fox, and Wood, (Quætius, Woodrow ?) call this a ford of the Inchinnan. This is a topographical mistake—there is no water of that name—it was the Cart." This is a rare discovery.

† Memoirs of Captain John Creichton, 1731, p. 111.

" challenges civilly, but at last they laid hands upon me,
" one upon each side, all of us on horseback. I grappled
" with both, and one of them and I went to the ground ;
" but I got up and rid myself of them both, by presenting
" my pocket pistols. After that, five came on me, and fired
" close at me without touching me, and I was like to get rid
" of them, till they knocked me down with their swords.
" As soon as they knew what I was, they seemed to be much
" troubled, but durst not let me go."*

The Earl, after his apprehension, was first conveyed to Renfrew, and afterwards to Glasgow, from which place he was sent to Edinburgh, under a strong guard, where he was beheaded on Tuesday, the 30th June, 1685. He met his death with pious fortitude. On the night previous to his execution he penned certain " soft, pleasant, and affecting lines," for his own epitaph, which, who lists, may read in the author above quoted.

"Look to the left bank of the Cart," &c. Mr. Brown here assumes that the Templars had a Commandery in the parish of Inchinnan, and the site of it he takes to have been on a hill almost due south from the church. Whether they had any such considerable establishment in this quarter, I cannot determine. Certain it is, however, that the church was a vicarage belonging to their order,† and besides it, they had very considerable possessions in this parish, as well as in other parts of the county. If they had a commandery, I think it is more likely to have been situated either where the farm steading of Inchinnan, or that of Greenhead, (which I believe was also called Greenend,) now stands. The Templars were introduced into Scotland in the reign of David I., and soon acquired considerable property, "there being scarce a parish wherein they had not some lands, farms, or houses." According to Spottiswood, their principal residences were at

---

* Woodrow's History, Vol II., p. 536, 537.
† Carlisle's Topographical Dictionary, voce Inchinnan.

The Temple in Mid-Lothian, Balantradoch in the same shire, Tulloch and Aboyne in Aberdeenshire, Mary Culter in Kincardine, Oggerstone in Stirlingshire, St. German's in East Lothian, and Inchinnan in Renfrewshire.* When the order was suppressed in 1312, Inchinnan along with many other of their possessions and sources of revenue, was conferred upon their rival order, that of the Hospitallers or Knights of St. John of Jerusalem. The principal residence of this order, was at Torphichen.† At the Reformation, by charter from Queen Mary, dated 24th January, 1563, Sir James Sandilands, the last preceptor of the Hospitallers in Scotland, got the lands, belonging to his order, erected into a temporal Lordship, with the dignity of Lord Torphichen and St. John. And the Temple lands in Renfrewshire, afterwards erected into a Regality, called the Regality of Greenend, were by him disponed to Bryce Sempil of Cathcart.‡

---

* Spottiswood's account of the religious Houses in Scotland, subjoined to Hope's Minor Practicks.

† Mackenzie's Lives, Vol. II. Spottiswood ut supra.

‡ Vide Special Service of Bryce Sempil of Cathcart to his Great-Grandfather, 2d December, 1725.—*Crawfurd's History of Renfrewshire.*

Mr. Crawfurd is very confused and careless in the account he gives of the Templars. He uniformly confounds them with the Hospitallers, or Knights of St. John. That stupendous folly which poured European armies upon the shores of Syria, gave rise to many orders of religious knighthood, the two most distinguished of which were the knights of St. John the Baptist, of Jerusalem, and the Knights Templars or Red Friars. The Knights of St. John, were instituted about the year 1099 by Gerard of Tholouse, their first Grand Master. They occupied a Hospital dedicated to St. John the Baptist, which had been first reared for the accommodation of Pilgrims, by the piety of some Neapolitan merchants. They wore a black habit, with a white cross of eight points, in token of the eight beatitudes. They took the vows of chastity, poverty, and obedience. Their office in common with that of the Templars, was to defend the holy sepulchre, to succour pilgrims, and destroy infidels. After Jerusalem was won by the victorious arms of Saladin, and the Christian powers at length compelled to evacuate the whole of Palestine, the Hospitallers successively occupied the Islands of Rhodes and Malta, and hence have been first styled Knights of Rhodes, and, latterly, Knights of Malta. They were approved soldiers, and did good service for Christendom.

"Yon farther hills are traced by the Roman wall and moat."
Alluding to the wall of Antoninus, which, beginning at Aber-

The Templars began under Hugo de Paganis and Godfredus, of St. Omers, in the Year 1119. They agreed in profession with the Hospitallers. Baldwin assigned them apartments nigh the Temple, from which circumstance they derived their name.* Their habit was a white cloak with a red Cross.† This order was at first exceedingly poor; and, in memory of their original poverty, their seal bore two knights, riding on one horse ;‡ "and hence it was," says Fuller, "that if the Turks took any of them prisoners, their constant ransom was sword and belt; it being conceived that their poor state could stretch to no higher price."

In every part of Europe these orders acquired immense property, and enjoyed great privileges. The Hospitallers are said to have had 19,000 Lordships or Manors, and the Templars 9,000.

The unjust and cruel suppression of the last mentioned order, by Philip the Fair, and Pope Clement the V. gives a melancholy interest to the story of the once powerful and proud Templars §. "The Historie thereof," observes Fuller, "is but in twilight not clearly delivered, but darkened with many doubts and difficulties." As a pretext for their abolition, they were charged with impiety, and every species of monstrous crime. Witnesses were suborned to substantiate the charges, and the Knights themselves, after being weakened by long imprisonment, were subjected to the torture, and confessions were wrung from their lips. These confessions were afterwards used as the grounds for their condemnation. The details of the foul and infamous conspiracy against the lives and property of this celebrated and unfortunate order, are truly hideous.

---

* Qui quoniam juxta templum Domini mansionem habent, fratres militiæ Templi dicuntur.

† Tandem vero post IX. annos in Concilio, Tecras celebrato instituta est eis regula and habitus albus a papa Honorio assignatus. Postmodum vero tempore Eugenii Papæ cruces de panno rubeo suis assuerunt mantellis a parte sinistra, ut esset eis tam triumphale signum pro clipeo, ne fugerunt pro aliquo infideli tanta talique protectione communiti, utque sic signati a cœteris religiosis viris valerent discerni.
Matthew Paris.

‡ Qui primo adeo pauperes, licet strenui fuerunt, quod unum solum dextrarium illi duo habuerunt ; unde propter primitivæ paupertatis memoriam & ad humilitatis observantiam in sigillo eorum insculpti sunt duo unum equum equitantes—*Mat. Paris. See also Gough's Sepulchral Monuments--Fuller's History of the Holy War.*

§ Anno M°. iii. c x° ordo Templariorum *uno die* per papam tam in Anglia quam in Francia extinctus est. Sprotti. Cronica. This may give an idea of the suddenness and secrecy with which the members of the order were arrested ; but it was not till 1312, that the Council of Vienna *finally* abolished the order. And it was in the following year that James de Molay, the Grand Master, was burned at Paris, along with many of the knights.

corn, crossed the country, and, terminating at Dunglass, formed the northern boundary of the Roman province of Valentia.

Stanza 18.

"For *turning* kings and wooden trenchers round;" even as Kilmarnock, in the present day, is celebrated for its manufacture of blue bonnets and striped worsted night-caps, so, in times of yore, so says tradition, Paisley was famous for the fabrication of wooden trenchers. It is also rumoured that one of our kings, meditating a visitation to his loving and loyal lieges, the Bailies of this Burgh, they, on learning his intention, were, incontinent, put into a wonderful consternation, lest the whole goods of their common weal should be devoured in entertaining his Majesty, and thereupon they most unceremoniously begged him to defer the purposed honour, till another and more fitting season.* His Majesty, indignant at this inhospitable request, accordingly *turned* on his heel, and shook the dust from his feet. This report may be true or false for ought I know. But, to the glory of the town be it said, that when it was known that the consort of our Scottish Solomon, James VI., intended to be in these parts, the Bailies magnanimously and unanimously concluded, 1st. That a painter should be sent for to decorate the kirk—and, 2d. That a wright should be conduced with to big, mend, and repair the ports of the Burgh.

How magnificent in their conceptions, how loyal in their hearts, our Bailies be! But still more unequivocal testimonies of their unaffected loyalty were shewn in the address which they presented to his present Majesty, previous to his arrival into Scotland. They invited him solemnly to visit the tombs of his ancestors! His Majesty not finding it convenient at that time to render up the ghost, declined to accept of this lugubrious invitation to the House of Death.

---

* There must have been a *Bailie Hume* then as well as now.—*Printer's Devil.*

Stanza 19.

"Pap-in! thou beveridge of the Gods!—Pap-in!" Isaac speaks here like Apollo himself. I could bet a groat to a sixpence, this line was written ere the fumes of his meridian tankard had quite evaporated. Of the virtues and nature of Pap-in, allow me, courteous reader, to give thee a taste. 'Tis a wholesome and generous beverage, compounded of whisky and single beer, the which is usually quaffed in wooden bickers, caups, or quaighs;—and, by the worthies cognominated *Corks*, who habitate in the various streets and crooked windings of this ever-to-be admired town, it is held in much and deserved esteem. Of the exact quantity of aqua-vitæ which goeth to the pint of single beer, I have not been able to learn that there is any positive canon; that being held a matter indifferent, and regulated solely by the taste, and peculiar habits of the toper. To the unformed and rude palate, the taste of this nectarious fluid, is somewhat disagreeable; but, by degrees, it becometh sweet and pleasant, diffusing through the whole heart, a kindly warmth, tickling the spleen, and wonderfully invigorating and refreshing the head, breeding therein many pretty fancies and sage observations, worth their weight in gold. A neophyte ought to be sparing in his libations, for it is seductive and intoxicating in the extreme. But the seasoned bag may be filled without fear of bursting.

Stanza 20.

"This town is noted too for rhyming men." Yea, it is greatly celebrated as a nursery for poetical genius. The fame of many of these, to be sure, hath not travelled beyond the skirts of their own town, but that is owing to the want of taste in the reading public. It may be asked, Is there any one whose religious feelings have not been warmed and cherished by the devotional effusions of worthy Mr. James Maxwell, the first on record who assumed the enviable title of Poet of Paisley? or is there one now living, whose heart hath not leaped with the rarest delight, as he heard the late William Glassford pour forth his sparkling and exhilarating lyricks! In William died the office of Civic laureat. Since his lamented departure none hath been bold enough to assume the title. He whose muse produced the pithy lines given below, the only lines, 'tis believed, he ever did produce, but lines which convey so much sterling and substantial truth, in so brief a compass, as to make ample amends for having written so little, is the only one, if he still lives, who should lay claim to the dormant dignity.* It is worthy of note, that Greenock, the second town in the shire, has produced no rhymers of any account; but this may be ascribed to the perpetual fogs and rains with which that Bœotia of Scotland is afflicted—making the inhabitants of a dull melancholious humour, very much alien to any thing like a poetic temperament.† Never did the united genius of Paisley display itself in more concentrated vigour and transcendant effulgence, than when Mr. Lawless *honoured* " *The Friends* of Liberty " here with his presence, and helped them to empty a few bowls of weak toddy. Then it was that the said Mr. Lawless, Editor of an Irish Newspaper, was destined to receive a gift, which, so long as it lasts, will prove a monument of Paisley politics, poetry, and taste. It was a cup formed of alternate staves of Queen Mary's Yew at Cruickston, and Wallace's Oak at Elderslie, the which was finely garnished with silver,

---

* There's no cheat,
In real meat.
Knox.

These two lines, pregnant with the most important truths, occur in the advertisement of a Concert some years ago, for behoof of the author, John Knox, twister in Paisley.

† A rash assertion: Look into its Newspaper, Mr. MacDirdum, and be convinced of the contrary. Moreover, some of its natives have written such excellent morsels of poetry that they be too good for this generation, but are printed and laid past in secure repositories to delight and astonish posterity.—*Printer's Devil.*

and on a small tablet of the same metal there was engraved this precious and delectable poesy :

" I'VE SHADED QUEEN MARY,
" I'VE SHELTERED BRAVE WALLACE,
" AND THINK IT NO LESS GLORIOUS
" TO HONOUR A LAWLESS."

At first this cup, with its inscription, was said to be presented to Mr. Lawless, as a mark of esteem by *The People of Paisley* ; but it at length struck some of the cooler heads, that 150 individuals could scarcely, with any degree of modesty, take upon themselves a designation that was common to a population of 40,000 : and *Mr. Lawless* had to be content with having it told him, that the cup was presented by a number of the people of Paisley, who admired *his principles*.

"In *Plunkin* which runs off the *Causeyside*." The street called Plunkin, is by the Genteel denominated Orchardstreet. What the etymology of *Plunkin* is, may be as difficult, for ought I know, to resolve as the etymology of Paisley itself, and that is sufficiently puzzling. Both of them might poze Dean Swift, who was fruitful enough in devising whimsical etymologies. The Causeyside was at one time a small clachan in the neighbourhood of Paisley, and took its name from its vicinity to the Roman Causeway which was at this place. It is now a street of manufacturer's warehouses.

Stanza 22.

Corks, a fancy term for manufacturers. "To bluid the Cork," to procure money at the warehouse—Vide Causeyside Slang Dictionary, *voce* Cork, a work of great learning and utility, at present in the press.

"I'd dangle like the bell," &c. The arms of the renowned city of Glasgow are well known, and the legend thereof hath passed into a nursery rhyme :

"This is the tree that never grew,
"This is the bird that never flew,
"This is the bell that never rang,
"And this the fish that never swam."

An explication of these mystical symbols will be given by way of appendix to a New and Improved Edition of the small Chronicle entitled "An account of His Majesty's visit to Scotland, in so far as the City of Glasgow was concerned."

Stanza 25.

The Abbey of Paisley, founded by Walter the Steward of Scotland, in 1160, grew to be one of the richest and best endowed monasteries in the Kingdom. In 1485,* its muni-

---

* At the north-west corner of the wall which is the angle formed by the present Lawn-street and Incle-street there was placed and still is to be seen, the following Inscription:—

𝔗𝔥𝔞 𝔠𝔞𝔩𝔩𝔦𝔱 𝔱𝔥𝔢 𝔞𝔟𝔟𝔬𝔱 𝔤𝔢𝔬𝔯𝔤 𝔬𝔣 𝔰𝔠𝔥𝔞𝔴𝔢,
𝔄𝔟𝔬𝔲𝔱 𝔪𝔶 𝔄𝔟𝔟𝔞𝔶 𝔤𝔞𝔯𝔱 𝔪𝔞𝔨𝔢 𝔱𝔥𝔦𝔰 𝔴𝔞𝔴𝔢;
𝔄 𝔱𝔥𝔬𝔲𝔰𝔞𝔫𝔡𝔢 𝔣𝔬𝔲𝔯 𝔥𝔲𝔫𝔡𝔢𝔯𝔢𝔱𝔥 𝔶𝔥𝔢𝔶𝔯,
𝔄𝔲𝔠𝔥𝔱𝔶 𝔞𝔫𝔡 𝔣𝔶𝔴𝔢 𝔱𝔥𝔢 𝔡𝔞𝔱𝔢 𝔟𝔲𝔱 𝔟𝔦𝔢𝔯:
* * * * * *
𝔱𝔥𝔞𝔱 𝔪𝔞𝔡𝔢 𝔱𝔥𝔲𝔰 𝔫𝔬𝔟𝔦𝔩 𝔣𝔲𝔫𝔡𝔞𝔠𝔦𝔬𝔟𝔫.

The line "Pray for his salvation," was obliterated, according to Semple, between the years 1710 and 1735. We have, for the *first* time, given an exact and *literal* copy of this inscription, so far as the want of a character representing the Saxon *th*, would permit us to do. The inscription is still perfectly legible, but it is erroneously copied by Crawfurd, Pennant, Semple, and Robertson.

Spottiswood mentions another inscription, "In one of the corners of this curious wall, towards the outer side, there was a niche with a Statue of the Virgin Mary, with this distich engraven under her feet :—

Hac ne vade via, nisi dixeris Ave Maria,
Sit semper sine væ, qui tibi dicit Ave.

The part of the church, too, which is yet standing, the authors above-named have uniformly called the *Chancel*, although any person at all acquainted with Ecclesiastical architecture knows it to be the *Nave*. This error has been silently corrected by the learned and reverend author of the article 'Paisley,'

ficent abbot, George Schaw, surrounded the church and monastery with a lofty wall of hewn stone, upwards of a mile in circuit. This wall was adorned at frequent intervals with goodly statues of cunning workmanship.* The great tower of the cross church, was built at immense cost by John Hamilton, another abbot, who was afterwards promoted to the See of St. Andrews. This tower, on a former occasion, and ere it was well completed had, from its weight, and the insufficiency of its foundation, given way. † It is impossible to say precisely at what period, or from what cause, it again fell. Crawfurd mentions that it went to decay about the time of the Reformation, and nothing is more likely than that it should suffer along with other ecclesiastical edifices, from the fury of ignorant fanatics and iconoclastic mobs, goaded on by interested and disaffected individuals. The account which tradition gives of its destruction is, that during the first effervescencies of the Reformation, the fabric of the Cross church was materially injured, and shortly afterwards its tall spire, said to have been 300 feet in height, having been struck by lightning, in a violent thunderstorm, fell, demolishing, with its ruins, the roof of the choir at the same time. The walls of the choir were, from time to time, taken to erect other buildings, and this sacrilegious plunder did not end till they were reduced to their present height of seven feet.

It does not appear that there has ever been a south transept to the church; the sounding aisle, a small chapel enter-

---

in Dr. Brewster's Encyclopædia. In a note subjoined to that article the author laments that no account is given by any of our legendarian historians, of St. Miren, but we have corrected him in this particular, as he will find by consulting the sketch of the Saint's life, appended to these notes.

* Quod (monasterium) magnificentissimo muro, quadro penitus lapide, pulcherrimis ac crebro eminentibus statuis ultra mille passus undique cingebatur.—*Leslæus.*

† Porro Pasleti immensis sumtibus Ecclesiæ turrim, mulli apud nos secundam extruxit Joannes ultimus archiepiscopus S. Andrew, quæ antea parum firmo nixa fundamento, vix dum absoluta mole sua conciderat—*Ibid.*

ing from the cloister court, seems to have answered that purpose.

Paisley was one of the four holy places in Scotland to which pilgrimages were made. The church was dedicated to St. James the apostle, and St. Miren the confessor.

Stanza 26.

According to Winton, Robert III. is interred in the Abbey of Paisley :—

> A thousand and foure hundyr yere,
> To tha the sext al reknyt clere,
> Sanct Ambros fest intil Aprile,
> The ferd fallis, bot in that quhile.
> That fest fell on Palm Sonday,
> The quhilke before Pasche fallis ay.
> Robert the thrid, our Lord the King,
> Maid at Dundonald his endyng,
> His Body wes had than to Paslay,
> And wes entyrit in that Abbay,
> The quhilk his Eldris devotely,
> Fondyt and dowyt rechely.
> Thare entyrit his Body lyis,
> His spyrite intil Paradys.*

Crawfurd mentions that his father, Robert II., is interred here also. It is probably nothing but a typographical mistake; for Robert II. was buried at Scoon. Mr. Robertson, who takes upon him to make trifling corrections on the Historian of Renfrewshire's text, has overlooked this substantial error.

The wives of Robert II. Elizabeth Mure and Euphame Ross, were, however, interred here, as also his mother,

---

* Wyntownis Cronykil, Book IX., Cap. 26.

Margery, daughter of Robert the Bruce, and Walter the Steward of Scotland.*

Stanza 28.

The town is much indebted to the taste of the late Dr. Boog, for restoring the Abbey to something like what it was. By his exertions the western front was stripped of the mean buildings which blocked up part of its fine windows, and beautiful porch: and the sculptured effigy of Queen Bleareye, which long lay exposed and neglected, was under his superintendence, cleaned, and transported from the cloister-court to the sounding aisle.

Stanza 38.

From imperfect information, or from irritation of feeling, Mr. Brown does much injustice to a very worthy and in-

---

* Schyr Waltre Stewart, that worthi was,
At Bathgate a gret seknes tas,
His Iwill ay woux mar and mar,
Quhill men persawit be his far,
That him worthit nede pay the det,
That na man to pay may let;
Schrywyn and als repentit weill,
Quhen all wes doyn him ilk deill
That Crystynman nedyt till have,
As gude Crystyn the gast he gave.
Than men mycht her men gret and cry:
And mony a knicht, and mony a lady,
Mak in apert rycht iwill cher,
Sai did thai all that euir thai war:
All men him menyt commonaly,
For of his eild he was worthy.
Quhen thai lang quhile their dule had maid,
The corss to Paisley haiff they haid
And thair with gret solempnyte,
And with gret dule erdyt was he.
God for his mycht his saule bring
Quhar joy ay lestis but ending!
    Bruce, Buke XIII. apud Jamieson.

genious man, to defend whom I am obliged to be rather more minute on the affair of the bell, than its importance may warrant. The late High Church bell was a great favourite with the Causeyside Corks, being hung in the steeple for their particular accommodation ; for at the time of its suspension, the principal merchants of the town, living in the beloved and bustling quarter above-mentioned, it, instead of it being swung east and west, as bells generally are, was swung north and south, for the purpose of its pleasant tones reaching their ears in a clearer and fuller stream, while they lazily sunned themselves and daikered to and fro before their respective warehouses. When the bell therefore met with its misfortune, namely a villainous rent occasioned by its perpetual clapper-clawing, morning and evening, all those who dwelled in Causeyside, the Plunkin, and parts adjacent, to a man, sympathized in its fate. An application was therefore made to our worthy friend, (who being cunning in all manner of stringed instruments, and other instruments of music, was deemed the fittest to undertake the delicate job of patching up the bell's reputation,) that he should examine the same, and do thereunto what to him might seem meet. Accordingly, with all due deliberation, various experiments were made upon bells of smaller calibre, such as table bells and weaver's bells, and the result of these experiments was, that a cracked bell might be improved in tone, by sawing off, or otherwise reducing the asperities on the edge of the crack. This result being obtained, the experiment was tried on a more magnificent scale, namely, on the bell itself, and Candour must allow that its tones were considerably improved, although there was no getting away with its dull clanking broken-pot sound. When I think of this bell's misfortunes, and compare them with those of the Port-Glasgow bell, I cannot but rejoice in the superior sagacity and prudence of my townsmen. It is a matter of authentic history, that the Port-Glasgow bell was most beautifully gilted and painted, no doubt to gratify the taste of the rooks, or whatever other birds might chuse to frequent the steeple. But this unadvised step most woefully impaired its tones. When this was discovered, with a rashness more calamitous than even the painting, the alarmed citizens instantly took down the bell, and boiled it to rags in a cauldron of oil. Unhappy experiment! fatal precipitation! they might have tarred and feathered it as well—for no sooner was it again hung up, after its boiling, than they found that the paint and the oil had insinuated themselves more subtilely into the pores of the metal, and utterly destroyed its sonorousness. Port-Glasgow, like Pisa and Bononia is celebrated for its crooked steeple. A freezing horror shoots through the heart of the passer-by as he looks up and beholds the impending spire nodding destruction to all beneath it.

To return to our own bell. When it was found unfit for duty it was cashiered, and a new one was subscribed for by a number of patriotic individuals, whose names, it is said are recorded to after ages in the books of the Burgh. This bell was hung in the steeple, with all due solemnity, in August, 1823, where heaven grant it may long abide. 'Tis a right lusty, long, loud, and heavy-tongued bell; and, from the manful mode in which it performs its duty at Matins and Vespers, men call it *Roaring Tom*, *Big Tom*, *Jolly Tom*, and a hundred other fair and honourable epithets.

Stanza 42.

Andrew Lindsay is truly an interesting character. He is a man of genius, and, what is better, he is a man of sterling worth: he has been all his life-time temperate, contented, and cheerful. He lost his sight, we believe, in infancy, by the small-pox. For his station in life, he received a good education, but was obliged to betake himself to that common refuge of blind men—the profession of a musician. He for long played the first fiddle at all the assemblies, balls, &c. in and round Paisley.

If we cannot call Andrew a learned, yet he is certainly an accomplished man, for he has made considerable proficiency in the French, Latin, Greek, and Hebrew Languages, and has, occasionally, we believe, taught all of them. In the pursuit of his favourite objects, he betrayed all the enthusiasm and ingenuity of resource, as to means, which are peculiar to men of genius, and which enable them successfully to persevere in tasks which ordinary men would at once shrink from, or very soon renounce, in despair. Except the Latin, (for Andrew attended the grammar-school of this town,) he mastered the other languages with which he is acquainted, almost solely by his own unaided exertions. In accomplishing this he had, of course, many formidable obstacles to surmount. The want of a person to give him the sounds of the various words and letters, was not the least of these. This difficulty he removed in a curious way. He managed to teach his mother, an uneducated woman, and, at the time, pretty far advanced in life, to pronounce all the languages, with which he sought an acquaintance, not excepting the Greek and Hebrew.

Andrew is now about seventy years of age; and is consequently quite unfitted to strike up either reel or country-dance. On this account, for his profession never yielded him more than a bare livelihood, he is now in a very destitute state. He has by no means, however, been quite forgotten by his townsmen, for, some time ago, a considerable number of humane gentlemen contributed a sum for his relief; and we hope—we are sure—that more will be done in this way. To suffer such a man as Andrew Lindsay, however humble he may be in life, to end his days amongst us in misery, would entail a lasting disgrace on the town, we may say, on the county.

We had almost forgot to mention that Andrew used to be a keen florist, and has walked many miles to *see*, as he expressed it, a fine flower.

Andrew's somnolent feats too, should not be forgotten. Mr. Coleridge has certainly the advantage of Andrew during their waking hours, but, when both are sound asleep, Andrew is the greater man of the two. Mr. Coleridge can only make *rhymes* in the land of Nod, but Andrew, when there, can play such merry springs to them in the land of the waking, as to render it impossible for any one to sleep but himself. As one instance of this out of many; a gentleman informed us that at a private dance which he attended, a number of years ago, and when Andrew was the sole minstrel, on one of the reels being lengthened out considerably beyond the ordinary time, the usual signals for stopping the music were given once and again, but to no purpose; seeing the musician would take no common hint, the dancers tried the more broad one of ceasing to dance: to the astonishment of the whole party, however, the music still went on, correctly and spiritedly too, when, upon going up to Andrew, to ascertain the cause of this extraordinary conduct, he was found *fast asleep*, in which state he must have been playing for, at least, 5 or 7 minutes, perhaps much longer. This is a wonderful instance of the power of habit.

HISTORIA STI. MIRENI CONFESSORIS.

"The supinity of elder days," says the learned Sir Thomas Brown, "hath left so much in silence, or time hath so martyred the records, that the most industrious do find no easy work to erect a new Britannia;" and I may repeat the observation as equally just and applicable to the difficulty which the most industrious head will find, in erecting a history of the blessed Confessor, Saint Mirenus. Meagre and unsatisfactory are the annals which time hath spared of this holy man : his name alone may be said to live in history ; for the praise-worthy actions of his long and well-spent life have long since sunk into silent forgetfulness, and the remotest tradition hath preserved no echo, however faint, of that fame which at one time, no doubt, filled the land with the odour of his sanctity.

The kingdom of Stratcluid was the field of Saint Miren's labours, and the destruction of that kingdom in the year 972, temp. Kenneth IV. and the flight of a great portion of its inhabitants to Wales, about the year 872, may account for the non-existence of any native records regarding the Saint. But I am not without hopes that some curious searcher into antiquity may hereafter discover some fair manuscript of virgin vellum, containing a history of his life, in all likelihood compiled by that noble and pious prince Dunwallon, the last king of the Stratcludenses, who went to Rome in the year 972, and who died there.

Mirenus was a monk of Greece, and in all probability he was a native of Patras in Achaia, where he first distinguished himself for his piety and love of letters, and where he resided until he left that city in company with Saint Regulus and other holy men : yet still the place of his nativity must remain in doubt, and sorry am I to say that of his parentage nothing is known, and of the era of his birth, equally little. This is to be the more regretted, because the ancient document which furnishes the first notice of the venerable Confessor has been impugned on the score of its chronological accuracy, by the acute historian who first gave it to the public. The document referred to is part of the Register of the Priory of St. Andrews, written about the year 1140, and is entitled " Historia Beati Reguli et fundacionis ecclesiæ Sancti Andreæ." * From it we learn that Mirenus was one of the holy men who, under the conduct of St. Regulus, imported the sacred reliques of the apostle, St. Andrew, into Scotland. As the history of the transmigration of the Saint's bones is curious, we shall abridge it for the satisfaction of the reader.

In the year 345, an angel appeared to the holy men who guarded the reliques of the Saint, and ordered their bishop, St. Regulus, to visit the sarcophagus, where these were hid, and abstract therefrom three fingers of the Saint's right hand, his arm, from the elbow to the shoulder, his knee-pan, and one of his teeth. This St. Regulus did, and secreted the precious bones. And time it was for him to do so, for the next morning the Emperor Constantine, with a great army, came and laid waste the city of Patras, where the body of the Saint had reposed ever since his martyrdom, and unceremoniously carried along with him to Rome, the scrinium which contained the remainder of the dilapidated Saint's bones. From Rome, the Imperial Collector of Reliques proceeded to the island of Tyber and Collossia, from which he purloined the bones of St. Luke the evangelist, and of Timothy, the disciple of the blessed Paul the apostle. With these holy and revered spoils he then returned to Constantinople.

---

* See appendix to Vol. I of Mr. Pinkerton's Early History of Scotland— also Appendix to Dr. Jamieson's History of the Culdees.

In these days, Hungus, the son of Ferlon, a great king of the Picts, was engaged in war with Athelstane, King of the Saxons. On the night before the armies joined battle, St. Andrew appeared to Hungus in a dream, and assured him of victory on the following day; but Hungus, having no acquaintance with the Saint, asked him the following questions, Quis est tu? et unde venis? Whereupon the shade of the apostle made this response: "Ego sum Andreas apostolus Christi, et nunc de cœlo veni a Deo missus revelare tibi, quod in die crastino expugnabo inimicos tuos et tibi subjugabo; et læta victoria potitus ipse cum exercitu tuo incolumis reparabis. Et in regnum tuum Reliquæ meæ afferentur; et locus ad quem deferentur cum omni honore et veneratione celebris erit, usque in ultimum diem seculi." The Saint then took his leave, and the King awoke from his dream, the particulars of which he immediately communicated to his followers, who joyfully swore to hold the apostle in the utmost reverence, provided the event of the battle proved as felicitous as had been predicted. Next morning the Pictish and Saxon armies joined battle, and Hungus proving victorious, had the satisfaction of cutting off Prince Athelstane's head, and thereafter of fixing it upon a stake above the principal gate of his Capital.

Not long after this splendid victory, an angel again appeared to St. Regulus, and commanded him to embark with his companions, taking with them the bones of the Saint, and to steer their course northward. St. Regulus obeyed the injunctions of the heavenly messenger; but as it is not our purpose to follow him in his wanderings by sea, or wayfarings by land, which occupied the period of a year and a half, we shall only mention, that, after many perils, he at length arrived in Scotland; and his arrival having been announced by the Apostle himself, as mentioned before, he was kindly and hospitably entertained by King Hungus and his people. The grateful King likewise made large grants of lands to the holy pilgrims, who founded a church at Chilrymont, and dedicated it to the Martyr of Patras;

and therein they, with fitting solemnities, deposited his osseus remains, namely, the three fingers of his right hand, his arm from the elbow to the shoulder joint, the pan of his knee, and the only tooth which had escaped the keen search of the relique-hunting Constantine.*

According to Boece, Lesly, Hollinshed, Spottiswood, M'Kenzie, and others, the memorable event above recited, occurred in the reign of Hergustus, and, as will be observed, these historians vary in the date they assign to this transaction, though all concur in placing it in the fourth century.

It is evident that the writer of the "Historia Sti. Reguli" has ascribed to one monarch what should properly be given to two, and he may have had interested motives for so doing, which I leave to Mr. Pinkerton to discover, and with whom I also leave the task of completing his series of Pictish Monarchs, by the insertion of this Hergustus, and whom I beg, for the sake both of us have for truth, that he do not confound him with Ungust II. son of Vergust. I believe Mr. Pinkerton's reason for not crediting the preceding account, has its origin in the fact that Hungust II. circa 821, was a great benefactor to the church of St. Andrews, and indeed to him Mr. P. ascribes its foundation. But if Winton's words have any meaning, or if many other authors' words have any truth, it would appear that this Hungust only enlarged and enriched it by various munificent donations. By Winton it appears he had erected the church lands of St. Andrews into a Regality, and probably built a new chapel, to which the Saint's reliques were transferred :

>Than fwrth in hys devotyowne,
>Ekyd the Dotatyowne,

---

* There is a little difference in the Catalogues given of these bones among authors. Boethius, in addition to the above account, gives three toes of the left foot, but says not a word about the tooth, lib. VI. fol. CVIII.; and Major speaks nothing of the toes, but gives Regulus the credit of carrying off the whole set of the apostle's teeth in place of one solitary tusk, Lib. I. Cap. XV.

> Of Sanct Andrewys Kyrk in Fe,
> With landis in Regalite.
> Syne Sanct Andrewys Relykis thare,
> Wytht honowre gret ressaywyd ware.*

In this justling of dates then we may exercise a discretionary power, and place Saint Mirenus in that era, which, in our judgment, appears to be the most eligible for the scene of his activity. For my own part much would I incline to fix the period of his arrival in Scotland about the time when

> Wes Saynt Martyn in his flowris,
> And other sundry Confessowris,
> Til hym were contemporane.

And, by extending his life to a comfortable length of days, he would thereby be made a companion and coadjutor to St. Ninian, St. Patrick, Palladius, and other devout men of celebrity.

But I need not perplex myself, or the reader, with fruitless conjectures on this topic, but shall follow the thread of my narrative as smoothly as I can, without entering upon any debateable ground, where hard blows are rife, and honour is scant. When Regulus had established himself at St. Andrews, those of his followers most eminent for their piety and gift of speech, were sent on missions to divers parts of Scotland, to preach the gospel. Saint Miren was appointed to the West, and after long travail he arrived at the place where Paisley now stands. It had been recently evacuated by the Romans, and was then in the possession of a potent chief, whose name hath not descended to posterity, but who, being much captivated by the winning manners of the Saint, allotted him a small field on the south side of the town, by the brink of a clear and pleasant rivulet, which field, though

---

* Winton, Buke VI.

now built on, was long known by the name of St. Miren's croft, and which rivulet still bears the name of the Devotee who lived on its banks. Here St. Miren passed his latter days, distinguished for his innocency and piety, working many miracles, and enlightening the natives wonderfully by his conversation. It is reported, that of all those who flocked to his cell, none more frequently came than Merlin the prophet, or shewed more delight in his company. Merlin then lived betwixt Renfrew and Govan, on the banks of the Clyde, at that spot which is still called Merlin's ford, but, notwithstanding the singular pains which the Confessor took with that Visionary, it is believed that he died wedded to all his superstitious and heathen idolatry. There were, however, four holy men who became his disciples, namely, Barchanus, Malcolmus, Petrus, and Alanus; these throve wonderfully under his eye, increasing in all manner of profitable and pious knowledge; and, after his death, they erected the Chapels of Kilbarchan, Kilmalcolm, Kilpeter, (now called Houstoun,) and Kilallan; where they respectively abode, to the great comfort and commodity of the people of those parts, who, to this day, possess some slight smack of the austere virtues ingrafted among them by these venerable Culdees. Though marriage, in those primitive days of the church, was not forbidden to ecclesiastics, it does not appear that Mirenus ever united himself to a wife, nor does it appear that he much affected the society of Saintly Virgins, like St. Patrick and St. Cuthbert; and in his voluntary seclusion from the vanities of the world, it does not overpass the bonds of conjecture to suppose that he would solace his spirits by perusing the works of eminent authors, and even employ much of his laborious leisure in composing others himself. Indeed, from the catalogue of his numerous works which hath miraculously reached our days,[*] it appears

---

[*] In the old *Charter Chest* of the Abbey, which has furnished our much esteemed friend, Mr. R. A. Smith, with some fine reliques of ancient psalmody, we also discovered this curious muniment. The list is long and interesting, but we have not room to mention any of his works, except the

that he was a man of universal acquirements, and well skilled in sundry languages— of rare eloquence, singular industry, and profound and various erudition.

When he departed this life, it is hard to say, and where his bones are deposited, it would require a second Sir Thomas Browne to discover. Probable, however, it is, that he would be buried within the precincts of his cell, and when the Monastery of Paisley was built, such of his reliques as were then unconsumed, would be removed there, and enshrined in a coffer of some precious metal. But the pains taken for their preservation, has belike been the innocent cause of their too premature decay; for now, nought is known of their fate, and the place where they once lay, is blotted from the page of authentic history, and the voice of tradition whispers nought of them. In his person, Mirenus was somewhat above the middle size, of a slender make, but clean limbed and active withal. His eyes, methinks, would be of a piercing gray, somewhat large, for the most part looking upwards to Heaven, in fits of contemplation and prayer. His hair would be of a comely brown, and it would cluster about his brow, which was high and commanding. His aspect was noble and somewhat saddened by deep thought, but there was ever a winning and

---

following, viz. *Libellus de Virtutibus præstantissimis Trottelli Radicis*, and which we notice because the famous *Trottel Root*, (which grows in great abundance in the neighbourhood of Greenock,) would appear to have been as well known in those early days as in the present, and consequently cannot be considered as a newly discovered article of economical food, as announced in various Magazines and Newspapers. From an experienced agricultural chemist, we learn that the best compost manure for the *Trottel* is this: To one bushel of *Snail Shells*, such as somewhile ago, showered from the skies upon, and swamped a vessel near the coast of Newfoundland, add half a bushel of dried *Frogs*, well impregnated with *Gourock Copper Ore*, and two bushels and a half (if such a quantity can be found) of a lately discovered mineral, entitled *Thomsonite;* the whole to be calcined in the furnace of the Tremendous American Frigate, named, on account of its horrible instrument of warfare, the *Devil*, (by the by, this nautical Gorgon is now blockading the principal port of the Isle of Utopia,) and then to be well slaked in an *Innerkip Thunder Plump.*

gracious smile upon his lips. For this description of Saint Miren's outward appearance, I am indebted to the seal of the Abbey of Paisley, where his true effigies is most lively insculped, and which may be consulted with advantage by any one, who shall hereafter undertake to write his life. He there appears, grasping in his right hand a pilgrim's staff, which is topped with a cross, while his left hand is resting on his side, immediately above the scrip which is slung across his shoulders. He is rising a little on one foot, as if to give additional height to his figure, and greater majesty and solemnity to the address which he seems about to deliver, his whole countenance, in the meanwhile, beaming with unutterable intelligence. On the right and left of the Saint, and immediately above the respective coats armour of the Steward of Scotland, and Earls of Lennox of old, may be seen the cross of St. Andrew floating in the firmament, such as it appeared in the eyes of Hungustus II. previous to his victory over Athelstane, and which is there engraven, as commemorative of the share which the holy Confessor had in the custody and safe conduct of the Apostle's bones.

I have now finished all I meant to say regarding the blessed Confessor St. Miren, but I cannot conclude without noticing another devout man who lived somewhile after him. This was Convallus, one of the two disciples of the blessed St. Kentigern.* Convallus resided in Inchenan, where a famous monument was erected to his memory, and which was long visited by the religious.† The large stone, which is now called Argyle's stone, was the pediment of a cross erected to the memory of that Saint, and near to the site of

---

* The other was named Baldredus, a worthy and pious man, but as he betook himself to the Bass, he does not concern us at present.

† Et Convallus divi Kentigerni discipulus, cuius reliquiæ celebri monumento in Inchennan haud procul a Glasguensi civitate a Christiano populo hactenus magna habentur veneratione.———*Boece Lib. IX. Fol. CLXXVII.*

the cell which he occupied.* That stone, in days of yore, was the commencement of the Paisley race-course. The riders started there, and proceeded due east to the Causeyend of Renfrew, from which they held the king's high-way to the Wallneuk. It was described then as the grey stone called St. Conallie's stone.† Further we mean not to discourse of Convallus, having it in contemplation to publish his life at length, and to give the oration he pronounced at the funeral of King Aidanus, with notes, shewing the exact fulfilment of divers prophecies he then delivered, touching the realm of Scotland.

---

* When we took notice of this stone before, we did not advert to the ancient name which it bore, and which we take the merit to ourselves of having first discovered.

† In April 1608, "It is concluded that ane silver bell be made, of 4 oz. weight, with all diligence for an horse race, yearly to be appointed within this Burgh, and the bounds and day for running thereof to be set down by my Lord Abercorn, Lord Paisley, and Kilpatrick."

But it was not till twelve years afterwards, namely, 13th May, 1620, that the "act setting down aue horse race" was passed by the Bailies and council. It was then concluded and ordained, "That yearly, in time comeing, their bell race shall be run on the sixth day of May, in manner following, viz. To be started at the grey stone called *St. Connallie's* stane, and, from that, right east to the little house at the Causeyend of Renfrew, and from that the king's high-way to the Wall nuik of Paisley, and what horse first comes over the score at Renfrew shall have a double angel, and the horse and master thereof that first comes over the score at the said Wall nuik of Paisley, shall have the said bell, with the said Burgess arms thereupon, for that year, together with the rest of the gold that shall be given in with the said bell, (the quantity of gold is afterwards specified, and by whom contributed,) except a double angel that shall be given to the second horse and his master that comes next over the score to the foremost." The act further provides, that the horses to run must be dieted within the Burgh, and their riders weighed at the Trone, before walking their horses to the place of starting, and weighed again after the race, to ascertain whether they have kept their weight, and that the riders shall also cast the dice " for their places in out-leading, and the wand hands." It also enacts that " an after-shot race shall be run yearly, from a score at the Sclaitts of Ellerslie to another score at the Causey head of the said Burgh of Paisley, by horse of the price of 100 Merks money, for a furnished saddle, which shall be yearly presented by the Baillies of Paisley, present and to come, at the score at the said Causey head."

See Records of the Town Council of Paisley.